M

DATE DUE

MAY 2 3 2002	
JAN 0 5 2008	
FEB 1 0 2008	

DEMCO, INC. 38-2931

JAN 1 5 2002

The
Judas
Economy

The
Judas
Economy

The
Triumph of Capital
and the
Betrayal of Work

William Wolman
and
Anne Colamosca

ADDISON-WESLEY PUBLISHING COMPANY, INC.

Reading, Massachusetts · Menlo Park, California · New York
Don Mills, Ontario · Harlow, England · Amsterdam · Bonn
Sydney · Singapore · Tokyo · Madrid · San Juan
Paris · Seoul · Milan · Mexico City · Taipei

Many of the designations used by manufacturers and sellers to distinguish their products are claimed as trademarks. Where those designations appear in this book and Addison-Wesley was aware of a trademark claim, the designations have been printed in initial capital letters.

Library of Congress Cataloging-in-Publication Data

Wolman, William.
    The Judas economy : the triumph of capital and the betrayal of work / William Wolman and Anne Colamosca.
       p.   cm.
    Includes bibliographical references and index.
    ISBN 0-201-44209-4
    1. Work.   2. Downsizing of organizations.   3. Capitalism.
4. Competition, International.   5. Economic history— 1990-
I. Colamosca, Anne.   II. Title.
HD4851.W65   1997
330. 12'2—dc21   97-11935
                                                              CIP

Jacket design by Andrew Newman
Text design by Kenneth J. Wilson
Set in 10.5-point Garamond by Carlisle Communications

1 2 3 4 5 6 7 8 9-MA-0100999897
First printing, May 1997

ALTHOUGH THE EARTHLY IDEAL OF SOCIALISM-COMMUNISM has collapsed, the problems it purported to solve remain: the brazen use of social power and the inordinate power of money, which often direct the very course of events. And if the global lesson of the twentieth century does not serve as healing inoculation, then the vast red whirlwind may repeat itself in entirety.

—Aleksandr Solzhenitsyn
New York Times
November 28, 1993

Contents

Preface   ix

1   Introduction: The Race Without a Finish Line   1

PART 1   THE TRIUMPH OF CAPITAL

2   Capital versus Work: Divorce, Post–Cold War Style   13

3   The New Leviathan: The Global Labor Pool   33

PART 2   THE BETRAYAL OF WORK

4   Downsizing or Cultural Revolution?   57

5   A Passage to India: The Case of Bangalore   87

6   Have the Elite Workers Had It?   107

PART 3   SAVING CAPITALISM FROM ITSELF

7   Can We Depend on Wall Street?   141

8   A New Crisis of Capitalism?   167

9   Conclusions   197

Endnotes   223

Index   233

Preface

A PREFACE ALWAYS GIVES AUTHORS A CHANCE TO REVIEW their own book.

First, our point of view. Both of us have had long careers in business journalism, and we have done graduate work in economics and economic history. The totality of our experience has made us great believers in the dynamism of the free market, and in the unparalleled power of capitalism to promote economic growth. Particularly after our reporting in Bangalore, we love the energy of a booming market economy.

But we also believe that both history and current experience demonstrate that left to its own devices, laissez-faire capitalism is extremely vulnerable to instability and perfectly capable of producing recessions or worse. There is, moreover, much evidence that capitalism can easily descend to a level where the system, in the words of Russell Baker, serves mainly to "comfort the comfortable and afflict the afflicted."

A well-ordered system, therefore, depends on striking a series of appropriate balances: between the market and state regulation, between capital and work, and between creditors and debtors. Our analytical—and political—position is exceedingly easy to describe. We occupy the extreme middle of the road. If we lived in an era or were citizens of a country, say India or Greece, that still places too much faith in government, we would be rabid supporters of free market reforms. But the problem in the leading industrialized nations of the world is exactly the opposite. We wrote this book because we believe that the victory of the free market ideology in the cold war has upset the kind of balance between the market and the state that promoted unparalleled prosperity in the advanced countries in the three decades that followed the end of World War II. This book is dedicated to the proposition that an appropriate balance can—and must—be restored.

This book is partly about the relations between labor and capital since the end of the cold war, and such a discussion immediately leads us into a semantic problem. Since the days of Karl Marx, the words *labor* and *worker* have carried heavy emotional and dialectical baggage, but these connotations have absolutely nothing to do with our analysis, and we are anxious to shed them. We mean for *labor* to be synonymous with *work,* and we use the word *worker* to refer to a person who earns his or her living mainly through the use of muscle, brains, or wit; we use the term *elite worker* to describe contemporary people with highly paid skills and professions. To us, those who earn their living from work have a great deal in common, even if they make as much as Ken Griffey, Jr., for swinging a bat or as little as the average author for writing a book. One important exception: you still count as a worker to us if you are living on a pension after devoting your life to honest work, even though your retirement funds may be invested in stocks, bonds, and real estate. It is the need to *work* for a living that distinguishes most people from capitalists, people who earn their living primarily from the ownership of *assets.*

Finally, because our book deals mainly with what has happened to the world economy since the end of the cold war, an issue of dating arises. A good case can be made for designating either 1988 or 1989 as the year when the cold war ended. The claim that the cold war ended in 1989 rests on the fall of the Berlin Wall on November 12 of that year. Yet we chose 1988 because on December 7 of that year Mikhail Gorbachev announced that over the next two years the USSR would unilaterally cut its military force by 500,000 men and 10,000 tanks, approximately 10 percent of the total Soviet manpower and 25 percent of the Red Army's tanks in Eastern Europe. His decision astounded the world because at the time the United States was still embarked on President Ronald Reagan's huge arms buildup. Yet the Soviet Union had made a major move to dismantle its military. The cold war had ended.

Many people helped us invaluably in thinking through the book, especially as the ideas we were dealing with were challenging to conventional wisdom. We would especially like to thank Bill's colleagues at *Business Week* for providing a sounding board for a set of ideas with which they were never in total, and seldom in even partial, agreement. *Business Week* senior editor Seymour Zucker and editorial page editor Bruce Nussbaum were particularly helpful and tolerant. A special debt of gratitude is owed to Chris Farrell, a longtime economics editor of *Business Week* who is now chief economic and financial correspondent for Minnesota Public Radio. Chris gave unstintingly of his open and wide-ranging mind to help us formulate the basic structure of this book.

We also had the benefit of our close friendship with Raymond F. Smith, for many years a sterling U.S. diplomat, who played an important role in the U.S. Embassy in Moscow in the period during which the cold war ended and the Berlin Wall came down. We are also grateful to Ann Miller, a Columbia University Ph.D. in social work, with broad experience the developing world, who helped us understand the true nature and power of its middle class. Thanks are also due to Istar Schwager, an educational psychologist with a Ph.D. from CUNY's Graduate Center, who unstintingly shared her unique insights with us when we felt the need to discuss our book as it developed. Chris Houzopoulos and Priscilla Pong provided us with the opportunity to do some of our writing at Cape Sunion overlooking the Temple of Poseidon, an experience we would recommend to any writer. Our friend George Donas gave us much moral support.

We would have been overwhelmed by India but for the help we received from three leading experts on that country's economy. Professor Jagdish Bhagwati of Columbia University led us to believe that we were on the right track in our comparison of the middle classes in the developed and developing worlds. He also told us who to see during our trip to India. We would also like to thank Ambassador Shyamala B. Cowsik for making herself available when we began our inquiry into India's software business. Vijay Kumar helped us immeasurably, and we thank him for his numerous suggestions and many hours of expertise. Kumar is a partner in Coopers and Lybrand whose practical knowledge of Indian business and businessmen was invaluable in developing the contacts needed to write this book and in finding the right questions to ask the leaders of the Indian software industry. Mr. Kumar's Coopers & Lybrand colleague in Bangalore, "Dash" Ashok and his wife Revathy, a senior executive with AMP in India, helped us understand the tremendous energy of Bangalore. Our children, Flor Lucia Wolman, seventeen, and John Luis Wolman, eighteen, traveled to India with us. Seeing the country through their eyes opened our eyes. Flor was a splendid editorial assistant.

Columbia University economic historian Jacobus Smit inspired us with his unique insights into the early days of capitalism in his course "Origins of Capitalism."

Our agent Joe Spieler, of the Spieler Agency, did everything an agent is supposed to do—and more. His hardheaded editing helped us to take our analysis to its logical conclusions. Henning Gutmann, our editor at Addison-Wesley, was invaluable in helping organize, focus, and refine our ideas into their final form. Maggie Carr, our copy editor, did yeoperson service. Beth Burleigh Fuller, our production editor at Addison-Wesley, could not have been more dedicated to getting this book done.

The usual disclaimer is particularly relevant to this book. We are the only ones responsible for what it says.

The
Judas
Economy

CHAPTER 1

Introduction: The Race Without a Finish Line

AMERICANS WHO EARN THEIR LIVING FROM WORK ARE IN A race without a finish line. Since the cold war ended in 1988, they have worked hard enough to produce some kind of an economic miracle. Yet they live in an economy where their standard of living stagnates and in which they can find no peace. Those are the ironic consequences of America's great victory in the cold war.

The betrayal of the American worker is becoming evident. Those who work for the great multinationals are being told that their companies have been pared down to fighting weight ready to take on all competition, foreign and domestic. Those who decided to escape from the corporate world and strike out on their own are being assured that the computer and the Internet have put the independent entrepreneur on a competitive par with the corporations they left or from which they were booted. Yet more than five years into the economic expansion of the 1990s those who earn their living in the United States had received the most meager wage gains of any economic expansion since the Great Depression, and meanwhile corporate profitability has reached unprecedented peaks.

Politicians are promising American workers some sort of redemption, assuring them of safety from the vicissitudes of economic life. Yet at the same time they promise that government will take its hands out of workers' pockets.

The assurances given to American workers by their bosses as well as by politicians are untruths, whether uttered consciously or not. The triumph of capital in the cold war has tilted the playing field against those who earn their living from work throughout the industrial world. As capital trots the globe, those who earn their

1

living from work are in the grip of global economic forces that promise no peace and limited prosperity. That is already true not only for ordinary workers who have felt the lash of the new global competition. It will also soon be true for the elite workers whose incomes have so far held up well, whose accomplishments have been widely celebrated, who have been assured that their future is safe, but who will soon be experiencing severe economic pressure.

America's economic troubles result from a refusal to face up to the true implications of victory in the cold war. The effects of that victory are widely discussed in terms of their impact on economic events in what was the Soviet Union, in Western Europe, in China, and in the Third World. What is ignored in serious discussion, however, is the impact of that victory on America itself. We would argue that understanding the impact of cold war victory on the United States is the key to understanding every major economic trend now in operation in the United States, indeed the entire global economy.

Capitalism's victory over the socialist system was as sudden as it was complete, and it will rank in significance among the epic transformations of economic history, equal in scope to the European discovery of the Americas or the Industrial Revolution. The victorious ideology has quickly become a supreme force whirling through the world economy. Like a twister, capitalism is changing the political and economic structures of those countries, both developed and developing, that had been hostile to the market. The market is now God; economic planning is the devil incarnate. Free market ideology has finally ridden to total victory in the four-hundred-year clash between the competing claims of the market and the state, which first ignited when modern capitalism developed in the Dutch Republic during the early 1600s. The collapse of the Soviet Union brings to capitalism something it had always sought but never before achieved: a withering away of all the important ideological opposition to the idea that the free market is the ideal way to organize society.

As country after country relentlessly moves toward a promarket economy, in these remarkable years, Western capital is discovering and courting brand-new populations of workers to manage, create and teach. White ethnic Europeans throughout the United States and Europe are, as always, more than free to compete, but for the first time in capitalism's four-hundred-year history, there is no longer anything intrinsically special about their role in the system. They are eminently replaceable—except for the most innovative, the most aggressive, the most creative among them. For the first time, although it is not widely advertised, Western capital is no longer wed to the idea that Western labor—particularly well-educated labor—has to be a partner in the brave new world of twenty-first-century capitalism.

Surely, those who earn their living from work deserve a better fate. After ten tough transitional years, their handiwork, the American economy, has in the mid-1990s reemerged as the most vital and innovative economy in the world. Capital, the erstwhile partner of work, has flourished; in 1995 and 1996 alone the stock market rose by a staggering 60 percent. Hundreds of new companies, the locus of wondrous new technologies, have appeared on the National Association of Securities Dealers Automated Quotations system, or NASDAQ. And although the rise in wages was the feeblest of any business cycle upswing since the end of World War II, the unemployment rate magically seemed to shrink in mid-1996, the fifth year of an economic upswing.

Perceptions of prosperity were buttressed by the propaganda barrage during the 1996 presidential campaign. In politics, upbeat fantasy contended with upbeat fantasy, as the Democrats sought to convince the public that all is on the right track, and the Republicans sought to convince the public that all would be well if only they would vote for the same kind of across-the-board tax cuts that produced the twin economic disasters of the 1980s—swelling balance-of-payments deficits and soaring foreign and domestic debt.

Nor was that the end of efforts to paint a smile on the statistics. Stung by what appeared to be the telling criticism of Pat Buchanan in the early Republican primaries, the corporate public relations machine, which had long been extolling the curative powers of massive downsizings, changed its story. Upbeat stories began to appear about new, integrative company approaches to "win over" employees. There was also an attempt to blame the troubles of American workers on their own inadequacies: "If you can't make it," the message seemed to be, "you are a whining, ineffective, loser adrift in a sea of prosperity and winners. Obviously, you haven't positioned yourself properly in the job market."

And the cheery story of the Democrats "sold" during the election year, at least, because it does have a surface plausibility, and it appears to be in tune with history. For the post–cold war American worker, the very system in which he or she works seems to have been vindicated on a global scale. In the aftermath of the fall of the Berlin Wall we have witnessed what looks like instant proof of the superiority of free market capitalism: vast state-owned industry dinosaurs from Budapest to Marrakesh have been disassembled and spun into market-oriented companies.

And the new global economy *is* exciting, and full of possibilities. Twenty-five-year-old traders ride off to brand-new stock market outposts all over Asia and South America to begin their own brave new world. Elite students at Harvard, Haverford, and Yale head to Asia in droves during the summer months the way they used to go to Paris to study, or join the Peace Corps, or fight for civil rights. "My adviser found me a bank job in Bombay," says an elated Haverford junior dressed all in white in the middle of Philadelphia's railroad station. "I feel a little like a character in a Masterpiece Theater plot." And the editor-in-chief of an international financial publication claims he couldn't find a good freelancer in New York anymore: "They've all picked up and moved to Hong Kong." While Asia's economic success story was certainly being plotted well before the end of the cold war, it was the blast of free market frenzy worldwide after the Soviet Union's collapse that made Asia an especially seminal experience for the most adventuresome of those coming of age in the 1990s.

Even the glamor is now in the global markets. Inevitably, television plays a vital role in the commercialization and mass appeal of the new global economy. Bankers and bond traders alike salivate every time the inflation rate jiggers up or down a fraction of a point, and their views become instant fodder for TV analysts. Increasingly large audiences, many of them retired or part-time workers who have already lived through two or three downsizings, sit glued to their TV sets for hourly updates on everything from Japanese over-the-counter stocks to Austrian bonds. Never before has so much Wall Street expertise been handed out to so many so fast. Never before have so many people, pinched with debt, tuned in to make quick killings with the mere flick of a remote control button, backed up all too quickly by a nine-digit punch-in call to an ever-ready broker. And for those too eager players who make the wrong stock picks on the inevitable wrong days, the fun painfully fades as they cope with losses alone. Like the gambling casinos that are attracting larger and larger crowds across the country, Wall Street and its ever enlarging coterie are a wonderful playground—at least for those with large amounts of capital at hand to ride out the valleys.

The reality is, of course, that there has been no return to tranquility or long-term safety, nor will there be. In the new pro-market world, capital moves wherever it sees its best opportunities, leaving behind those who earn their living from work. At the very time that new technology is exploding and the cost of transferring information is tumbling, opportunities for capital have never been greater. Corporations are hunting down well-educated workers in countries with emerging economies, just as they sought out blue-collar workers in the past—because they will work for less than their Generation X and baby boomer counterparts in the developed world. It is an environment where corporations will seek out the best talent anyplace in the world. Virtually every profession—academia, medicine, law, architecture, and accounting—will undergo radical change as professional workers lose control over their lives to mobile capital. These are the *true* dynamics of the post–cold war marketplace. Despite the economic recovery of the mid-1990s, there is a strange peeling away of life as Americans have known it since the 1950s.

And without radical changes in the way the industrial world controls capital flows, the race will never come to an end for those who earn their living from work. Surely that is the lesson we learned from what happened during the two "prosperous" years of the mid-1990s, when the economy was in the late stages of a recovery and the unemployment rate fell close to 5 percent. Though there were wage gains in those years, real median family incomes at the end of 1996 were still about $2,000 below what they were in 1988, the year the cold war ended. It is disturbing that the growth in workers' income was exceptionally weak while corporate profits were expanding and the economy was "recovering." It is even more disturbing that job market trends in the mid-1990s pulled down new groups of workers. Although most women had experienced growing wages for ten years, the bottom two thirds of women in the workforce saw their wages decline between 1988 and 1995. In the 1980s families managed to offset stagnant and declining wages among men only by working longer and sending more family members to work, but this trend has apparently reached close to its maximum capacity.

Family income has fallen in the 1990s, a period when jobs have become less secure and less likely to offer health and pension benefits. And despite the sharp rise in the stock market (in which middle-class holdings are paltry in any event), the net wealth of the typical middle-class family (the value of tangible assets such as houses and cars, as well as financial assets, minus, of course, debt) has also fallen.

Nor should better-educated workers imagine that they have been, or will be, spared. The signs of trouble first appeared in the wages for entry-level jobs. Though the cost of education is soaring, male college graduates with one to five years of experience earned 9.5 percent less in 1995 than in 1989, and when corrected for inflation, the decline is more like 15 percent. Their female counterparts were earning 7.7 percent less in 1995 than in 1989 — 13 percent less after correcting for inflation.

These are harrowing indicators of what is to come for America's elite workers. It is not surprising, therefore, that our "elite workers"—the top 20 percent of the workforce—are experiencing escalating job stress. Supposedly inoculated against economic insecurity by a good education, global problem-solving skills, and high IQs, they simply were not supposed to face these pressures. "Experts," from futurists Alvin and Heidi Toffler to former Labor Secretary Robert Reich, to *Bell Curve* coauthor Charles Murray, have promised that while the rest of America's workforce might suffer mightily in global restructuring, the elite top 20 percent would be spared. But it is beginning to look as though this prediction was way too optimistic for large parts of even this "gifted" population, many of whom did not blink ten years earlier when analysts simply wrote off millions of American blue-collar jobs because these workers were no longer globally competitive.

Neither the elite workers nor anyone else will find salvation in the new technology of the information age. Many policy makers, economists, and businessmen have cited a technology-driven increase in the demand for "educated" or "skilled" workers as the most important force behind the recent trend in wages. Yet the evidence that will be presented in this book suggests that the overall impact of technology on wages and employment is no greater as America approaches the twenty-first century than it has been in earlier eras of rapid technological change. There is no evidence that the impact of technology on wage growth was any greater in the first half of the 1990s than in the 1980s or the 1970s, or earlier periods for that matter. Productivity growth has been lackluster thus far in the 1990s, not what we would expect if we are wedded to the idea that technology is the primary force inducing a widespread restructuring of the economy.

A new phase of global capitalism, rather than technology, explains the post–cold war features of the American economy. The formidable imbalance between the opportunities open to capital and those open to workers will continue to undermine those who earn their living from work despite assurances that once the United States puts its financial and emotional house in order, all will be well and back to normal. There is a reluctance to acknowledge that the world has changed profoundly since the 1950s. Instead, Americans lash out wildly against the federal government, those deemed lacking in morals, illegals sneaking into the country under cover of darkness, or welfare mothers. Even though they have chosen the wrong targets, their anger is justified: everyday pleasures, such as pride and contentment in one's job, are slipping away and now often seem unattainable.

Americans who earn their living from work have led the race to become competitive again, but they seem fated to be returning to the starting line again and again. They are looking from the outside at a prosperity in which they have no part and working in a job market in which they can find no peace. In the economy, the reality is a growing imbalance between capital and work, between debtors and creditors, between state regulation and control and unfettered free enterprise. In each instance, those who earn their living from work are coming out losers. In each instance the political process reacts to manifest problems with total denial.

A hardheaded look at the world suggests that the betrayal of work is only beginning. In the global economy of the mid-1990s no country can stay ahead for very long without continuing strenuous effort on the part of corporations to cut costs, reorganize their workforce, and shed employees. And no country surges to the head of the field without inviting rapid retaliation by its rivals. The resurgence of the U.S. economy in the mid-1990s, the recovery of its competitiveness in a line of products from computer chips to cars to textile manufacturing has sent shock waves around the world. Japan, Germany, and other countries in the industrialized world, sobered by difficulties in many industries and humbled by slow economic growth, are also reengineering themselves. The appearance on the scene of vast numbers of elite workers in the emerging world, willing and anxious to work for less, is intensifying the pressure in developed countries to drastically pare down and cut costs. For the first time, waves of elite workers—in Bangalore, India; Guangdong Province, China; and dozens of other developing regions—have begun to compete head-to-head for professional jobs that had been the nearly exclusive fiefdoms of white ethnic Europeans in industrialized nations since the beginning of modern capitalism four hundred years ago.

The danger to those who earn their living from work in the United States may seem remote in the mid-1990s. It is not merely that the American economy has performed far better than earlier in the decade. Far more important psychologically has been a roaring stock market, which seems to give both lie to any warnings of potential trouble and life to visions of boundless wealth to anyone in a position to run with the bulls, in a market that has become the financial incarnation of Pamplona's Fiesta of San Fermin.

And opportunities to bet on the stock market have become far more easily available. Mutual fund advertising beckons from everywhere. Corporations are introducing 401(k) plans, profit-sharing plans, and stock options on a broader and broader scale. And, perhaps most important of all in influencing the national psyche, the idea that the problems of an underfunded Social Security system can be solved by investing part of the existing monies in common stocks has begun to exert a strong grip on the national imagination. What is being deemed safe for the Social Security system can surely be touted as being safe for everybody. What a payday for Wall Street!

Yet the probability is low that anyone who earns his or her living mainly from work can find salvation in stocks. It is not merely that anyone familiar with the great crash of 1929 knows that speculative episodes never come gently to an end. What is far more important (and subject to a far more cynical interpretation) is the notion that those who earn their living from work can find a place at Wall Street's table. The vast majority of stock in this country, after all, is held by the richest 5 percent of the population (see Chapter 8). These well-heeled folks are the beneficiaries of the great stock-market run-up, which is being fueled by more average working folks, those relative newcomers to mutual funds, 401(k) plans, and profit-sharing schemes.

Are these workers truly being given a chance to assure their prosperity through participation in the stock market, or are they really being courted as a ready market for the stocks that stockholders of entrenched wealth have ridden up and are getting ready to dump? Is the man who is selling the average worker his or her stock a benign financial uncle, or is he a reincarnation of the great short seller of the late 1920s, Joe Kennedy?

In today's world, the wild imbalance between the fortunes of the stock market and those of average workers is only the most vivid recent symptom of a free market economy that is favoring capital over work, and in some unfortunate sense one of the most superficial. For workers are being, and will continue to be buffeted for the most fundamental of all reasons: they are seeking to earn a living in a period that represents one of the great watersheds in economic history. The end of the cold war ushered in vast changes, fully equivalent in impact but opposite in effect to the great discoveries that followed the voyages of Columbus. For four hundred years, modern capitalism has raised the living standard of the vast majority of people in what became a Eurocentric developed world. But since the end of the cold war, powerful economic forces have been grinding away at the position of all workers in that world.

It is to an analysis of the forces that are at the heart of this radical betrayal of work that we now turn. Without understanding them, it will be virtually impossible for Americans to equip themselves for the twenty-first century, or for the United States to devise policies that will allow not only its giant corporations, but also its people, to flourish. It is dead certain that the outcome of the current economic policy debate will result in policies that do nothing to improve the life of average Americans. Yet if the U.S. government doesn't devise imaginative new economic approaches and become effective in working with its major international trading partners, Americans who earn their living from work—be it with muscle, intelligence, or wit—are running in a race they cannot possibly win.

PART 1

THE TRIUMPH OF CAPITAL

Capital versus Work: Divorce, Post–Cold War Style

> The change in world history after 1500 is quite without precedent. Never before had one culture spread over the whole globe. From the earliest observable stage of prehistory, the tendency had always been toward differentiation. Now the cultural tide was turning. . . . The remarkable transformation that began (and to go much further) was almost entirely a one-way process. Europeans went out to the world; it did not come to them.
>
> J. M. Roberts, *History of the World*

THEY COULDN'T STAND EACH OTHER, BUT THEY STAYED together because they needed each other. What has been said of many marriages has also been true of the relations between capital and labor throughout most of the modern history of the West European peoples. During most of these four hundred years of capitalism, Western capital and labor were locked in an icy kiss. It has been an extended, stormy and often embittered embrace that has lasted even though huge new pools of labor became available to European capital during the four-hundred-year expansion of the West European economy that followed the voyages of Columbus. As technology has been reinvented and diffused in each successive era of modern capitalism, first in the Netherlands, then in Britain, then in Germany, then in the United States, white ethnic Europeans have been at the cutting edge of change. As Western capital made new jobs available, educated Western workers in particular benefited greatly with each new advance; while those at the bottom of the economic ladder struggled mightily working for the railroad, in the factory, and doing the other tough physical labor that was vital to building and sustaining the core of each new phase of capitalism.

In the years of European expansion, European capital interests unequivocally wanted Europeans to administer the British East India Company and the Dutch West India Company. They needed European soldiers to impose order in Latin America and on the Indian subcontinent. They needed European sailors and traders to dominate China. There have been, of course, many conflicts between capital and labor throughout the history of capitalism, but in the past ordinary people could, albeit in painful and hazardous voyages, escape to new lands and could rely on heavy overseas investment to equip them with the tools needed to work. The ties that bound European capital and European labor were perhaps most vividly, and confidently, displayed during the age of imperialism in the period from the second half of the nineteenth century until World War I. Those were the years when Rudyard Kipling bragged, and complained, about the "white man's burden." They were also the years, as British historian Eric Hobsbawm notes, that "saw a new integration of the underdeveloped countries as dependencies into a world economy dominated by the developed countries." And in the United States, it was the Gilded Age that saw the new industrial economy engulf the entire continent.

Behind capitalism's drive for economic dominance lay the *joint* movement of West European capital and West European labor. There were exceptions to this convenient marriage. For example, when the British controlled India, they did encourage the development of a small group of anglicized Indian elites, but only out of dire necessity, to help out the handful of British trying to run a subcontinent that at the end of the nineteenth century already numbered 190 million people. In the end the British were replaced by these very "Westernized elites" who eventually became the leaders of a successful Indian liberation movement. But for the most part, up until recently it was the Europeans who continued to be the "special" heirs to the dynamic economic system of capitalism and the technology that evolved alongside it.

As this global system grew, there were substantial shifts among the European populations and the system's Americanized offspring. In the mid-nineteenth century what had been a stream of European out-migration became a torrent. Before 1845 it was rare for more than 100,000 immigrants to arrive in the United States each year. But between 1846 and 1850 the annual average emigration from Europe to the United States suddenly increased to more than a quarter million people; in the next five years the immigrant population in America mushroomed to almost 350,000 annually. Enormous as these migrations were, they were still modest by later standards. By the 1880s between 700,000 and 800,000 Europeans emigrated on average every year; in the years after 1900 between 1 and 1.4 million a year. Between 1900 and 1910, more people migrated to the United States than in the entire second half of the nineteenth century.

Within the United States population movements were also enormous, as the country's center of gravity continuously shifted westward. The proportion of the population to leave the states in which they were born for new states and territories continued to mount at least until 1895, when the last of the public lands in what became the contiguous forty-eight states were taken. But internal mobility continued high, as Americans trekked here and there for particular reasons, so census figures ebbed and flowed dramatically. A mighty emigration occurred from the Midwest to the new promised land, California, during the dark, dust bowl days of the 1930s; another mass exodus, this time of blacks migrating from the South during and just after World War II to find better wages and better skills; and most recently, the great movement of companies and workers to the amenities-based economies of Florida and southern California during the 1970s and 1980s.

Importantly, during most of the history of capitalism, the movement of people was matched by a movement of capital—monies used to invest in the economy. Even the size of capital flows roughly matched the number of people who were moving. Thus, in broad outlines, the flow of capital out of Europe followed the flow of people. The United States, the country to which people migrated in the greatest numbers, was the recipient of the greatest flow of capital to build canals, railroads, and other industries. Similarly, in the colonial orbit, the flow of capital from Britain to India was closely connected with the movement of the British into administrative and business positions in India, particularly into the Indian Civil Service, whose top ranks were made up mostly of British. The symbiosis between labor and capital was maintained, even while emigration provided an important safety valve for European workers displaced by invention and innovation. As the Industrial Revolution swept across Europe, the workers displaced by economic change swarmed into the United States; the Scots and the Irish into the American South and Appalachia; Germans to eastern Pennsylvania, New York, and Ohio; Poles to western Pennsylvania and Illinois; Scandinavians to Minnesota and the Pacific Northwest; Italians and Portuguese to the San Francisco Bay Area; and Basques to the grazing lands of California and

Nevada. As these people moved to new lands, their productivity increased, partly because of the enormous bounty of temperate-zone agriculture in North America, but also because industry and transportation (first canals and then railroads) benefited from the parallel migration of capital. The joint migration of labor and capital created a global economic elite with membership confined mainly to white ethnic Europeans. Non-Europeans—particularly black, Mexican, and Chinese laborers—were often used when domestic labor shortages suddenly appeared, particularly in the booming years between the 1870s through the 1920s. Thousands of Chinese workers were brought in as contract workers to help build American railroads in the 1870s. Many blacks continued to work southern fields as farmhands after the Civil War ended but left to fill industrial jobs in the North after World War I began. Mexicans took their places as agricultural workers. But it was inevitably white ethnic Europeans—from northern and western Europe—who rose through the job ranks to become America's nineteenth- and early twentieth-century managers and professionals because they had access to more schooling, family networks, and, ultimately, wage increases.

No one understood more clearly than the economist Adam Smith the enormous boost this movement of labor and capital gave to ordinary Europeans who derived their income from work. *The Wealth of Nations* was published in 1776, the year of the signing of the American Declaration of Independence. By then the migration of Europeans into new lands had been underway for some two hundred years, but the Industrial Revolution was still in its early stages. In his famous book, Smith compares the position of those who were earning their living from work in Britain with their counterparts in what were then still Britain's principal colonies in North America. Though industry was already on the move in Smith's day, the global economy was still primarily agricultural. For this reason, Smith's analysis of the differences in the wages paid for in Britain and America leans heavily on comparing the position of landlords and workers in the two countries. Nevertheless *The Wealth of Nations* is still an extremely lucid exposition of one of the basic forces now transforming the world economy in a way that is betraying those who earn their living from work in the industrialized world. Smith's pathbreaking idea was that the relative incomes (or rates of return) of landowners, capitalists, and workers depended on the relative scarcity of what they had to offer. In Britain, where labor was abundant, those who earned their living from work were under the shadow of an axe: a British economy where "rent and profit eat up wages," and "the two superior orders of people [landlords and capitalists] oppress the inferior one." Unlike in Britain, where capital had increasing control over a relatively large workforce that had to bid competitively for shelter and daily wages, in the "new colonies"

> the interest of the two superior orders obliges them to treat the inferior one with more generosity and humanity. Waste lands of the greatest natural fertility, are to be had for a trifle. The increase in the revenue the proprietor expects from their improvement constitutes his profit; which in these circumstances is commonly very great. But this great profit cannot be made without employing the labor of other people in clearing and cultivating the land; and the disproportion between the great extent of the land and the small number of people, . . . which commonly takes place in the new colonies, make it difficult for him to get this labor. He does not, therefore, dispute about wages, but is willing to employ labor at any price.

This relative scarcity of labor, identified so early by Adam Smith, became a pattern during long intervals of the history of capitalism. It has put its unique stamp on the economic history of the British and the other West European peoples—until the last quarter of the twentieth century, that is.

A NEW GLOBAL CAPITALISM

With the end of the cold war and the global triumph of capitalism, the patterns of migration to which Europeans and Americans have been accustomed suddenly came to an end. As the free market has catapulted around the globe since 1988, it has become increasingly clear that Western capital no longer needs to take well-educated ethnic Europeans along when it moves into the developing world. In fact, for both economic and cultural reasons, elite Western workers are often better left behind these days. There was, of course, already a thriving managerial class—particularly in East Asia—years before the cold war ended. But only since 1988 has capital become really freed up from its centuries-old contract with Western labor— particularly professional labor, which can now be found anywhere on the globe in a highly motivated, talented, less expensive form than back home. A combination of socialist-backed educational systems, hard-won professional track records made abroad, and a pent-up, frustrated middle class in many new market-centered economies has produced large populations of elites in developing countries, eager for good work, and Western capital is finding this workforce justly appealing. In fact, Western capital has begun to compete hard with capital from other parts of the world to buy members of this new workforce, in increasing numbers, and in places where economic growth is moving off the charts. The result: the end of a four-hundred-year symbiotic relationship between capital and labor in the developed world. For while the mobility of labor has diminished, the mobility of capital has taken a quantum jump.

The new, and largely unexpected, ability of capital to move across the seas without trailing either workers, managers, or administrators in its wake has stood conventional economics on its head. Economic analysts suffer from a not wholly justified nostalgia for the European age of imperialism that came to an end with the outbreak of World War I in 1914. Scholars in other fields no longer look at this time favorably: political historians, because national rivalries culminated in a pointless war; Marxist historians, because they see the period as a high point of the exploitation of labor; and emerging world intellectuals, because they see the time as a painful episode of colonialist oppression and economic degradation.

Conventional economists, in contrast, see in the late nineteenth and early twentieth centuries their holy grail: a benign combination of currency stability (produced by the gold standard), price stability (mainly the product of huge new supplies of food from the United States, Canada, Australia, New Zealand, and Argentina), and rapid economic growth (produced by the stream of invention and innovation that poured forth in the late stages of the Industrial Revolution). Transportation costs fell, too, during this time, and with the underdeveloped world firmly in the control of Europe, and to some extent the United States, international trade grew astonishingly, producing, at least for the West European peoples, remarkable results. In the United States the outcome was indeed magical. Between 1865 and 1914 the country enjoyed its most rapid growth ever: a 3.9 percent annual growth in real GNP between 1870 and 1913. The advance of real wages was even more impressive, with an annual growth rate of 4.1 percent. All this was accomplished without inflation. Between 1870 (by which time the impact of Civil War inflation had been erased) and 1914 wholesale prices in the United States increased by less than 1 percent per year.

Though there was a brief flurry of international investment in the 1920s, the years between the two great wars marked a retreat from dependence on the global economy. The gold standard was gradually abandoned, and countries pursued "beggar thy neighbor" trade policies imposing tariffs, quotas, and other trade restrictions in a futile attempt to shore up domestic employment. The consequences were disastrous in every conceivable way.

When World War II ended, the democratic states among the victorious Allies had a deep longing to restore a vibrant international economy. They established international institutions—the International Monetary Fund (IMF), the World Bank, and the General Agreements on Tariffs and Trade (GATT)—under whose auspices the world economy began to revive in the late 1940s and the early 1950s. This vigorous effort to reintegrate the global economy (outside the Communist bloc, at least) gathered strength in the ensuing decades, producing a smashing success, beyond the wildest dreams of the most ardent economic internationalists.

The sudden collapse of Communism raised the power of global capitalism to new heights. In a narrow sense, the victory was over a state, the USSR, which had represented a grotesque perversion of the appropriate role of government in economic life. But in a broader sense, the sudden and total collapse of the Soviet empire also damaged the case for milder forms of state intervention, ranging from democratic socialism to such gentle free market reforms as America's New Deal. The ideological losers in the cold war were not only the heirs of Karl Marx and V. I. Lenin, but also the traditions of such social democrats as Germany's Fredrich Ebert and Helmut Schmidt, and the legacies of American reformers like Franklin Delano Roosevelt and Lyndon B. Johnson who embraced free enterprise, at the same time believing that the people needed a measure of protection from its excesses.

By the end of the 1980s, the global reach of capitalism had evolved far beyond its scope during the age of imperialism. With sweeping speed the victorious ideology changed the political and economic structures of those countries, in both the developed and developing world, that had been hostile to the market. The ideology of the free market continues to triumph, even though opposition to its harshest manifestations is intensifying around the world. Russian Communists made a bid to return to power but were beaten back in the election of July 1996. In the mid-1990s many Western countries, from Portugal in 1995 to Italy in 1996, elected parties on the Left that promised they would modify the harshness of the market. Within the old Soviet bloc, Communists are returning to power, as in Hungary. Even in the United States, there seems to be some backing away from the extreme free market stance that appeared to be in ascendance with the election of Republican majorities in both the House and Senate in 1994 that were dedicated to rolling back the role of government in the economy.

But in an important sense, a movement should be judged not by the policies espoused by its own zealots but rather by the effect that it has on its opponents. And in this sense, the great capitalist wave seems to have lost little of its power. In the mid-1990s, eight years after the total triumph of capital, no significant political movement, no matter how leftist its roots, has sought to totally turn the clock back and readopt a socialist development model.

THE DIVERGENCE OF FORTUNES

The consequences of the victory in the cold war have been widely discussed in terms of their impact on economic events in the former Soviet Union, in China, Eastern Europe, and the rest of the developing world that were once client states for Communism. But the consequences for Western Europe and the United States have not yet been understood, possibly because they are so unexpected, but more likely because the new global economy differs so radically from the days of colonial imperialism and the gold standard, and even the post–World War II halcyon years. In the late nineteenth century, the Eurocentric world flourished while Third World Countries stagnated, and some, such as India and China, actually declined. In the new post–cold war global economy, what was the Third World has been energized while the developed world has languished. The expectations of many of those in the developed world who have hoped the new global economy will bring prosperity have been disappointed. And, for the first time in capitalist history, Western European elites have not automatically been enlisted to reap the rewards of globalization.

For the emerging nations of the world, the decision to abandon socialist planning has proven to be, in many instances, an act of liberation. Economic growth had, of course, been more rapid in the developing world than in the developed world throughout the 1980s as more and more countries adopted free-market models. But with the end of the cold war, the margin by which developing world

Table 2-1

Economic Growth in the Developing World: Annual Rate of Change in
Real Gross Domestic Product, 1979–1996

Country	1979–89	1989–94	1995	1996
India	5.90%	3.87%	6.2%	5.7%
China	9.78	10.63	10.5	9.7
South Korea	7.75	7.56	9.0	6.8
Hong Kong	7.18	5.25	4.6	4.2
Singapore	7.18	8.87	8.8	6.5
Taiwan	8.06	6.47	6.0	5.5
Malaysia	5.9	4.23	9.6	8.2
Philippines	2.06	1.53	4.8	6.5
Thailand	7.32	8.91	8.6	6.5
Argentina	−.75	6.26	−4.4	2.7
Brazil	2.86	1.25	4.2	2.8
Chile	3.3	6.64	8.6	6.7
Mexico	2.16	2.98	−6.2	4.0
Industrialized Economies	2.70	1.72	2.1	2.2
Developing Economies	4.05	5.15	5.1	5.6

Data: DRI/McGraw Hill

growth leads developed world growth widened considerably. Between 1989 and 1996, as Table 2-1 shows, the growth rate of the developing world has been over twice as fast as that of the industrialized world. In the decade ending in 1989, the developed world grew only one and one-half times as fast as the developed world.

The growth rate of some of the important countries of the developed world is almost miraculous. The numbers truly speak for themselves. Since 1989, China has grown over 10 percent per year. The growth of India has been more erratic, slipping back in the early 1990s from the growth rates of the 1980s, but then spurting again in 1995 and 1996.

Among the less populous countries of east Asia, Singapore grew by over 8 percent per year in the 1990s, and growth has also been strong in South Korea and Thailand. And in 1995 and 1996, the Philippines appear to have climbed aboard the Asian growth wagon.

In Latin America, Chile has enjoyed a growth rate that puts it in the same league as many developing countries in Asia. In contrast, the growth record of some other important countries, Argentina, Mexico, and Brazil among them, has been marked by roller-coaster ups and downs. But as Table 2-1 shows, the adoption of free-market development models has raised their average growth rates.

It is important to grasp the level of energy that the free market has unleashed in the developing world. When coupled with the availability of a technology that has had over two hundred years to improve since the industrial revolution, the pace of economic development has quickened. Britain needed nearly sixty years to double its output per person beginning in 1780. It took Japan thirty-four years starting in the 1880s, and in South Korea it took only eleven years after 1966. Commenting on this speedup of growth among countries that start down the path to industrialization, Jeffrey D. Sachs, a developmental economist at Harvard University, says, "At the turn of the century, stellar growth meant 4 percent a year. Now it means 10 percent plus." Stanford Business School professor Henry S. Rowan has noted the same huge growth potential for the developing world. "A process is underway," he says, "that promises within one generation to make most of the world's population a lot richer than it is today."

But numbers on economic growth that look so wonderful for the emerging world tell only half the story. The developed world has experienced a sharp slowdown in growth. Indeed, even before but especially since the end of the cold war wages have stagnated, and unemployment has emerged as a major problem throughout the industrial world. The slowdown in growth is evident in virtually every industrial country, as Table 2-2 shows, and the economic recovery that began in the United States in 1991 has been the weakest since World War II.

In the United States, the rate of growth is slower than at any time since the Great Depression. And despite repeated forecasts of recovery, the growth rates of key European economies, as projected by the International Monetary Fund, continue to be dismal. Throughout the 1990s Germany, the supposed industrial powerhouse of Europe and the linchpin of efforts to forge a single European currency, has had an economy characterized by painfully slow growth. Yet the IMF cut its estimate of 1996 German growth to 1 percent, down from its estimate in October 1995 of 2.9 percent growth, and at the same time unemployment rose above 11 percent. France, battered by many of the same forces afflicting Germany, is forecast to grow at only 1.3 percent in 1996; this forecast was shifted downward from an earlier prediction of 2.7 percent. For the fifteen-member European Union as

Table 2-2

Growth in Per Capita Gross Domestic Product
in the Developed World, 1979–1994

Country	1979–89	1989–94
Australia	1.8%	0.9%
Canada	1.8	−0.2
France	1.6	0.6
Germany	1.9	1.3
Italy	2.4	0.8
Japan	3.4	1.8
Netherlands	1.3	1.5
Sweden	1.8	−1.0
United Kingdom	2.2	0.4
United States	1.6	1.1
Average*	2.4%	n.a.

* Weighted by 1990 population excludes the U.S.

Data: Economic Policy Institute

a whole, the IMF projected that growth for 1996 would be 1.8 percent, down from the earlier prediction of 2.8 percent. And Japan is essentially suffering the same fate as the other industrialized nations, experiencing a bitter recession in the mid-1990s and able to mount only a weak and halting recovery after that.

THE BITTER DIVORCE

Just as there has always been a sharp difference in fortunes between the developed and the developing world, there has been a sharp split between the reward to capital and the rewards to work *within* the developed world. The new global economy has been exceptionally generous to those who own capital, but for those who earn their living from work this economy has brought stagnant incomes, job instability, and economic anxiety.

Location, location, location explains the divergence in the value of real estate. But mobility, mobility, mobility goes a long way toward explaining the divergence of fortunes within the developed world. In the old global economy, capital and labor moved together. In the new global economy, developed world capital globe-trots in a freewheeling way that was never before possible. Those who earn their living from work stay at home, sullen, confused, fending off ongoing assaults to their jobs and their quality of life. In today's economy work and capital no longer have anything like the mutual self-interest that was characteristic of the heady earlier episodes of capitalist global expansion. Once in a while, but not very often, Western labor momentarily takes the upper hand when wage rates rise a few pennies an hour. Often, in these brief intervals, all-controlling capital is likely to go bonkers, and Wall Street takes a sharp nosedive to show its disgust. In the summer of 1996, for example, stocks retreated on the news that inflation-adjusted wages made minute gains after twenty years of decline. It was only after the financial markets began to realize that the wage gains were marginal, even though the unemployment rate had dropped to below 5.5 percent, that stock prices stabilized. Wall Street was beginning to learn the major lesson of the new global capitalism: countries can achieve large increases in employment only if labor remains cheap by international standards. In fact, it is highly likely that the United States has managed to grow faster than either West Europe or Japan in the mid-1990s because its economic policies serve to strictly limit the gains that workers can make.

There are no such restraints on capital, and profits are soaring. Countries once hostile to foreign capital are suddenly throwing out the welcome mat, opening their arms to the relatively unhindered play of demand and supply. Countries that once viewed private securities markets as cesspools of exploitation and socially damaging speculation are calling in officials of great Western exchanges to help them set up securities markets of their own. Countries that before the end of 1988 placed faith in government ownership are suddenly undertaking privatization in vast waves, and they invite Western capital in to finance the transition. In Russia itself some 60 percent of all property had passed into private hands by 1994, and similar privatization movements are taking place across the globe.

This sudden thirst for capital in the developing world applies to both direct investment (the building of plants and the installation of equipment in offices as well as factories) and for portfolio investment (the purchase of stocks and bonds issued in the emerging world). Since the late 1980s both kinds of capital have been moving from the developed to the developing nations in rising amounts, again with ethnic European managers who historically organized and managed the new, profitable businesses retaining less and less of a connection to the capital.

Many statistics document the outflow of capital from the developed world in general, and the United States in particular, to the less developed countries. The best single measure is probably the net flow of global capital into the developing countries. That flow hovered around an annual level of $50 billion in the first half of the 1980s and then began to soar as the cold war wound down. By 1993 net capital flows into the developing world more than doubled to over $110 billion a year.

There is every reason to believe that the developing countries will continue to draw an increasing share of worldwide investment funds. According to estimates prepared by DRI/McGraw Hill, the share of world investment going into the developing world will climb rapidly over the next fifteen years. At present, investment in the developing world is running at about 55 percent of the rate of investment in the developed world; DRI/McGraw Hill's analysis indicates that figure will rise to 125 percent by the year 2010. If these projections hold true, the level of output in the developing world will equal the level of output of the first world by the year 2010. In 1996 the gross domestic product (GDP) of the developing world was about 55 percent of the combined product of the developed countries. By 2010, DRI/McGraw Hill estimates, it will reach 98 percent, or approximate parity.

Net investment flows into the developing world are of two kinds. The story of direct investment, spending mainly by the great multinational corporations for plant and equipment in foreign countries, has become a familiar one. The other flow, portfolio investment (money invested in the stocks and bonds of foreign companies), is less familiar. In the 1990s such investment has grown more quickly than direct investment. DRI/McGraw Hill data show that the flow of equity capital from the developed to the developing world has surged twentyfold since 1988—a lot of it coming from individual investors. By 2010 emerging economies are expected to account for 44 percent of world stock market capitalization, as compared with only 15 percent now, according to DRI/McGraw Hill estimates. Despite the worries in 1995 brought on by Mexican bankruptcies, more and more investment banks, brokers, and mutual fund companies are keeping track of foreign currencies, political situations, and little-known foreign companies, making it easier and more comfortable for the money managers in the developed world to put their investment money into the developing world. A growing number of people have begun putting their money into global mutual funds and American Depositary Receipts (ADRs), which took the American equity markets by storm in 1995. Backed by the stocks of foreign companies, these ADRs, about 1,200 of which were traded on Wall Street by 1996, have risen in value by more than 50 percent since 1990.

Investment in the emerging nations abroad has also been driven by privatization, one of the icons of the new global religion of capital. Prodded by the World Bank and the International Monetary Fund, thousands of government-run businesses across entire continents were swiftly privatized. The market began taking over in places as different as rural Morocco, where King Hassan laid off thousands of government workers in state-run industries, to the countries of Eastern Europe, where literally millions of workers lined up to sign over for cash vouchers they received when public companies they worked for became private. The money involved in privatizations was enormous. DRI/McGraw Hill estimated that the total value of global privatizations reached over $300 billion in 1994, and that it will reach over $900 billion by the year 2000.

The forces driving portfolio investment in the emerging world are intense, just as they were in late-nineteenth-century America, and they are no more likely to disappear than were the robber barons who created the great steel and railroad industries a hundred years ago. The great downsizings by corporations in the developed world in the 1990s only induce their employees, or in some cases their former employees, to invest good chunks of their own remaining capital abroad. These individual investors respond to the same incentives as their bosses, or former bosses: projections that show that the biggest money can be made developing infrastructure and industry in the Pacific Rim and Latin America. But it takes a while for them to realize, because of capital's "spin," that investing what little capital they have and then watching the financial markets on TV from their own living rooms will probably be the limit of their participation in this twenty-first-century global boom.

Capital, of course, flows two ways, and there has been an important offset to the capital outflow from the United States. As wages in Europe and Japan rose in the 1970s and 1980s, a wave of direct investment hit the United States. German, Japanese, and even British and French companies began to locate new plants in the United States, both to take advantage of the value created through the purchase and construction of assets made possible by the cheap dollar, and to benefit from low U.S. wages. By far the largest share of the new foreign investment went into the American South to take advantage not only of low wages, but also of a weak union movement whose ability to organize is hampered by right-to-work laws. And for Japan the construction of production facilities providing American jobs helped to reduce political fallout over their huge trade surpluses with the United States. Great new enclaves of foreign-owned companies have appeared in the United States. Especially in the South, Japanese companies such as Honda and Toyota and German companies including Mercedes Benz and BMW became the centers of whole new industrial complexes that attracted cheap labor from the countryside and from small towns where disguised unemployment had been a problem for many years.

This flow of investment into the United States was hailed by many economists as evidence that the globalization of production did no damage to American workers but, in fact, provided net benefits. And it is perfectly true that as long as U.S. wages remained relatively low, foreign investment would continue to flow into the United States.

But that is precisely the point. Now the United States is like any other country in that to attract foreign investment it too must keep labor costs down. It is highly significant that the opening of China and other parts of Asia to capitalist development brought with it a fundamental change in the international economic strategy of Japan. For the most part, that country no longer looks to the United States as a highly desirable place to locate new facilities. The "new" post–cold war Japan instead focuses its growth strategy on Asia rather than North America. It is simply cheaper to produce there; besides, Asian consumers are not yet maxed out on credit like Americans are. And, indeed, since the end of the cold war, both German and Japanese investment has been growing far faster in Asia and in Latin America than in the United States. Japanese direct investment in the United States has slowed almost to a trickle; the $12 billion for 1994 was a scant one third of the level of ten years earlier.

In the post–cold war world, the movement of workers has been almost exactly opposite to the movement of capital. The migration is not mainly of ethnic West Europeans abroad but of people from the emerging world into the developed countries. In the United States the trend is legal and illegal immigration from Latin America and an influx of both students and permanent workers from Asia. In Western Europe the peoples of North Africa seek menial jobs on the Continent, while highly skilled and educated emigrants from Eastern Europe doggedly search out positions in Britain, France, and Germany.

The impact of migrations from the developing world has been particularly powerful in the United States, a country historically reluctant to curb immigration. Since the end of the cold war, the best available statistics indicate that about 1 million immigrants, including 200,000 illegals, arrive each year. These new immigrants account for a growing share of total population growth; between 1980 and 1990 immigration made up 39 percent of the increase in population as compared to 33 percent in the 1970s and only 11 percent in the 1960s. Unlike past waves of immigrants, these new immigrants are mainly from Asia and Latin America. In 1991, for example, Asia provided 35 percent of immigrants, Mexico 24 percent, Central and South America 11 percent, and Europe only 12 percent.

This wave of new immigration has come at a time when the majority of the American-born population, whose history has long been one of constant movement, suddenly appears to have become very immobile. Data on internal migration is hard to come by, but the most basic measure of family mobility shows the immediate effect on families of the changed position of American labor. Census data noted that in 1980, 24 percent of all American families moved to new homes; by 1990, only 16 percent of American families moved. (Even more striking are statistics showing that those who moved in 1990 ended up closer to their original homes than those who moved in 1980. Over the span of time there was also a drastic decline in the proportion of the American population that moved to new states each year.) These numbers point to a dramatic decline in the mobility of the average American. If many people feel left at the starting gate, they have reason, and the psychology of being left behind is particularly difficult for members of a society accustomed to movement.

The divorce between labor and capital that has occurred in the developed world has not come to pass in the developing countries. Today people from developing countries who are educated in the American university system have an exciting new frontier to go to: their original homeland, and capital is going with them. Yet newly formed global corporations in the emerging world are also gradually beginning to locate facilities in the developed world. But there is an important sense in which there has been a role reversal between the developed world and the developing world in the relation between capital and work.

South Koreans provide a cutting-edge example of the change. Suk K. Lee, former chairman of the Korean-American Chamber of Commerce in New York, returned to South Korea a few years ago to start a cable television company with other New Yorkers of South Korean origin. Mr. Lee is far from alone. A Cornell University professor became chairman of the life sciences department at a South Korean university and staffed his entire department with Korean-American professors. A second-generation Korean American said he would probably move to South Korea after graduation from law school "because a Harvard law degree goes much further in South Korea than it does in America." Although there is a heavy inflow of immigrants from Asia as a whole, over the last five years the number of people in South Korea who received immigration visas to the United States has fallen by more than half, from about 25,500 in 1990 to about 10,800 in 1994, according to the Bureau of Consular Affairs of the U.S. State Department. The flow of people returning over the past four years, according to the South Korean Ministry of Foreign Affairs, has been between 5,000 and 6,500 per year, compared to only about 800 in 1980.

What explains the dramatic backflow? For the past decade, South Korea has enjoyed the kind of heavy capital investment that previously occurred only in the Eurocentric countries of the world, and Japan. As Korean companies have rapidly established manufacturing bases in China, Vietnam, and Indonesia, American and European companies have invested heavily in joint ventures with these Korean corporations. Hyundai Motor, Samsung Electronics, Daewoo, LG Electronics, and other Korean companies have all attracted vast amounts of Western capital. But Westerners are hardly moving to Seoul to run them.

LIFE AFTER SEPARATION

The post–cold war divorce between capital and labor has had ramifications that have spread throughout the developed world, and of the most surprising kind. We already know about blue-collar woes. But consider what has happened to middle-class managers. It is often argued that they are disappearing from the great multinationals because of new technology that eliminates their historic role as the organizers of the information that top executives need to make decisions. This is partly correct.

But what is also true is that the explosion of the global labor supply has greatly reduced the need for a cadre of middle managers to impose industrial discipline on lower-rung workers. Instead of relying on stern bosses to keep workers' toes to the line, companies now make it obvious that they can—and will—move their facilities elsewhere,

where emerging world workers, once shunned as not up to the job, are now every bit as able as, and certainly as willing as, developed world workers to perform the tasks of industry. This reality underlies all the talk of worker "empowerment" resulting from "teaming" and attempts at less hierarchical management. Though these changes are certainly in full flood, top management in the developed world also knows that it no longer needs its workers and makes then acutely aware that corporate/industrial flight to the developing world is entirely possible. Over the long run, such flight is a much cheaper approach than enforcing industrial discipline by paying middle management salaries at developed-nation levels.

Multinationals, once shunned as colonialists by the developing world, have been courted as never before since the Soviet empire dissolved. With all its problems, Russia has attracted nine thousand companies with foreign ties between 1991 and 1995. China, the most successful of all, attracted $34 billion in 1994 alone. The twenty largest multinational corporations already had high percentages of total assets invested abroad by 1993, according to the United Nations World Investment report of 1995. Royal Dutch Shell had just under $70 billion of its $100.8 billion total invested internationally; Exxon had $47.4 billion of $84.1 billion; IBM had $44.1 billion of its $81.1 billion total; and General Motors had just under $37 billion of its $167.4 billion total capital assets. And this is only the beginning. Most analysts expect this capital shift to continue. While it was true that developing nations represent huge markets for Western firms, it is also true that a lot of these goods were already being produced and marketed for Coca Cola, Pepsico, Motorola, Eastman Kodak, and so forth, by the population pools that would be consuming them—those in the developing world.

In addition, an increasing amount of available global capital is now being controlled by emerging market multinational companies, which are growing at a stunning rate. Direct investment outflows from developing countries were 5 percent of the world total from 1980 to 1984, 10 percent from 1990 to 1994, and 15 percent in 1994, according to the UN World Investment Report. The rapid growth of the Asian "tigers" and their own indigenous corporations has become a model for many nations. After generations of economic frustrations, the middle and upper classes of the new nations following the original tigers are not about to introduce what they see as affirmative action for Western European and American job candidates. "What is usual," says one Asian expert, "is for an American or European to come into an office for a year or so, and then, after he has shared his knowledge, be told discreetly that his services are no longer required. People all over Asia really want to run their own shows these days. They've waited for a long time."

Long-term trends portend escalating troubles for upper-echelon Western workers, and at the very least a continued drag on their wages. A World Bank study predicts that the export of services by the developing world will exceed its export of goods by the year 2010. Innovation in telecommunications has reduced the cost of shipping data and professional services directly into the huge markets of the developed world, and this has had a sharply negative effect on the earnings of many U.S. professionals. Those who forecast the future of technology, such as the Semiconductor Association and the Internet Society, suggest that the computer revolution is only beginning to reduce the cost of data transmission, which is making the export of such jobs possible.

Optimists continue to point to the large number of high-tech companies and consultants sprouting up along America's coasts, in California and in Washington, along with a newly emerging Boston hub. They point as well to the Rochester, New York, Eastman Kodak Company, with its various spin-offs, a reenergized IBM, and vital, ongoing global forces in the American heartland, such as Motorola. These companies do, in fact, along with hundreds of new biotechnology companies spread out around the country, make up more than their share of the backbone of America's future. But as a whole, even high-tech industry will continue to look abroad. "We don't think of ourselves as an American company," says a top Hewlett-Packard executive. "We don't have a corporate policy of moving in or out of the United States. We consider each business situation separately." Already 40 percent of Hewlett-Packard's workforce and 54 percent of its sales are outside the United States. Employees in Eastman Kodak's Rochester headquarters have been through some rough times over the last few years, and many are happy just to have kept their jobs. At the same time, Kodak in China has grown from nine employees in 1994 to more than two hundred by mid-1996. By the end of 1996 Kodak China will have eight offices and nearly three hundred employees. Kodak China manager John Tseng's goal is to overtake competitor Fuji within two years.

An Intel executive points out, "I see the same level of skills in Malaysia as in the U.S., even up to Ph.D.'s. And if you can get the job done cheaper elsewhere, you're at a disadvantage if you don't." A nine-year-old California company, Conner Peripherals, a manufacturer of disk drives listed on the New York Stock Exchange and considered a leader among the newer high-tech companies, has almost completely leapfrogged U.S. employment during its quick growth. It opened a plant in Singapore, then later a lower-cost one in Malaysia—now the company's largest—and most recently one in China. Currently, 90 percent of Conner's production and 75 percent of its 11,400 employees are located outside the United States. Aluminum Co. of America, or Alcoa, has remade itself into a globally integrated giant over the last ten years. "We're not geographically bound, and that includes the Americans," says sixty-one-year-old Paul O'Neill, chairman and chief executive officer, responsible for the overhaul. In a recent list of two hundred people deemed ready for senior positions, there is no country name listed next to the employee name, or any indication of where they work in Alcoa's international operation. "It just says this is a list of people who are ready," says a top operating officer.

We would love to share the optimism that still characterizes much economic debate. Most economists readily grant that the developing world will grow more rapidly than the already industrialized countries. As economies mature, they say, economic slowdown comes with the territory. They go on to argue that even though First World growth will slump compared to emerging world growth, the industrial countries will grow faster than if what was the Third World were still stagnant. We may be that lucky. But the proposition that rapid growth in one country or one part of the world benefits everyone else could turn out to be the exact opposite of the truth.

CHAPTER 3

The New Leviathan: The Global Labor Pool

BABY BOOMERS. GENERATION X. THE DEMOGRAPHIC FORCES that will gradually, but relentlessly, attack their security are already visible. It is not merely a matter of the sheer *number* of people on the planet. It is the vast *labor pool* that global capitalism has tapped into that is the new leviathan. As capital has become more mobile in the wake of the dissolution of the Soviet empire, the number of workers ready and anxious to find work in the new global market has exploded. The effect, which is barely being felt so far, and which will get worse, is to greatly weaken the competitive position of those who earn their living from work in the advanced countries.

The magnitude of the global increase in workers available for global market production since the end of the cold war has yet to sink in, either in the intellectual community or among average Americans. The triumph of capitalism has brought about historically great demographic changes, fully comparable, but opposite in effect, to the last great and sudden series of events that changed the demographic fortunes of the white, West European working class: the age of discovery that followed the voyage of Columbus in 1492. And like that great transformation, it has radical consequences for the relations between work and capital.

The serious nature of the decline in the demographic position of Western workers is easy to grasp. In 1989, 248 million Americans were part of a select industrial-world population of 900 million fully participating in a free global marketplace—some 23 percent of the world's population. Each American was in effect competing with 2.8 people in the industrial world.

The end of the cold war radically increased the number of competitors. The year 1994 is the latest year for which reasonably

Table 3-1

The Global Middle Class

Key Regions	Population (in Millions)	% Middle Class	Middle Class Population
United States and Canada	279	83	232
Western Europe	378	78	295
Eastern Europe	347	69	239
Latin America	447	19	85
Middle East	259	13	34
Far East	1,812	31	562
South Asia	1,130	8	90
Africa	664	5	33
World Total	5,316	29	1,570

Data: DRI/McGraw Hill. Data are for 1990.

comprehensive data on world population are available. By that time, when the free market had penetrated all but the most remote and obdurately communist parts of the world, 260 million Americans faced potential competition from 5.6 billion people around the globe—essentially each American competing with about 21 people.

For many members of the managerial classes since the 1950s in the United States, Europe, and Japan, theirs had been a more than comfortable existence. Each member of the American middle class faced competition from 2.7 members of the middle class in the industrial world. Advanced world elite workers, by virtue of their limited numbers, were able to almost monopolize the rewards of four hundred years of capitalism.

But with the free market suddenly sweeping the globe after the end of the cold war, workers from the developed world are now facing competition in a much more intense, explosive way from middle-class mind workers around the world (Table 3-1). American multinationals, which are doing immensely well in the new post-cold war period, are hiring considerable numbers of these educated workers abroad in joint venture companies and through independent contracting, particularly in Asia. In fact, it is very difficult to determine how many such hirings there have been, since much of this information is not public knowledge.

Only after the collapse of the Soviet Union did those populous Asian countries that were not part of the original group of economic "tigers"—China, Indonesia, Malaysia, Vietnam, and India—begin changing at dizzying speeds. China's retreat from Communism and early attempts at privatization actually began in 1978 and evolved gradually under Deng Xiaoping's guidance. But it wasn't until the early 1990s that Westerners, along with the overseas Chinese, began pouring large amounts of money into China with a growing confidence that the promarket revolution would prove permanent, and, eventually, over a billion Chinese would enter the promarket economy. These newcomers would be tapped as both the world's largest new consumer market and capitalism's newest vast and talented labor force.

The other untapped Goliath of Asia, India, had an economy that had been badly damaged by its relationship with its former political ally the Soviet Union. Indian goods remained globally uncompetitive because of India's undemanding but claustrophobic Soviet customer. As a result, many Indian businessmen simply failed to improve their products because there was no real need. When the Soviet collapse came, expensive, imported capital equipment was needed to quickly modernize Indian production, so that India could attract new customers. The cost of this overhaul hit India hard, but it was partially met by a reform probusiness government, which came into power in 1991, headed by Narasimha Rao. Rao moved quickly—by Indian standards—to begin privatizing and reenergizing Indian industry. Multimillion-dollar deals were eventually closed with Western conglomerates such as General Electric and Enron. With these changes, 920 million Indians slowly began to enter the global economy, prompting some analysts to predict that despite India's formidable problems, it too could have its own golden age, similar to that of the United States forty years earlier.

On the other side of the globe, the Pinochet dictatorship, despite its many grotesque human rights violations, had turned Chile into a highly successful export-oriented economy (with a deeply weakened labor movement)—creating the perfect setup for the cold war wind-down. Following Chile's lead, its neighbors—Argentina, Peru, Brazil, and Venezuela—also adopted aggressive promarket reforms while working hard to increase their visibility as high-profile post-cold war global players.

In all, the size of the globally competitive population rose from under 1 billion to over 5 billion in 1994, and the size of the globally competitive world middle class grew from about 725 million to a figure something over 1.2 billion. These significant leaps in numbers have a certain science fiction quality and come to signify qualitative change. Around the world, indigenous well-educated managerial classes—the likes of which the world has never seen before—have aggressively begun making their presence felt as promarket reforms have been put in place, changing the demographics of the professional labor force forever.

IF CITIBANK MOVES ABROAD, ARE OTHERS FAR BEHIND?

This new global labor force is seeking jobs in a much-changed business world. Innovative spin-offs of Western corporations compete everywhere with indigenous and Japanese multinational companies. It was the Americans who understood instinctively—after long years of grappling (often unhappily) with affirmative-action programs back home—that to be effective, they needed to hire those who best understood the cultures in which American companies were trying to compete. John S. Reed, chairman and chief executive of Citibank, has gambled that Citibank's future in many ways, lies abroad, in Asia and, increasingly, in South America. In contrast, Citibank began to see its domestic share of the credit card market, by far its most profitable business, shrink from 25.6 percent in 1994 to 22.1 percent in 1995. Citibank's biggest breakthroughs in the 1990s have been in those countries where the banking industry is least developed, such as India, Pakistan, Indonesia, and the Philippines. The consumer business in emerging markets, while accounting for only 12 percent of Citicorp's assets, brought in 22 percent of its operating profits in 1995, and John S. Reed is gambling that these profits will grow even faster in the years to come.

Although Citibank had a presence in India before the end of the cold war, it wasn't until the early 1990s that the bank began making a push to become that country's largest foreign banker, setting up branches throughout the country, the likes of which had never been seen before on that subcontinent. Citibank offered Indians installment credit for the first time to buy cars at the same time that Japan's automakers were introducing cheaper cars in India, around 1993. India's increasing middle class is all the more appealing because Citibank is able to charge higher interest rates in India and several other Asian markets—between 24 to 40 percent annually—because for customers there the only alternative, at this point, is to go to local loan sharks who charge even higher rates.

The American bank immediately began hiring well-educated local talent to manage its operations—many of whom are constantly being poached by other foreign companies or local Indian operations trying to expand beyond their local base. By the mid-1990s some rumors circulated that Citibank would eventually move its headquarters to Asia, perhaps even Bombay. The company also set up a top tier of Indians— along with executives from such countries as Argentina and Pakistan—as senior management back in New York, as part of its plan to tap the mushrooming earning power of the emerging world's middle class.

But Asia, although a major factor in Citibank's plans, is far from its only international growth center. Recently it hired two hundred Bahrainis to run an Islamic bank, Citi Islamic Investment Bank, whose lending practices would conform to Islamic religious principles. The first Western institution to inaugurate such a bank in the Persian Gulf region, Citibank needs to find a way to become profitable in the region while conforming to Islamic law, which forbids the charging of interest. (Islamic banks, unlike their Western counterparts, make money by financing trade and construction projects in partnership with their depositors. Both the bank and its depositors traditionally share in any profits or losses.) By adapting to Islamic customs and hiring Islamic talent, Citibank is able to compete in the rapidly growing Arab banking network, which over the last decade has managed to control more than $150 billion in assets worldwide, and which has an estimated growth rate of about 15 percent a year.

In the same week in July 1996 that Citibank hired the Bahrainis for the Citi Islamic Investment Bank, Smith Barney created a joint venture with a Korean bank to form a new brokerage and underwriting company based in Seoul, with an initial capitalization of $62 million, to be managed largely by Korean employees. These are just two examples of Western capital moving overseas, separate from Western labor. But both instances are harbingers of what will happen more and more in the twenty-first century, as elite workers in the developing world reap the rewards of high economic growth in their nations, fueled by both indigenous and, importantly, Western capital.

These days, thanks to advances in data communications, it is almost instantly possible to farm out any kind of work—engineering, architecture, banking, even medicine—and get daily feedback from the most highly skilled practitioners in every field, around the world (in Chapter 5 we show how this is already happening in Bangalore, India). Much has been made of the large number of high-paying jobs recently created in the United States as a result of advances in computer capabilities, but a high percentage of them are in business services and are vulnerable. In a few brief years, such jobs will easily be duplicated, at much lower prices, by individual contractors—accountants, data processors, graphic artists, brokers—anywhere in the world.

As the professional jobs heretofore held by Westerners have begun to move overseas, there is at least one short-term economic victory. Many Western manufacturing industries have once again become competitive globally, and factories are already moving back to hire the best skilled workers that can be found at competitive wages. But for the elite workers in the West, the shock of losing their preeminence has yet to fully hit. They have never found themselves in this place before, and their reaction so far is one of denial: they want to go on believing that, because of their advanced skills, they can carry on their lives in a secure state. Yet a growing minority of professionals is beginning to realize the magnitude of the threat posed by the brave new world of capital triumphant—the significance of the new global demographic mix, buoyed and supported with revolutionary technologies, such as the Internet, that vastly reduce the hiring barriers once posed by distance. These two developments are just on the verge of creating a truly international labor market, featuring head-on competition for wages and skill, even for cognitive elites.

The industrial world has had trouble enough dealing with the appearance of much smaller new labor forces on the scene, and much smaller middle classes, in the 1960s, 1970s, and early 1980s. With the reintegration of Japan into the world economy in the late 1960s and 1970s, workers of the developed world had fits when jobs were lost to the Japanese in industry after industry, first in shipbuilding, then in photographic equipment, then in autos, and, finally, home electronics and machine tools. And Japan had a population of only a little over 100 million people! The other Asian countries now becoming substantially integrated into the global market economy also have relatively modest populations and, like Japan, are located on the periphery of the Asian land mass. Like the industries of Japan, those of South Korea with 44 million, Taiwan with 21 million, Singapore with 3 million, and Hong Kong with 6 million people have already displaced millions of workers in the developed world. Yet the East Asian economic miracle is only a small foretaste of what, demographically, is coming.

THE GROWING MIDDLE-CLASS WORKFORCE IN THE DEVELOPING WORLD

Their political churning and angst have been much publicized, but China and India, have, nevertheless, begun their move to global center stage, with Russia waiting in the wings. In the seven short years since the end of the cold war, by 1995 the United States was already running a whopping $30 billion trade deficit with China, though only one Chinese province, Guangdong in southern China, has begun the climb to developed-world status. In India only about 8 percent of the population, or 70 million people, had achieved middle-class status by 1995. The middle class was also small in Indonesia with 26 million people; Malaysia had 1.4 million; and the Philippines had 5.5 million. In the former Eastern bloc countries, which have many well-educated workers, the proportion who have achieved middle-class status is much higher—about 20 percent of the population of 347 million.

Based on these current numbers alone, the precariousness of the competitive position of American workers is considerable. Projecting ahead, it gets much worse. Between 1996 and 2025 the world's population is expected to grow at about 1.7 percent per year, with 95 percent of the growth taking place in the developing world. Such disproportionate growth will produce startling changes in the global distribution of population. The growth rate of Europe's population is projected at about .22 percent per year; that of the United States is projected at about .32 percent. By contrast, population growth will be 3 percent per year in Africa, 2.4 percent in Asia, and about 2.2 percent in Latin America.

Another important as an indicator of potential competition for U.S. labor—both blue collar and managerial—is the projected growth of *urban populations* in the developing world. Urban populations are far more likely to attend university and to enter the global workforce than are rural populations. At the same time there is no denying the overwhelming poverty in many cities in the developing world. But the energy, the excitement, the lure of new careers and new money are also there for anyone to see in the pubs of Bangalore or the real estate offices in Shanghai. With their enormous populations—8 million in Shanghai, 3.3 million in Bangalore, 8.3 million in Mexico City, 3.8 million in Jakarta—the eternal question of "how to make it" in these cities gives them a verve, a panache that is striking in its post-cold war zeal.

The workforces in these cities will grow rapidly. Over the next quarter century, the proportion of people in China, India, and Latin America who will live in cities is likely to increase from about 30 percent to an average of 50 percent. This projection alone implies an increase in the urban population of the emerging world from about 1.4 billion today to 4.1 billion by 2025. By then the metropolitan population of Mexico City will be an estimated 24.4 million; of São Paulo, 23.6 million; Bombay, 15.4 million; and Shanghai 14.7 million.

Westerners are often tempted to write off the great urban centers of the developing world as almost beyond hope. It is true enough that there are many poor in these cities, that the cities are polluted, and that their urban infrastructures are grossly inadequate. But these strained metropolises are the locus of a new workforce that is adept at production in ways previously reserved for workers in the developed world. The vitality of these cities, in fact, should make the existing business capitals of the industrial world nervous. Since real estate prices can often provide the best index to what cities or regions of the world economy are becoming hot, let's compare prices in large cities in the developing world to their counterparts in the developed world. As of 1996 the cost per square foot of office space was far higher in Bombay and Shanghai than in New York, London, Zurich, Frankfurt, or even Tokyo. It is these positive indicators that will count in the long run. By 2025 the huge problems of these cities will likely be easier to solve because city resources will be bolstered by rapidly growing tax bases. New York, London, and even Tokyo may not be so lucky.

Taipei, the capital of Taiwan, has already evolved as an important Asian model for this kind of change. In *Cities and the Wealth of Nations,* architect and critic Jane Jacobs describes the economic transformation of Taiwan from a country that had existed, like Puerto Rico, on transplanted industries from the West because labor could be bought cheap. The Taiwanese realized at some point that "if our cheap labor can be put to use by foreigners, we should be able to put it to use for ourselves." With the capital city playing a major role as a center for local growth, the Taiwanese used the skills and experiences they had learned from working in transplant factories, together with indigenous capital put up by local investors to build light industry. As Jacobs points out, "[A]s new niches opened up, Taipei was developing a real foundation for symbiotic and versatile production on its own behalf. The networks of symbiotic enterprises became capable not only of supplying one another, and exporters as well, but also of replacing with their own production some of the producers' goods being imported, as well as some consumers' goods." In varying ways, Taiwan's experience, with Taipei as an economic linchpin, is now being replicated around the world. Bombay, despite all its horrors, is busy expanding as a regional financial and entertainment hub. Santiago serves as a center for networking Chile's international food export business. Shanghai is setting itself up to be one of the great reborn cities of the world in finance and manufacturing. The vitality of these bustling "world cities" comes from the upbeat members of their middle class, hustling hard to be at the center of twenty-first-century capitalism.

LESS ROOM AT THE TOP

Given the energy of the emerging world metropolises, as international competition evolves, the elite workers of the industrial world will face a serious threat. By "elite workers" we mean well-educated middle-class workers (in some places in this book referred to as the "cognitive elite," or the top 20 percent of the workforce). Breakthroughs in digitization and computer technology have combined with the new worldwide labor force to create a daunting challenge to these professional workers. Harley Shaiken, professor of labor and technology at the University of California at Berkeley, says, "In the 1970s capital intensive, highly automated production seemed to be linked to industrial economies like the United States, and the jobs that went off-shore were low-tech, low-productivity jobs like sewing blue jeans and assembling toys." Now, says Shaiken, "with computers, telecommunications and new forms of cheap transport, highly advanced production has been successfully transplanted to third world countries."

Western elite workers—perceived by many intellectuals as an "overclass" immune from international competition—have so far been the main beneficiaries of the "knowledge revolution." The popular view that the top rungs of the occupation ladder in the advanced industrial countries have been strengthened rather than weakened by the spread of the global market is understandable. It is indeed this class—the educated, skilled, well-fed, healthy, hardworking, prosperous professional and managerial workers—that has been the main beneficiary of modern capitalism. This class created the Industrial Revolution in Britain, was responsible for the emergence of the great nineteenth-century industries of Germany, and created modern mass production and management practices in the United States. The only serious competition it has faced so far has come from Japan, where the creation of a Western-style economy has been that country's lasting achievement of this century.

The Western economic elite has always been a small class and continues so to this day. In the United States the number of workers defined as upper echelon was about 29 million in mid-1995, or about 23.2 percent of the total labor force of 132 million. These are workers defined by the U.S. Census Bureau as professional, technical, and kindred workers (18.4 million) or as managers, officials, and proprietors (10.5 million). The view that this small and privileged class will retain its power and income is naive. On the contrary, the erosion of the dominant position of these Western elite workers is likely to be the most important historical fact of the next half-century: their enameled rice bowls are about to be broken by a surge of competition from the developing world.

Although the number of elite "knowledge workers" in the emerging world is still a tiny proportion of the labor force in those countries, it is growing extremely rapidly. The attitude, and qualifications, of this class is exemplified by an eighteen-year-old economics student from Beijing who recently won a full scholarship to Vanderbilt University and who says earnestly, "I feel very lucky, my English score was not very high in the SAT's, but I scored an almost perfect score on the math section. A lot of the math on the test we had in elementary school. The hardest part for me was remembering back that far." If all goes well, this student expects to return to Beijing with an MBA in five years to work for a large Chinese corporation and eventually start her own business. Ironically, a tough Communist upbringing has produced a capitalist psyche with a no-holds-barred attitude toward competition—no matter what the personal cost. "My mother had three abortions before she decided to have me. Then she left for the United States to study at Columbia for five years on her own. I was brought up by my father and his mother. I want to do even more than my mother has."

The DRI/McGraw Hill study of the global middle and upper class clearly shows why upper-echelon Americans and Canadians will come under enormous pressure as we showed in Table 3-1. It compares the demographic status of the U.S. and Canadian middle class with that of the middle class in other parts of the world. As this decade opened, some 83 percent of the American population belongs to the middle class. By comparison, only 11 percent of the population, or 199 million people, in the Far East, which includes China, were middle class. The figures for the South Asia region (including India) are 8 percent and 90 million people respectively.

Forecasts of the size of the world middle class are of course problematic. But on conservative estimates its size is likely to triple by 2025. On this assumption, a ballpark number for the world middle class population by 2025 would be about 3.7 billion. Each member of the American middle class would then be competing with 15 people in the world middle class as compared to about 5 today. At that point the American middle class will no longer seem such a special repository of knowledge and skill. It will face competition on a scale it is not prepared to meet given its charmed history of having almost exclusive access to the skills needed to apply new scientific and organizational knowledge to production. In the new global scene, members of the professional and managerial classes of the industrial countries will face displacement on the same scale as that experienced by manufacturing workers in the 1980s and 1990s. And on any realistic assumptions about population growth, the assault by waves of skilled new workers from the emerging world on the elite workers of the industrial world has barely begun.

Indeed, history will show that the position of the U.S. workforce elite is beginning to decline at just the moment when its power is being celebrated on both the Left and the Right. The pay of college-educated men, for example, outpaced inflation in the 1980s. But thus far in the 1990s it has *fallen* and remains 1 percent below its 1989 level, according to an analysis of the U.S. Bureau of Labor Statistics data. A host of professions that thrived in the 1980s are now treading water, according to a survey by Robert Half Associates, a job placement firm. In nearly 80 percent of the 142 professions that the Half organization surveys in accounting, information systems, and commercial banking, workers received below inflation raises in 1995, indicating that the real income of these workers is falling. New college graduates are beginning to experience something similar. Since 1991 starting salaries have risen more slowly than the rate of inflation for most of the seventy college majors tracked by the National Association of Colleges and Employers, which surveys some 350 college job placement centers each year. For the economy as a whole, male college graduates with one to five years of experience earned 9.5 percent less in 1995 than in 1989. Their female counterparts were earning 7.7 percent less in 1995 than in 1989.

Why is this erosion taking place? The cutting edge of the world information age has been in the United States, led by its most creative scientists, engineers, and entrepreneurs. And each successive new wave appears from sources, again, mainly in the United States, as television, telecommunications, phone systems, cable, and biomedical companies all bump each other around trying to figure out what will be the next great "bundling" of global services. Networked into all of these giants, of course, are the "whiz kid" companies that pioneer each new layer of technological products, which are then drawn into this whirlpool of cyberactivity. A high percentage of the creative talent in these innovative businesses comes from the United States, often from centers of technological creativity such as Stanford, MIT, Carnegie-Mellon, the North Carolina Research Triangle, and a few others. One would think that these twenty-first-century scientists and mathematicians would produce more than enough jobs to help employ many educated workers in the United States.

But anywhere you go in Asia nowadays—China, India, Taiwan, or Singapore—you can find highly skilled workers designing interactive CD-ROM programs, producing programs that map three-dimensional images to diagnose brain disorders, designing digital answering machines or interactive computers for children. The "back-end" work of product development—the painstaking job of turning a conceptual design into blueprints, computer code, or working models, and testing the final product—is increasingly being done in Asia these days. Citibank taps local skills in India, Hong Kong, Australia, and Singapore to manage data and develop products for its global financial services. Hewlett-Packard encourages each of its manufacturing sites around the world to become the global base for its product. Penang, Malaysia, has become a global center for many components used in HP's microwave products and has taken over responsibility for computer hard-disk drives from Palo Alto. More and more, specially trained Filipino accountants do much of the grunt work in preparing tax returns for multinational firms. All this overseas work is easily transferred via satellite links, computers, and e-mail.

In fact, pioneers such as Citibank and Hewlett-Packard are only the beginning of the trend toward corporate "outsourcing" (or contracting outside of the company) of highly skilled labor. Well-paying back-end jobs such as software designers, draftsmen, librarians, and mechanical engineers, in which many Americans make their livings are barely in the first stages of being transported globally. Most companies haven't yet figured out how to be as innovative as Citibank and Hewlett-Packard. As they do, many more high-skill jobs will be transported abroad. In Bangalore, trained medical transcriptionists with university degrees decipher American medical jargon and transmit transcripts overnight to Virginia hospitals, which need the work to be highly accurate and done quickly in order to discharge patients. The Bangaloreans get paid roughly one tenth the $25,000 average salary of full-time medical transcriptionists in the United States. And some in the large southern Indian medical community are currently hard at work trying to figure out how to use the same high-speed data lines to create more upscale medical jobs for their increasing population of university graduates. More and more, high-skilled cyberspace jobs will also be done throughout Latin America as well as in Asia. In addition, those involved in this first wave of cyberspace skilled labor are working very hard to move up from "back-end" production jobs to the creative, frontline jobs, many of which have been monopolized, in the last generation, by American "whiz kids" and foreign "whiz kids" working in the United States.

WILL WAGE "CONVERGENCE" SAVE US?

Most economists deny that competition with low-wage workers abroad is a problem for Americans. They tend to view calmly the movement of capital into low-wage areas and expect its effects, in the end, to be benign. Their argument, essentially, is that the wage advantages that make newly industrializing areas effective competitors with the established countries of the world will disappear over time. And it is certainly true that these earnings differentials have had a tendency to diminish in the past. As capital moves to low-wage areas, the employment rate tends to rise, and wages are pushed up. Certainly wages in many foreign countries have been rising faster than in the United States, reducing the gap between the cost of labor in developing countries and American labor and the gap between the prices of goods in developing countries and in the United States.

Economists see the process by which earnings in less developed areas catch up with wages in the advanced countries as an aspect of *convergence.* In this view over time the advantage that low-wage countries have over high-wage countries erodes. As capital moves into the less developed countries, increasing productivity there, exports to the developed world rise, generating more demand for work in the once disadvantaged areas, and increasing wages there. In an environment of reasonably free trade, the process of convergence proceeds to a point where wages in the developing world catch up with wages in the developed countries.

Particularly reassuring to many economists is the experience of the United States in its trade with Western Europe and Japan after those areas began their post–World War II reconstruction. Wages were far lower in those countries than in the United States at the time, far lower, indeed. But by the beginning of the 1990s, wages in Japan and Europe had caught up with American wages, and now wages are higher in those countries than they are in the United States. And although they have yet to equal wages in America, wages in many of the other countries in Asia are catching up.

Don't worry, say most economists. In their view, wages in the other emerging countries will catch up with those of the United States too, and there is nothing wrong with capital moving abroad because rising prosperity in the emerging world will also increase demand for U.S. goods and services, thereby increasing American production, employment, and productivity. We do not dispute the first tenet of this argument: the probability is that rising wages and increased demand for American products in the developing world will, in the long run, bring *some* benefits to American workers. We also join conventional economists in hailing the sharp growth in American exports of both capital goods and consumer products to the developing nations, particularly those nations that are growing rapidly.

Nonetheless, we do not believe that these developments will bring the benefits to the United States that many economists claim they will. The full impact of rapid growth abroad on jobs and incomes in the United States cannot be measured in terms of the growth of U.S. exports; rather it should be gauged by what happens to the margin between the quantity of goods that the United States exports and the quantity of goods that the nation imports. And by both measures that margin, the balance of trade, has been deteriorating because American imports are growing faster than American exports. While American industry is becoming more competitive in some product lines, it is losing competitive advantage for products that have an even greater total value. The widely celebrated American export boom is impressive, but the less celebrated import boom is more telling. Between 1990 and 1996 the margin by which U.S. imports exceeded U.S. exports was almost $1 billion. And because U.S. imports have been growing faster than U.S. exports, it is likely that the international position of American workers is not improving but deteriorating. That is a major reason why there is no end in sight to wage stagnation in the United States and in other industrial countries.

The optimistic view of America's ability to prosper in the wake of the new demographic revolution is, in our view, anchored in the past.

The demographics of a world where the growth of the free market labor force is in hyperdrive are far different from those during the cold war, before the free market held unquestioned sway. Because of the seismic impact of the rapid worldwide spread of available skilled labor, the process by which wages will become equalized around the world is almost certain to progress extremely slowly. It is only among the economic tigers on the periphery of Asia and in one province in southern China (Guangdong), and elsewhere just among select members of the middle class, that the process of wage convergence has advanced with any degree of speed. Yet developments in these areas are, as we have seen, but harbingers of what is about to happen in mainland Asia, in Latin America, and in the old Soviet empire. There are several military analogies for the challenge facing American workers, trying to keep their wages up: consider what the French army faced when Napoleon tried to conquer Russia, what the Germans faced when they tried to subdue the USSR, or what Japan confronted when it tried to conquer China. Each of these armies could win battle after battle, but when the clashes were over, they still faced wave after wave of fresh troops. Similarly, industrial world workers may succeed in winning battles with particular countries, but after those battles are over they still face new assaults from wave after wave of workers who will be entering the new market economy.

There should be no mistaking where the logic of a totally free, totally integrated world labor market leads. Think of the process of arbitrage, the dynamic by which values are equalized in markets throughout the world, forcing the rate at which the dollar trades for, say, the yen to be the same in London as it is in Frankfurt, the same in New York as in Shanghai, the same in Jakarta as in Guangdong Province. In a similar fashion, the labor market will be equalized so that the same rate is paid for the same kind of work in Manila as in Minneapolis, in New Delhi as in New York, in Seoul as in Cincinnati. The very same forces that pit the exchange rate of the dollar against other currencies will eventually guarantee that a programmer earns no more in Boston than in Bangalore, a certified public accountant no more in Baltimore than in Beijing, or an architect no more in New York City than in Kuala Lumpur.

Nor is there any way for those in the industrialized world who earn their living from work to really escape the assault of the market. On the eve of a fight with a skilled defensive boxer, Tony Pastor, the great heavyweight champion Joe Louis once said, "He can run, but he can't hide." And so it is with all those who earn their living from work. There is no way for them to hide from the relentless market process, except by producing idiosyncratic work—usually involving creativity—that no one else seems able to duplicate easily. It should not be imagined that one can avoid the impact of foreign competition by choosing to work in an industry in which imports do not provide direct competition. No one will commute from Penang, Malaysia, to take a job flipping hamburgers at a McDonald's in Peoria, Illinois, nor will casino dealers in Reno face competition from would-be dealers in Rangoon. But such jobs and wages in the United States depend on hamburger joints and casinos having a ready supply of customers, and in turn the willingness of customers to spend money depends on the wages that they, their neighbors, and their countrymen can earn.

Competition from workers abroad will affect those who earn their living from work, no matter what their occupation. The wages in those industries that are successful in the global economy, in turn, will call the tune, and wages in virtually every labor market will follow that piper. International wage competition affects income levels in all occupations, and it is not a force from which anyone can easily hide, no matter how he or she may earn his or her living.

IS THE IMPACT OF THE NEW TECHNOLOGY OVERRATED?

Our view that the new demographics of the world labor force and the divorce between capital and labor are the defining characteristics of the new global capitalism is not the conventional view today. Most analysts argue, instead, that it is our technological revolution, the information superhighway and all it implies, that explains the growing inequality between the top 20 percent of the labor force and the remaining 80 percent, as well as the wage stagnation afflicting most workers.

That the new technology is being blamed for the wedge that has opened up between the wages of the many and the wages of the few shows up in analyses from both the Left and the Right. The attack on those who earn their living from work has been fully supported, indeed aided, abetted, and legitimized, by American intellectuals of all political stripes. There is a widespread conviction among intellectuals that the majority of American workers deserve their fate. The problem, the thinkers say, is that the vast majority of Americans are simply not equipped to function in an age dominated by the knowledge revolution.

This argument has a huge surface plausibility, backed as it is by an imperfectly understood set of statistics. The returns to "skill," appear to have increased. The incomes of college-educated workers have risen faster than those of high school graduates, and among high school graduates wages have risen faster than among high school dropouts. The incomes of those with high measured IQs have risen relative to those with low IQs, and the incomes of "knowledge" workers have increased compared to the compensation of those who work with their hands. In 1993, for example, the average annual earnings of male college graduates were 70 percent higher than those of high school graduates; in 1979 the difference was only 42 percent.

Given such huge pay differentials, many analysts have drawn drastic conclusions about what the knowledge revolution means for the employability of the majority of American workers. Their widespread conviction is that the emerging "knowledge economy" is creating a new elite worker expert at analyzing words and numbers, at ease in a global community linked by computers, but that most Americans are not prepared to fit this new role.

Many argue that the inequality in wages will only widen as new computer and telecommunications technologies sweep the workplace. Observing from the Left, Jeremy Rifkin, head of the Foundation on Economic Trends, writes, "America is a house divided. There's the knowledge sector and everybody else." Dozens of other liberals and conservatives alike have dwelt on the dark side of the knowledge economy, among them former Labor Secretary Robert B. Reich who warns, "We are on our way to becoming a two-tiered society composed of a few winners and a larger group left behind, whose anger and resentment is easily manipulated." Is this gloomy view justified? Is it really true that current technological change explains the stagnant wages of four out of five Americans and that growing pay differentials can only enrich a "cognitive elite" while leaving the remaining 80 percent of Americans in the dust, as conservative authors Richard J. Herrnstein and Charles Murray argued in *The Bell Curve*? Although this view is popular, it is most likely wrong.

In reality, technological innovations have come and gone, but it is the swelling labor pool in the emerging world that has, in an unprecedented way, vastly diminished capital's need for the labor force of the industrialized world, and caused the work of this labor pool to be increasingly devalued. Particularly since the cold war ended in 1988, the economic incentives of capital to make concessions to both blue-collar and, most recently, white-collar management jobs has totally withered away. As a consequence, the victory of capital in the cold war has attenuated the gradual improvement in the status of work, a trend that persisted for four hundred years. While it is true that certain categories of workers have gained significantly from technological changes of the 1980s and 1990s, there is no serious evidence, when it comes to the impact of technology on the distribution of income, of any difference between the current knowledge revolution and earlier technological waves beginning in the late eighteenth century.

The wage erosion, of course, started before the end of the cold war. Throughout the 1970s and 1980s, the diffusion of technology began having a substantial impact on the 80 percent of jobs not held by the top 20 percent of Western workers, or the "cognitive elite." Major parts of this sector of the workforce began adjusting to the idea, as painful as it was, that they were being deserted by capital, which had sought the embrace of a more pliant and cheaper labor force in the developing world. But beginning in the late 1980s, as white-collar workers at increasingly higher executive levels began disappearing from the workforce, it has slowly become apparent that the dual impact of globalization and late-twentieth-century technology breakthroughs has metastasized, and the top 20 percent of Western workers are now at risk as well. And more than that, this global diffusion is only in its very early stages. Commentators who insist that the advances in technology of the late twentieth century are so radically different from those of other earlier eras and that as a result a large part of the population will in effect fall off the global radar screen and out of competition are wrong. What they have failed to take into account are the historical antecedents to today's "cognitive elite."

There is a predictable life cycle to the enjoyment of wealth by a particular sector as a result of technological gains. When hybrid species of corn were first introduced in the 1920s, educated farmers who were able to follow the sophisticated watering and fertilizing demands of the species were largely the ones who benefited. But this knowledge gradually spread throughout the corn belt, and by the mid-1950s hybrids accounted for 95 percent of corn acreage, and average yields per acre had quadrupled since the 1920s.

More striking still is what can be learned from the period from 1870 to 1929, when the use of coal and iron in the Industrial Revolution gave way to the use of chemicals and electricity. As now, there was widespread intellectual pessimism about America's economic future, and ethnic battles were frequent. Social Darwinism, the notion that the rewards from laissez-faire capitalism justly went to the fittest, gained support among industrial plutocrats; while populism spread among farmers and workers. The discrepancy in incomes widened precipitously, especially as the new giant industrial corporations competed for "skilled," but scarce, office workers, while business leaders and policy reformers worried about the shortfall in "skilled" labor.

But by 1929 dramatic improvements in education and the spread of easy-to-use office technology had brought down the wage premium paid to educated workers. High school graduation rates rose from around 13 percent in 1913 to almost 50 percent by 1940. Typewriters, address machines, dictation machines, mimeograph machines, and other innovations made many office jobs far simpler, and skill differentials declined. But the skilled elite barely complained about their lost premium because, in the words of Claudia Goldin, an economist at Harvard University, "Strong productivity growth substantially increased the real wages paid to most Americans."

There is no essential difference between the latest wave of technology (the "knowledge economy") and the new inventions that arrived between 1870 and 1929. Just as before, economic wealth is being created by research, discovery, and worksite know-how. The foundation of the knowledge economy is the information infrastructure of computers, software, and telecommunications equipment; the pace of expansion is feverish. From 1984 to 1993, the percentage of workers using computers rose from 25 percent to 47 percent. High-technology equipment has become so embedded in manufacturing and service industries that some 80 percent of economic activity generating gross domestic product now involves information technology in a significant way, according to Michael Dertouzos, director of the Laboratory for Computer Science at the Massachusetts Institute of Technology.

We disagree with the prevailing view that the present technological revolution need leave most Americans far behind. Any explanation of the slump in American wages that argues that the United States has more than its share of dim-witted workers, or that our labor force is ill-educated or ill-trained either by world standards or by the standards of the past, ignores history. There is nothing unique about what is happening to the labor force today. How a science-based society such as ours defines "skilled" changes throughout time. Middle managers were the heroes of the permanent "technostructure" described by John Kenneth Galbraith in the *New Industrial State* and by William H. Whyte in *The Organization Man,* but the class of middle managers that rose to power in the 1950s has been under severe pressure for over a decade. The middle-rung occupants of management have become redundant as "downsizing" and "reengineering" have worked their way through corporate America.

Occupational catastrophe has been with us since the Industrial Revolution. The invention of the spinning jenny in 1767 greatly increased the supply of yarn and raised the wages of weavers to a point where they were wearing top hats on the streets of Bradford in the English Midlands. But when the flying shuttle revolutionized weaving in 1773, the practitioners of what had been a "skilled" craft suffered. In the history of American transportation, railroad engineers were among the aristocrats of labor in the 1890s, earning ten times the average wage, just as airline pilots have been earning a huge "skill differential" for fifty years (but their wages are now eroding). Samuel Gompers, founder of the American Federation of Labor in the late nineteenth century, was an "aristocrat of labor" when he plied his trade as a cigar roller. His successors, women now working in Tampa, are probably lower on the occupation scale than Bizet's Carmen.

Dire warnings about the impact of technology on labor as a whole have been common throughout history—and have always proved wrong. The jobs lost in declining industries or among workers using obsolete technologies have always been replaced by new jobs in new industries using new technologies. There has never been an instance in history when the increase in productivity resulting from invention and innovation has failed to lead to a rise in overall wages or standard of living. The increased productivity that results from invention raises the real incomes and spending power of those who benefit from the new technology. The spending is then diffused throughout the economy, raising income and growth.

In the past, the diffusion of technology and its effect on highly skilled wages stayed, for the most part, neatly within the Western world. But since the dramatic end of the cold war, the new technology has quickly spread outside, so the gains of technological breakthroughs are no longer reaped solely within the industrial world.

So by itself, the current new wave of technology should prove an economic elixir, as have earlier advances, but because of the little-understood but dramatic impact of the end of the cold war and the globalization of labor, the usual economic gains have escaped those who earn their living from work in the countries of the developed world, including the United States. As we will argue in Chapter 7, the conservative policies that have swept the globe with the triumph of capital have held back economic growth in the developed countries of the West. Economic history suggests that rapid growth in productivity leads to rising employment and wages only if rapid economic growth follows in its wake. But this time around there has been a huge expansion in the globally available labor force, both skilled and unskilled, in the less developed world, thereby preventing those who earn their living from work *anywhere* in the industrial world from reaping the benefits of the growth in productivity. Capital migrates to low-wage areas, and the only way that it can be kept in the developed world is if wages in the developed world are kept low.

Despite the disdain in which it is held by the worshippers of the cognitive elites, there is every evidence that the American labor force is equipping itself to benefit from the current spurt in productivity growth with amazing speed and effectiveness. The proportion of high school graduates enrolling in college jumped from 49 percent in 1980 to 62 percent in 1992. The ratio of bachelors degrees awarded to the population aged eighteen to twenty-four rose a remarkable 29 percent between 1980 and 1990. Women, too, are meeting the demand for skill in the knowledge economy: more women than men are getting college degrees. Nearly half of all American businesses offer some kind of formal training to their workers. New entrants to the job market are considerably better educated than workers who are retiring.

In the past decade community and technical colleges, a major educational resource for poor and minority students, have become a vital link between employers and potential employees. Enrollment at community colleges and other two-year learning institutions has soared. The state of Missouri will spend some $20 million upgrading worker skills for local companies at its community colleges. Ohio has restructured its community college system so that no resident lives more than twenty minutes away from a local institution. South Carolina's sixteen technical colleges have trained more than four thousand manufacturing workers since 1991, placing more than 90 percent of graduates into jobs with a targeted employer.

Few appreciate how fast the skill level of the American workforce is rising; they also underestimate the huge advances toward making information technologies accessible to the masses. "Up until the early 1980s, the only people able to use personal computers were a very tiny elite. In some sense, this technology is democratizing rather than elitizing," says David Card, an economist at Princeton University. It could even be that in the long run the computer would create a technology and management structure whose implications are, in fact, a more equal distribution of income if appropriate economic and corporate policies were put into place.

Our contention is that it is the triumph of capital, not advances in technology, that has led to the betrayal of work for a growing number of people in industrialized society. In any event, there is no sign that wage convergence has brought major benefits to those who earn their living from work in the industrialized world. It is perfectly true that there are many examples of decisions to again build plants in particular industries—for instance, textiles, apparel, and even steel. Wage increases abroad have led certain corporations to locate plants in the United States once again as its labor has begun to look cheap in specific situations.

But if rising wages in some areas of the developing world have, in the net, brought benefits to the American workforce as a whole, we haven't seen any sign of it yet. U.S. wage gains have shriveled rather than increased since the end of the cold war. Real U.S. wages have actually fallen over the past seven years, the worst performance since the Great Depression. And when the net loss in fringe benefits is included, the negative impact of the end of the cold war is even more striking. Gains in wages have been shrinking in Western Europe and Japan as well, and unemployment has been rising there.

Did the average American benefit when the auto industry substantially migrated to Europe and Japan in the late 1960s and early 1970s? Many Americans did get cheaper and better cars. But what of the price—urban decay in Detroit, the disappearance of many decent jobs for inner-city workers? Are we really better off now than we were in the 1960s, when cars sported tailfins and downtown Detroit was a vibrant center of blue-collar life?

Honest answers to these questions suggest that the general assumption that growth in one country benefits the entire world is highly dubious. Indeed, the willingness of economists and public officials to count on wage convergence to bring employment or wage relief to workers in the United States and other industrial countries may be one of the great economic policy mistakes of this century, comparable to the federal government's unwillingness, before the election of FDR, to use government spending to fight the Great Depression in the 1930s. Yet the perceived "benefits" to American workers of global wage convergence continue to be among the hidden foundations of economic policy.

PART **2**

THE BETRAYAL
OF WORK

CHAPTER 4

Downsizing or Cultural Revolution?

PSYCHOLOGICALLY, AMERICANS WERE TOTALLY UNPREPARED for the impact of victory in the cold war. In the first six years that followed its end, the entire U.S. economy grew extremely slowly. Growth did accelerate in the mid-1990s, but wages remained essentially stagnant. Only profits and stock prices boomed. Instead of producing a feeling of security among American workers, the aftermath of the victory has brought a heightened sense of insecurity. Instead of being sweet, the fruits of victory are tasting bitter. Where were the American workers' peace dividends?

Despite a highly acclaimed "tight" labor market, which moved the unemployment rate toward 5 percent, median family income, measured in dollars of constant purchasing power, was in 1995 still 2 percent below where it had been five years earlier, and personal debt levels crept to historic highs. "Underemployment," a broader measure of the lack of employment success in the labor market, and a number rarely used by the media, measured 10.1 percent for 1995, according to the Economic Policy Institute, a Washington think tank. This much more troubling statistic takes into account part-time workers who could not find full-time jobs and "discouraged workers" who wanted jobs but had been discouraged by their lack of success and consequently had left the labor force and were no longer counted on the unemployment rolls. At the same time, the 10 percent of the population who are at the top of the economic ladder (which also owned 66 percent of the nation's equities) was making money hand over fist as the stock market continued its dizzying ascent toward 7000. And merger mania, strongly reminiscent of the 1980s, took on a new obsessive quality in the mid-1990s, which bothered barely a soul in the Clinton White House, characterized by what was, for a Democratic administration, an unseemly solicitude for the perceived interests of the corporate community.

Cynics might argue that the passionate love affair between the great American corporations and Washington politicians is rooted in the impact of campaign contributions on electoral success. That is surely 90 percent of the truth. But there is another reason why the great American corporation was generally held in such high esteem in Washington and, indeed, by large sectors of the media, the intellectual community, and among the public at large in the mid-1990s. It seemed to many that the American corporate sector had found the key to success in the new post–cold-war global economy. Wasn't unemployment far lower and economic growth much faster in the United States than in the other industrial countries? Did it not look as though the great American companies were besting their rivals in many product lines, not only in computers, chips, and software but also in more routine industries such as steel, textiles, and autos? Were not profits and stock prices booming? Surely the great corporations had done something right and were worthy of great respect.

Because of the power vested in the American corporate community (its advertising dollars supported the media, and its campaign contributions supported politicians) it was easy for the managers of big business to get their story across—and in a highly favorable light. And it was, of course, perfectly true that the years since the end of the cold war had seen a transformation of the corporate sector. But as the evidence in this chapter will strongly suggest, the metamorphosis of the American workplace has been neither benign nor beneficial. The notion that the downsizing movement has imposed much pain on many workers is hardly new or surprising. What is less clearly understood, though equally true and important, is that the pain has brought little if any gain: there is no serious evidence that the downsizing movement has led to a material improvement in the speed with which the efficiency of the American corporation is increasing or in the rate of growth in productivity in the American economy as a whole. Indeed, many changes introduced by management in the post–cold-war years read like a catalogue of the misbegotten.

We have searched both our minds and a few libraries to come up with the appropriate antecedent for the management philosophy that has gripped the corporate world since the end of the cold war. This movement has gone under the name of "reengineering." Instead of seeking explanations for its failures in the great market and demographic changes that have transformed the world economy, in the post–cold war years American business began turning inward, finding the main causes for failure in the inadequacies of its own employees and managers. This dark phenomenon, which has spawned a host of books, consultants' careers, and layoffs, is perhaps best understood in comparison with the violent Cultural Revolution that traumatized China—particularly its professional elites—in the late 1960s and early 1970s. The American version, of course, was not nearly as horrendous from a human rights perspective or economically disastrous as its Chinese antecedent, in which professionals were forced out of their careers to work for years in rural labor camps where they were physically tortured. But reengineering seemed to put many professional workers in America on the couch of a sadistic psychiatrist. And other similarities between the two movements are eerie. Both the Cultural Revolution and the reengineering movement set up emotional climates that conveniently blamed elite workers for all the problems. Although these workers were "denounced" for their inherent weaknesses and removed, their removal, on the evidence, did little or nothing to solve either nation's problems. America's reengineering movement failed to achieve its stated purpose: to increase the productivity of the American economy. Insofar as the competitiveness of the American economy did increase, it was primarily because wage growth had been strangled and the dollar had been debased. That, of course, means that increased corporate competitiveness was paid for by those who earn their living from work, in both stagnant incomes and a higher real cost of imported products.

THE PSYCHOLOGICAL ATTACK ON WORK

The Cultural Revolution tore China apart between 1966 and 1969 and traumatized an entire professional generation in China. It is vividly described in the 1993 autobiography by Ningkun Wu entitled *A Single Tear.* Wu, a Chinese academic, was deemed "reactionary" by those who had power over his career. By the middle of the 1960s it had become clear that profound economic problems had evolved under the leadership of Chairman Mao Tse-tung. The economy had suffered severe depression in the early 1960s and was having a hard time reviving. Mao became convinced that China's weaknesses could only be overcome by changing the Chinese character—specifically the character of the professional classes that ran the bureaucracies and universities.

The Cultural Revolution had initially been applauded as a way to cleanse an economy of its most "backward" elements and get it moving on the right track again with elite leaders—professors, managers, scientists—who were deemed "progressive." By loudly scapegoating large segments of the professional classes, China's leaders could conveniently shift the growing mass discontent with quality of Chinese life away from themselves and onto the unsuspecting shoulders of the "cognitive elites" who were busily teaching at universities, working in laboratories, and managing state-owned companies. Those who were smart enough to figure out this deadly new political game early on often served as cheerleaders for the Cultural Revolution, just as businessmen in the United States wanting to demonstrate their loyalty to growth and the future have unhesitatingly embraced reengineering. In Mao's world, reactionary elements were drummed out of their positions in public sessions during which they were discredited by their peers, and later they were ultimately dismissed from their institutions. This is what happened to Ningkun Wu; he lost his university position after being denounced by zealots of the revolution. In the course of America's reengineering zealotry, many members of the professional classes were also "argued" against, often in closed group sessions eerily similar to those in Mao's program.

In the United States the reengineering program was laid out in Michael Hammer and James Champy's 1993 best-seller, *Reengineering the Corporation*. The authors, management consultants for a Boston-based firm, CSC Index, called the book "revolutionary," and said they offered a road of purification and hard-hitting action to an American business community driven almost frantic by the erosion of its ability to compete in world markets during the 1980s. The new Holy Grail of reengineering forecast one endless barren winter for any company that did not deeply prune its old workforce, flatten its hierarchy, and grow anew. "Reengineering is new, and it has to be done," said Peter F. Drucker, the senior guru of management consulting. "The payoff is dramatic improvement in cost, quality, and customer satisfaction," said Robert E. Allen, chief executive officer of AT&T, a company that by the consensus of most business analysts has produced few such improvements during his regime as CEO, this despite spending $347.1 million on "consulting and research services" in 1993, up from $137.5 million in 1990. Businessmen went out to buy Hammer and Champy's missive for upheaval. It mattered little that the formulae described in the original 1993 book were shown to be inadequate by study after study or that the two books that followed *Reengineering the Corporation* readily granted the failure of the original model and proposed new solutions.

When AT&T announced that it was laying off 40,000 workers early in 1996, Hammer and Champy cheered them on, telling the *New York Times,* "This move shows incredible foresight. Other companies may not be as bold, but eventually other companies will follow suit in reducing their management ranks." At the same time, an AT&T spokeswoman suggested, "The idea is that everybody has been asked to step out into a parking lot." She explained that no one was being fired or even "laid off." Instead, she hastened to add that the employees not invited back in from the lot were those who had the bad luck to find themselves "unassigned." Nevertheless, they would be helped along by "facilitators" who would size up their skills.

The future of capitalism now seemed to hang on the notion that the individual no longer mattered very much. This of course, flew in the face of most profiles of successful "twenty-first-century-style" CEOs such as cable-TV giant John Malone of TCI, famous for having few if any real confidants when it came to making key decisions, for not working in groups, and for spending every spare moment alone with his wife and dogs in wilderness areas away from all people. Yet Hammer and Champy had decided that for the mass of professional managers, team decision making by "process" players was the only way to ultimate success. Those who did not see themselves as team workers were denounced—much as in China during the Cultural Revolution—as reactionaries who had not honed their skills for the revolution.

Mao's reengineering was not very different. Both revolutions put the responsibility on workers—professional workers—to reexamine and reshape themselves so that their institutions could thrive and move into the future. Implicit was the understanding that if failure occurred, the worker was to blame—not outside forces, such as technological backwardness or the horrendous inefficiency of centralized economic planning. "Inflexibility, unresponsiveness, the absence of customer focus, an obsession with activity rather than result, bureaucratic paralysis, lack of innovation, high overhead—these are the legacies of one hundred years of American industrial leadership," Hammer and Champy intoned. But in the end, no matter how integrative the workers became, the ultimate leaders, whether Mao Tse-tung or U.S. corporate CEOs, ended up with more power than ever before, and at least in Champy and Hammer's world, much more money. That was the beauty of an evolving plan in which the most expensive ingredient of the old twentieth-century industrial model—professional talent—had become demographically cheapened by a growing worldwide supply of workers. Reengineering became a built-in management process, to be used at the convenience of those who controlled capital, for the rearrangement and movement of this overabundant factor of production whenever possible. Those who remained in the worker ranks were physically controlled in demeaned workspaces—often taking the form of movable steel pods—which could be removed instantaneously along with the tenant if management deemed it necessary or desirable. In the United States, a country where labor had, in fact, been scarce for most of its industrial history, the trauma was deep.

Another striking similarity between the Cultural Revolution and the reengineering movement is the use of outsiders who were brought in to hurry the managerial "reactionaries" off the premises after they had been "argued against" by their career-conscious peers. In China student Red Guards usually set off the alarms against those being blamed, who were then handily sent off to distant villages to do agricultural labor as penance. In the United States it was often the newly minted management consultants, fresh out of MBA programs, who doubled as corporate America's Red Guards, calling on other workers to take part in the "criticism" in the name of cleansing the corporation.

Outplacement consultants, backup troops for the forward guard, were brought in to analyze employees' skills and grill them about what they had been up to over the last twenty years or so, as though the company itself had no idea who these people were, where they had come from, or what they did every day. Often sessions would include psychological tests designed to gauge workers' personality traits: extroverted, introverted, thoughtful, or driving. Sometimes, after these characteristics had been determined, the newly categorized workers would be asked to wear personality tags at management "camps" advertising their traits for all to see, again, in a strange parallel to large "character" Chinese posters displayed by the Red Guards against reactionaries in the late 1960s.

In groups, managers would be coaxed to discuss their personality traits honestly and open up to others during talk sessions. Later, some employees report, these sessions, and what was revealed in the process, was used against them. A mid-level manager at a mid-Atlantic drug company reports admitting that he had trouble not being overly sympathetic to the needs of those who worked for him. "I feel that a number of raise requests I made, and recommendations for promotion were turned down because upper management thought I was just soft on labor and not hard-driving enough. Yet this admission was coaxed out of me, and then put into a file, by a very seasoned therapist."

One manager working for a major East Coast multinational that has been strenuously reengineered during the mid-1990s was diagnosed by a series of tests as being quiet and introspective. This manager reports,

> But the way my corporation used it made a mockery of therapy. From my point of view, it was purely a management tool used to manipulate me and other colleagues, as a future means of cost-cutting. At a seminar discussing the results of these tests, I, along with other managers, was asked to wear a sign saying "introverted" which, I truly believe, designated me as someone targeted to be watched, and the results were put into my personnel file, I am sure. I know this sounds paranoid, but it's true, and I've never felt truly secure since the seminar took place. I may not be the noisiest guy around, but the truth is, I have tried hard to protect the people who work for me. I have tried hard to get some of them raises, and upper management doesn't like me for this reason. The truth of the matter is, it's an old-line company with few really new ideas or products, so in order to please Wall Street every quarter, they keep cutting back to the bone on labor costs. And basically the cutting never stops. We're currently going through a whole new round which will pare back another 5 percent of all workers—many of them managerial.

The processes set into motion during the Cultural Revolution and the reengineering movement started with the same intention— purportedly to improve key institutions. As Wu reports, in a passage describing experiences strikingly similar to those of the U.S. manager just quoted,

> [T]he Premier called on the nation's intellectuals, especially the high intellectuals [similar to our cognitive elites] to start on a course of thought reform. The intellectuals who had come from the old society were said to have been imbued with the mistaken thought of the bourgeois classes. He urged the university faculties of the two great cities to take the lead in carrying out thought reform among the nation's intellectuals. . . . Little did I know that the seven-hour report was nothing less than a declaration of war on the mind and integrity of the intelligentsia for the next forty years.

In the mid-1990s, Citibank began using a 360-degree "criticism" program to "assess" some of its managers. The subjects were critiqued by colleagues in positions above, below, and parallel to their own. "I feel that my assessment went pretty well, but it was still a very uncomfortable experience," reports one manager. "But I sat in on another meeting where the guy was totally creamed. My understanding is that our new managers overseas are not subjected to this kind of treatment." The Citibank program resembled the criticism Wu underwent many times at the hands of his colleagues at Beijing University. He remembers,

> I was ordered to sit in the middle of the room encircled by rings of clamoring and table-banging accusers. After the initial bombardment, questions about my past were fired at me. I gave factual answers. Soon I saw my accusers were well prepared. Their questions followed chronological order. Similar denunciation sessions became a settled routine for several days running. I was exhorted daily to confess or to surrender and reminded what the iron fist proletarian dictatorship could do to me or my family. I saw it was all psychological warfare yet my mortal flesh was weak. I wished I had some crime to confess so as to escape these . . . nerve-wracking threats. I wracked my brain to find crimes I had committed unwittingly but it was fruitless, and my head ached day and night.

Afterward Wu lost his academic post because of Red Guard reports. He writes:

> A few days later I was informed of my employment as a temporary contract worker. The contract was renewable every three months. It was less than a third of what I was paid before my expulsion, with none of the benefits available to full faculty and staff, neither was I eligible for free medical care. But I was not unhappy with my lot. I had learned to live by the sage proverb "he is happy who knows contentment with his lot."

Comparably, in the book *White Collar Blues,* Rutgers professor and chair of the Labor Studies and Employment Relations Department Charles Heckscher tells the stories of many American middle managers he has interviewed, many of whom have psychologically withdrawn and resigned themselves to just getting by after reengineering. None of these people, neither Wu nor his American counterparts, had the feeling that he could do anything but carefully toe the line. A bank executive from Doylestown, Pennsylvania, who has survived two mergers and three reorganizations, says, "I have two kids to feed. I used to love my job, but each successive reorganization has been managed by people who literally don't know anything. I stay because I can't find anything else at a comparable level in the area. I really detest going to work these days."

As a result of the severe anguish of living through the Cultural Revolution—being engineered and reengineered in and out of the Chinese work system the way Wu had been—Wu's generation lost many years of professional creativity. But the ultimate horror, it seemed for Wu, was the appearance of an old friend from the University of Chicago. This friend had been able to win a Nobel Peace Prize back in the United States, working under ideal conditions in a safe academic post. Ironically, this friend was royally feted by the same Communist bosses who had ultimately been responsible for destroying Wu's career. Wu's only mistake had been returning to China to teach instead of staying in the United States, where he had attended undergraduate and graduate programs as an exceptionally gifted scholarship student. When offered a job in China, the loyal Wu went home to help carry out the revolution. It wasn't until years later, when he was in his late sixties, that Wu was able to write his most acclaimed work, his autobiography. But as he points out, he was only able to do so because he had finally been given a safe, secure work haven at the tiny midwestern school in America where he had taken his undergraduate degree.

Wu was in that sense lucky. Such havens are not usually available to victims of revolution in the workplace, either in China or in the United States. Of course, there is no comparison between these revolutions in terms of scale—Ningkun Wu faced physical torture in labor camps that no constantly recycled-and-replaced American manager ever need fear. But the effect is similar. The overall psychological loss in the United States has been severe, and in many cases, permanent. Managers have lost both their sense of security and the freedom to be creative by experimenting and having the luxury of sometimes failing.

Businessmen from around the country zealously relied on Hammer and Champy's reengineering, it seemed, to convert their businesses for the new global economy. It all looked and sounded so good that even universities, hospitals, and just about any institution interested in increasing efficiency, began using Hammer and Champy's new prescription for change. The allure of the book was the simple-minded assurance that success was within the reach of all workers who promised to become less rigid, look inward, and transform themselves into parts of a "process" rather than continue on as mere individual workers. And according to these managerial prophets, *all* harsh external competitive climates could be easily conquered because the real problems lay with the workers themselves and the way they behaved in the workplace. If they could go with the flow, transform and retransform themselves, all would be well.

REENGINEERING AS BLACK COMEDY

But it hasn't gone well. The failures of the reengineering movement are visible for anyone to see in black-and-white, on the pages of its sacred texts. The CSC consultants Hammer and Champy are, as it turns out, fools who went where angels fear to tread, actually providing a list of companies that have followed their advice and are therefore presented as examples of successful corporate transformation, or at least of the successful application of their methods. In their first book, *Reengineering the Corporation,* Hammer and Champy single out for praise Chubb Insurance, Aetna Life and Casualty, Ford, Eastman Kodak, Wal-Mart, and the Gap. All are credited with faithfully carrying out what was proclaimed as the ultimate post–cold war management remake. The vicissitudes of business in an era of slow growth being what they are, it turned out that all but one of the reengineered heroes of 1993 were lackluster performers over the next three years. Neither Wal-Mart, nor the Gap, nor Ford, nor Aetna, nor Chubb was reengineered into overachievement; the stocks of all four companies were mediocre performers for 1993 to 1995, lagging behind the S&P 500 index and matching the average for their industry only in the case of Ford. Eastman Kodak did flourish for two years after 1993, but surely success at one out of seven companies could have occurred by pure chance, or it could be owing to factors that had little to do with reengineering programs.

The case of Wal-Mart is particularly instructive. The CSC consultants insist that "external forces" are never responsible for the failure of companies, since, if external factors "accounted for our dilemma, nearly all American companies would be in decline. But they aren't." Wal-Mart workers did go with the "flow," but the reality is that the Arkansas-based company had been hurt by "external forces." The company stock languished between 1993 and 1995, largely because its primary customer base—the lower-middle and middle class in the United States—suffered a severe squeeze in its wages. Assuming that the discount market would continue to grow, Wal-Mart stores had expanded too rapidly and consequently failed to do well in the stock market.

The transformation of the American workplace has exacted a heavy psychological toll. But what has been the result of the frenetic reorganization of the American workplace that has been put into place under the lash of stiff global competition? The intuitive answer, and the one that we would all like to believe, is that it has worked a miracle. Companies have, after all, slavishly followed the advice of the cadre of management consulting firms, whose gross fee extraction from the business community has been rising rapidly over the past ten years.

No matter what language is used to describe the effects, it is fair to say that the reengineering movement has been a sick joke. An American Management Association study of corporate downsizing efforts undertaken between 1989 and 1995 found that only about one third of the companies experienced increased productivity. These results are confirmed by earlier studies. A $2 million study of 584 companies conducted jointly by Ernst and Young and the American Quality Foundation in 1991 found that most reengineering programs achieve "shoddy results." In 1992 studies by management consulting firms, McKinsey and Company (of 30 quality programs) and Arthur D. Little (of 5,000 manufacturing and service companies)—both found that only about one-third of such programs had a significant impact on their companies' market success. The following year, both the Electric Power Institute (in a study of more than 300 large companies) and another management consulting company, Sibson and Company, found the overall success rate to be even lower (based on 4,000 focus groups, consisting of both employees and customers).

These studies showing the impact of reengineering on a company-by-company basis are reinforced by broad economic analyses. After a careful review of macroeconomic studies on the subject Stephen D. Oliner and William L. Wascher say that they "[c]ome away . . . skeptical that restructuring activity in the 1990s has lifted the pace of productivity growth much for the aggregate economy. Indeed," they conclude, "after nearly a decade of anecdotal reports of aggressive corporate restructuring, and downsizing, the economy's rate of productivity growth has barely improved."

Reengineering, it seems, like the Cultural Revolution before it, has suddenly fallen out of favor with those in power. Indeed, in a revealing post-Thanksgiving Boston seminar (in 1996), which companies paid $2,200 a head to attend for three days of advice, Michael Hammer pointed out that now the idea was no longer "so much getting rid of people. It's now getting more out of people. I wasn't smart enough about that," he admitted publicly. "I was reflecting my engineering background and was insufficiently appreciative of the human dimension. I've since learned that's critical."

In fact, his firm, CSC Index, has been scrambling to overhaul its reengineering practice as corporate America increasingly views the associated strategies as unproductive. "Reengineering is dead," says one consultant. "It's considered to be a disaster." Management consulting firms, meanwhile, are forging ahead revamping their services, often focusing and capitalizing these days on having companies increase the service sides of their businesses as General Electric has been doing successfully. But none of this really seems to have changed the way in which the corporation functions. Outsourcing and restructuring continue to exact a heavy toll even in the tight labor markets of the mid-1990s.

Those who earn their living from work can put up with a lot if they see some visible improvements as a result of their efforts or even as a result of some painful psychological adjustment. But nothing is more degrading to workers than to be told that some disruption of their working life has improved the efficiency and profitability of the firm that they work for, and to know deep in their hearts that nothing is further from the truth.

When the costs and benefits of the reengineering movement are eventually totaled up, the evidence available to date strongly suggests that although it has succeeded in increasing the profitability of American business by providing a rationale for suppressing wage costs, reengineering has not led to any improvement in the rate of productivity growth. It has opened the way for a huge surge in corporate profits, even though it has not brought an overall increase in the growth rate of the efficiency of business operations.

The scapegoating of professional workers did more for America's corporate leaders than it did for China's leaders. And the leaders of the reengineering movement in the U.S., the management consulting firms, have, like the Energizer bunny, gone on and on and on. In a sales pitch whose psychological message is unchanged, consultants still take the lead from the message on the jacket of the original *Reengineering the Corporation,* where Michael Hammer and James

Champy shouted out in fourteen languages around the world "Forget what you know about how business should work—most of it is wrong." And though the tune they sang a few years ago has been changed, the radical sales pitch remains the same:

> We do experience a missionary zeal when we write—or talk— about reengineering because reengineering to us is not just another business technique to improve an organization's bottom line. Rather, we believe that reengineering is the only thing that stands between many U.S. corporations—indeed the U.S. economy—and disaster. It is difficult to remain dispassionate under such circumstances.

Clearly, the zeal did not dissipate as rapidly as did the early message of reengineering or the fortunes of many companies that followed Hammer and Champy's advice. Indeed, as the authors' fame grew worldwide and their tactics for purging took on a life of their own, resulting in millions of destroyed careers, Hammer and Champy ultimately created conditions that still invite a comparison with the kind of zealotry and economic purification preached twenty-five years earlier by Chinese leader Mao Tse-tung.

MEANINGLESS MERGERS

Opulent though they may be, the fees exacted from business by management consulting firms are "as sounding brass, or a tinkling cymbal" as compared to the rewards that have been reaped by the investment banking community from the great merger wave of the 1990s. Again, the promise is that the resulting reorganizations will bring increased efficiency. But again the record is at best spotty, providing no decisive evidence that the great consolidation wave of the first half of the 1990s did a lot more to increase efficiency than did the disastrous series of "free-form" mergers that characterized the 1960s or the string of junk bond–financed buyouts of the mid-1980s, such as the famed RJR–Nabisco merger so vividly described in *Barbarians at the Gates.*

The post-cold war merger wave has been all-consuming. According to Securities Data Corporation, which keeps track of merger activity, the value of deals consummated in 1995 was about $522 billion, and it rose to $664 billion in 1996, both figures comfortably above 1988's figure of $248 billion. The stated rationale for the vast majority of 1990s mergers on the surface makes a lot more sense than did the explanations of the conglomerate merger wave of the 1960s or the gigantic junk bond-financed mergers of the 1980s. The talk has been about the advantages of consolidation to reduce competition, and of vertical integration—linking manufacturing with distribution—to take advantage of the new, bigger globalized market. But the evidence is that most of these mergers have fallen far short of their promise. Deals that were announced with much fanfare, such as AT&T's acquisition of NCR and Matsushita's 1991 acquisition of MCA, have since unraveled. Others, notably the acquisitions of drug wholesalers by big pharmaceuticals manufacturers as well as software and entertainment deals aren't producing the results the acquirers had hoped for.

The anecdotal evidence is supported statistically. An analysis conducted in 1995 by *Business Week* and Mercer Management Consulting Inc. indicates that companies did perform better in the wake of the 1990s deal making compared to those companies put together in the 1980s deals. Yet the analysis also concluded that most of the deals of the 1990s still haven't worked. The 1995 *Business Week*-Mercer analysis was not able to measure the productivity performance of the combined entities, but the stock market often provides a good measuring stick, with the performance and price activity of stocks being a proxy for the effectiveness with which a company uses its assets. On this basis, the study concluded that some 50 percent of all deals actually eroded shareholder returns, and 33 percent created only marginal returns. Even more significant is that, on average, companies that made no significant deals outperformed those that did—and by a fairly wide margin. Again, those employees who were told that the stressful mergers they were living through—or which ended up costing them their jobs—were necessary to increase efficiency can rightly feel they were also victims of the "big corporate lie."

The reason for all this misdirected activity is simple: the real motive of the reengineering movement is not to increase productivity but rather to extend the control that capital exerts over work to an entirely new level.

REENGINEERING AND PRODUCTIVITY

Elite workers in the United States should be embarked on a prosperous voyage. The demand for their products seems to be at an all-time high, at least as measured by the growth of exports, particularly to newly emerging economies. High-tech products, particularly, seem to be in almost unlimited demand. The computer *appears* to make work more efficient; technological change *seems* to be enhancing worker productivity at an unprecedented pace. Companies have been hell-bent on reorganization. Surely this zymotic activity should be energizing the workplace, making it far more productive.

Employment growth, as the Clinton administration shouted from the rooftops throughout the election campaign of 1996, was indeed spectacular during Clinton's first administration, with the creation of 10 million new jobs. And if that was not enough, the number of hours worked by the average American has increased even faster than employment has. More Americans are pushing themselves mentally and physically, working harder and longer than at any time in the second half of the twentieth century. But increased hours and employment tell only part of the story. As compared to other business upswings, real wages during this growth period have remained relatively stagnant.

The effects of the betrayal of the worker reach beyond stagnant income to more subtle, and in some senses even more disturbing, ramifications. Many who have lived through the endless, grinding machinations of reengineering have noticed that despite the drama and trumpeted successes, companies following the new advice have been enormously successful at only one thing—increasing profits, at least temporarily, at the expense of workers. And many workers who had survived reengineering found that the purported flattening of management structures lead to more, not fewer, procedures and controls.

The reengineering movement and the series of changes made in the way in which work is organized have, quite simply, led to the degradation of work—workplaces that are populated by psychologically withdrawn workers with low expectations about their own economic security and that of their children. Reduced expectations have shown up in many public opinion polls taken in recent years. Particularly revealing is a poll taken by the Lou Harris organization for *Business Week* in early 1996. Only 50 percent of the respondents expected their children to have a better life than they have had, compared to 59 percent in a poll taken in August 1989, just before the Berlin Wall fell. In the same 1996 poll the Harris organization asked, "For most Americans, do you think the American dream of equal opportunity, personal freedom, and social mobility has become easier or harder to achieve in the past 10 years?" Some 67 percent answered that it had become harder, as compared to only 31 percent who said it had become easier.

The reality of reengineering has begun to gnaw away at those who had earnestly embraced this newest form of management self-improvement. Ann Miller, a family therapist with a Ph.D. from Columbia University who had been based in Connecticut, has observed many reengineered families throughout the Stamford-Westport corridor. "Mostly, they are totally stunned," she says.

> Some have been laid off twice already and they are only in their mid-thirties. They have huge mortgages and a couple of kids. After they are laid off the first time, they definitely become more vulnerable in the next workplace. But they cling to the idea that this situation is only temporary. That things will go back to the way they used to be. From the carnage I've seen, and all the ongoing outplacement going on, I don't think so. The layoffs are done much more quietly though, these days, so as not to get any publicity.

Because it points to a future of diminished hope, in a nation that has historically been optimistic, it is this evidence of psychological damage that is especially chilling. And this pessimism is directly related to industry's response to the globalization of the market economy. In economics *hope* is spelled with a *p*—for *productivity*—simply because it is impossible for the living standard of average workers to rise rapidly unless productivity increases rapidly, particularly in a world where American workers face unprecedented competition from the leviathan labor force of the emerging countries. Yet there are no signs that massive downsizing or armies of consultants have done anything to increase the pace at which the efficiency of the workplace is accelerating. It is not the new technology of the information age itself that is truly surprising and threatening, but rather the failure of the information revolution to lead to increased productivity growth in the American workplace. Robert A. Solow, MIT's shrewd Nobel laureate economist, observed in 1989, "You can see the computer revolution everywhere, except in the productivity statistics." In 1995 he was still right. And if productivity growth continues pallid—the most likely scenario—American workers will face continued wage stagnation and workplace degradation.

Sad stories are seldom best told with dry numbers. Yet there is no way of getting a grasp on the failure of American management in the post–cold war era other than to face up to the drab picture painted in recent years by the trend of productivity growth in the United States.

Washington's official productivity data tell the story quite clearly. From the fourth quarter of 1993 to the fourth quarter of 1995, output per hour in the American business sector grew at an annual rate of 1.1 percent. That is only a little over one third of the 2.9 percent productivity growth rate that was achieved between 1950 and 1973, and only about half the historic rate of productivity growth in the United States—the 2.2 percent annual rate of improvement that prevailed for the hundred-year period that followed the end of the Civil War.

Economists who have studied productivity improvement distinguish between what they see as two distinct sets of causes. The first are those factors that can be quantified. Economists have demonstrated (mainly through the use of econometric models) that improvements in education and the quality of members of the workforce explain part of the growth in productivity, as does an increase in the amount of capital equipment with which each worker is equipped. But these easily measurable factors don't seem to explain the total increase in productivity, so there seems to be another, more mysterious and difficult to quantify source of productivity gains—the increase in knowledge. By convention, economists these days call that part of productivity gain explained by scientific and organizational discovery the "residual," the catch-all term for what is unexplained.

Because factors that are easy to quantify played the major role in the productivity growth in America after World War II, it is fairly easy to explain this trend until we get to the 1980s. The 2.9 percent productivity growth rate trend that prevailed between 1950 and 1973 came in above the long-term 2.2 percent average. After the immediate post-World War II adjustment (1945-1950), two important factors had a role in American productivity growth. The first was improved education, partly as a result of the GI Bill, which funded college for many ex-soldiers, and partly because the state governments that finance education emerged from World War II with bulging coffers and were able to increase their spending on education. Second, capital investment boomed, partly because of the need to make up for the hollowing out of production facilities after the depression and the war.

The causes of the slowdown in productivity growth that occurred in 1973 are similarly transparent. The OPEC oil embargo, and the quadrupling in the price of oil that followed it, was a giant setback for an industrial sector that was dependent on cheap energy for much of its growth. The high price of energy reduced the efficiency of the economy. Demographics also turned against rapid productivity growth after 1973. The average age of workers declined as the baby boomer generation, born between the late 1940s and the early 1960s, began to seek jobs, causing a decline in the level of experience in the workforce. At the same time, the number of women who sought and found work out of the home also increased. There is no reason to believe that women are less efficient than men, but many entering the job market at that time were, like the younger workers, inexperienced. These factors virtually doomed the United States to a period when the productivity growth rate would be less than the historic average.

But fundamental economic factors turned more favorable to productivity growth in the 1980s and especially in the 1990s. The baby boomers reached the age brackets in which workers are normally highly efficient. The rate at which women were entering the workforce slowed. And beginning in the 1990s there was an increase in the rate of capital spending, as business invested heavily in the computer revolution and the technology of the information age. If what has happened to productivity since the information revolution began is a measure of the impact of the "information revolution" on economic performance, we should be grateful for the preceding century of ignorance during which America's productivity increased twice as fast, at 2.2 percent per year! Based on the statistics, the impact of the information revolution has not been to increase the rate of productivity growth but to keep it at the same 1.1 percent rate that prevailed in the late 1970s and early 1980s, even while, as we have seen, the fundamentals that determine productivity growth had turned exceptionally favorable.

Nor is there any convincing reason to believe that the past ten years have been a period of base building in preparation for a surge in productivity growth as we move into the twenty-first century. The *Economic Report of the President,* submitted to Congress in February of 1996, contains a projection of productivity growth for the years from 1995 to 2002. That prediction was prepared by the president's Council of Economic Advisers headed by its then chair Joseph E. Stiglitz, a Stanford University economist who is an acknowledged expert on the economics of technological change. Its disturbing forecast: productivity will grow at a rate of 1.2 percent during this seven-year period, a razor-thin .1 percentage point above the dismal 1.1 percent figure of the years from 1973 to 1995. If the Council of Economic Advisers is to be believed, there is no imminent breakthrough in productivity.

WHY PRODUCTIVITY HAS STAGNATED

The failure of productivity growth to accelerate in the 1990s seems counterintuitive—contrary, that is, to the common impressions that can be drawn from everyday life. Indeed, there is much similarity between the story of contemporary productivity growth and the story of cancer cures so far in the 1990s. In the area of cancer many individuals can legitimately point to miracle cures and wonderful periods of remission produced by the latest medications and treatments. In a similar way, it is routine these days to be able to point to specific companies that at some point in time have experienced huge increases in efficiency, reaping the profit that accompanies such productivity. But just as there is no sign that the overall incidence of cancer is decreasing among the American people as a whole, there is no sign that the economy as a whole is experiencing an improvement in productivity. So the real issue regarding productivity is not how to spread the benefits of the latest technological revolution, but rather how to explain why the latest technological revolution and the accompanying efforts by American business to increase efficiency have, as the data surely show, failed.

History offers the most important clues. Certainly the computer has wrought miracles. But, as we have seen, technological miracles have been almost routine during the past four hundred years of capitalism. Take the ability to process and transmit information, for example, areas in which improvements in the present seem most striking. Is it really true that the invention of the computer has had more powerful and comprehensive effects than did the invention of the printing press or the spread of literacy? Is the Internet apt to be more remarkable in its effect than the spread of libraries and their accessibility to the masses? (It may be that by endowing libraries across the country, Andrew Carnegie created an earlier knowledge revolution in the United States whose scope at least matched that of the information revolution created by Bill Gates and his competitors.) Is it really the case that the ability to move information in milliseconds has had a more profound effect in increasing productivity than did the invention of the telegraph? Samuel F. B. Morse's invention of the telegraph cut the time it took to send information across the North Atlantic Ocean from twelve days to twelve seconds. It is easy for every age to overestimate the power and impact of its own technological miracles. But when we compare our computer creations against the miracles of the past, it may be that what is occurring in the present phase of capitalism is no more remarkable than the changes that occurred in earlier technological and "knowledge revolutions" that have produced wave after wave of rapid technological change during the entire four hundred years of capitalism.

For that reason we believe that the failure of productivity to grow substantially in the United States, and elsewhere in the developed world, since the end of the cold war lies in the unique characteristics of the present phase of capitalist development, a phase that has seen the emergence of a leviathan world labor force, a weakening in the ties between capital and labor in the industrialized world, and macroeconomic policies (see Chapter 7) that have doomed the developed countries to slow growth. It is in these unique features of the post–cold war economy, not in the character of the current pace of technological change, that we can find the explanation for the sluggishness of productivity growth.

We now live in a world where labor is abundant compared to capital. In the developed countries the effects have been stagnant wages and high real interest rates. But faced with a combination of global cheap labor and expensive capital, business is making the obvious, profit-maximizing choice: to use more labor (the cheaper factor of production) not more capital (the expensive factor of production). As a consequence, one of the basic trends that has increased wages in the developed world throughout the prior four hundred years of capitalist development—that the well-being of those who earn their living from work generally rises when each worker is equipped with more and more capital—has come to a screeching halt. In the past, living standards generally advanced because there were huge incentives to substitute capital for labor so as to economize on what had been the scarce factor of production, labor. But since the spread of the free market to the less developed world, the incentives have run the other way. Business now economizes on capital as compared to labor.

Again, appearance and reality come into conflict. Cocktail party talk, the blizzard of reports emanating from the brokerage community, and business press coverage of the American economy stress the wonders of the new technology of the information revolution. Television and the print press are full of pictures of workers in "clean rooms" dressed in trend-setting space suits, using equipment that looks as though it was designed for use on an atmosphereless moon. For most workers, however, the reality is quite the opposite. Since the end of the cold war, workers have been deprived of the aid of

Figure 4-1

The Falling Capital/Output Ratio, 1948–1995

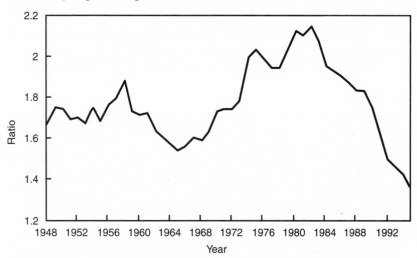

Data: *The State of Working America, 1996–97* (Armonk, N.Y.: M. A. Sharpe, 1997), 69.

technology to surprising degrees, simply because the rate of growth in the amount of capital available to each worker has been shrinking. And a worker without adequate tools is a worker who is degraded. The capital/output ratio is the statistical device that economists conventionally, and correctly, use to measure the average amount of capital that is used to produce a given output. If the ratio of capital to output falls, it is safe to conclude that an economy is producing the goods and services that it uses in a more labor intensive way. As Figure 4-1 shows, that critical ratio has been falling ever since the end of the cold war, and falling fairly sharply. The effect is a transformation: the workplace that was, however grudgingly, becoming more friendly to increased worker productivity has become a workplace that has turned distinctly hostile to productivity growth.

The incentive for business to substitute work for capital has been working with particular force since the end of the cold war. The notion that business is increasing the amount of toil needed to produce goods and services while economizing on the capital equipment that could be instrumental in achieving productivity gains, seems to contradict what most people would expect to happen in an economy widely praised for its rapid pace of technological change.

Yet the data seems to leave no doubt that the rate at which business is increasing its use of capital in production has decelerated—and

Table 4-1

Are American Workers Starved for Capital?

(Annual Growth**)

Period	Productivity* Output per Hour (Annual Growth Rate)	Capital Accumulation	
		Capital Services per Hour (Annual Growth Rate)	Equipment per Worker (Annual Growth Rate)
Pre-1973			
1948-73	n.a.	2.8%	n.a.
1959-73	2.9%	2.9	3.7%
Post-1973			
1973-79	1.1	2.4	4.2
1979-89	1.0	2.4	2.8
1989-94	0.9***	1.4	2.3

* Nonfarm business sector.
** Log growth rate.
*** 1989-94.

Data: *The State of Working America, 1996-97* (Armonk, N.Y.: M. A. Sharpe, 1997), 22.

decelerated sharply. Table 4-1 shows that the growth rate in two measures of the capital intensity of production—capital services per man hour and equipment per worker—has increased much more slowly since 1989 than it did in the earlier post–World War II years with powerful consequences for the performance of the economy. The decline in the rate of growth of capital used in production has been accompanied by a slowdown in the rate of productivity growth, as the first column of Table 4-1 shows. And because workers need capital to increase their efficiency, it is highly likely that the fall in the amount of capital used for each unit of production has also led to the slowdown in the growth of real wages.

The only good news in all this, for those who earn their living through work, is that an economy that uses less capital in production is also likely to use more hours of work. It is undoubtedly comforting that unemployment has fallen and that jobs have appeared to become more abundant in the mid-1990s, particularly in 1996. But in thinking about the future of work in America it is critical to realize that the increase in employment has come about because the growth of wages has been meager. And those who are raising loud hosannahs to high employment in the mid-1990s are neglecting the disturbing fact that job growth has been high because wage growth has been extremely slow. The implication is that since the end of the cold war, employment has risen in the United States mainly because labor is cheap as compared to capital.

Both history and literature are full of stories of men who metamorphosed into magnates because they controlled some scarce factor of production. Karl August von Wittfogel's penetrating study of medieval China demonstrates that those who were in control of water had instant power. James Clavell's *Shogun* was partly a vivid account of a fight over the control of the supply of silkworms in Japan. Lando Calrissian, a powerful character in *Star Wars,* controlled the mining of an element that was both scarce and vital.

Controlling capital today does not provide such a solid guarantee of making a fortune, but there is overwhelming evidence that the distribution of wealth in the United States has, in recent years, turned overwhelmingly favorable to those few people and families who control the flow of capital in the economy. Business executives who make the key decisions as to how to dispose of the most important segment of capital, the part that is actually used to purchase the technology and capital equipment that shape the workplace, have witnessed an amazing growth in their incomes, as compared to those ordinary mortals with whom they share the corporate workplace. According to *Business Week's* annual survey, between 1990 and 1995 the pay of corporate CEOs at the nation's 362 largest companies increased by 92 percent as compared to the 75 percent increase for corporate profits and the 16 percent increase for average workers. In 1990 the average CEO was paid $1.95 million, the average worker $22,976. That difference is, of course, gargantuan enough. But by 1995 the average CEO pay package had risen by $1.8 million to $3.75 million; whereas the average worker's pay had increased by $4,000, or .0004 million (four thousandths of a million). The level of CEO pay in the U.S. exceeds that in any of the industrial countries as Table 4-2 shows. In 1994, for example, CEOs in France, the foreign country that best treated its chief executives, earned only 64.7% of what their American counterparts earned. The figure for Japan was 60.2%, and for Germany 55.2 percent.

This widening discrepancy between the incomes of the captains of capital and the common workers has produced a chorus of denunciation of corporate greed, polite in the case of the business press, strident in the case of such right-wing demagogues as perennial Republican presidential hopeful Pat Buchanan. Yet one need not be a profound observer of American society to notice that although

Table 4-2

CEO Pay: An International Comparison, 1994

Country	CEO Compensation ($000)	U.S. Pay Relative to Foreign Pay (U.S. = 100)		Ratio of CEO to Worker Pay
		CEO	Worker	
Australia	$377.3	40.7	79.7	13.8
Belgium	544.7	59.8	134.3	12.1
Canada	399.3	43.0	91.7	12.7
France	600.1	64.7	99.6	17.6
Germany	512.7	55.2	159.7	9.4
Italy	421.8	45.5	94.5	13.1
Japan	558.5	60.2	125.3	13.0
Netherlands	458.0	49.4	122.3	11.0
New Zealand	163.0	17.6	52.2	9.1
Spain	415.9	44.8	67.0	18.2
Sweden	297.6	32.1	110.0	7.9
Switzerland	572.4	61.7	145.2	11.5
United Kingdom	483.8	52.1	79.6	17.8
United States	927.9	100.0	100.0	27.1
Non-U.S. average	$447.3	48.2	104.7	12.9

Data: Economic Policy Institute

corporate executives may have temporary monopolies on particular products or brilliant business strategies, they hardly have a corner on greed, a trait widely and equally distributed among the social classes. The executives' gargantuan incomes derive from their power over what has become an increasingly scarce factor of production, capital. It is the corporate chieftains who decide whether new plants and new jobs should be located in America or in Asia or Latin America. In a world where the competition for capital is intense, those who dispose of it are certain to be well rewarded. That's how markets have always worked in the past. It is how markets work now.

Though probably not the major cause of the persistent productivity slowdown, the increase in the proportion of income flowing toward corporate CEOs, and toward all workers in the financial sector, does have some negative effects on productivity growth. Money put into pay packages of top executives is not money spent on new capital equipment; Wall Street is not a capital-intensive industry, and the increase in its share of national income has probably come at the cost of many new factories, much new machinery, and much new technology.

But the soaring *incomes* of top executives are not the major issue in the great productivity slowdown. The soaring *power* of these business leaders is a far more important factor. Asceticism is seldom a characteristic of the powerful. The arrivistes to the corridors of great power have typically in the past increased the size of the establishment that serves them and of the forces that are employed in keeping them in power. Caesar did not voluntarily shrink his legions, Napoleon his army, or Harry Truman his CIA. By the same token there is no reason to suppose that the new captains of capital will behave any differently. And they haven't.

Indeed, today's captains of capital stand squarely in the ranks of those who have achieved great power in the past. There has been plenty of talk about downsizing, about companies that have become lean and mean, about organization structures that have become flatter and less hierarchical. And plenty of people have been fired. But a careful look at labor statistics shows that more administrators are surviving the axe than production workers.

Today's top managers have used their power in the old-fashioned way, by *fattening,* not flattening, their administrative apparatus. In a book published posthumously, the late David M. Gordon, long associated with the New School for Social Research in New York, succeeded in "exploding" what he called "the myth of managerial downsizing." Gordon's research focused on a phenomenon that he called "bureaucratic burden," and he argued that because of this burden "that instead of decreasing, the size of the supervisory force in business has increased." His analysis is based on the employment and earnings data published by the U.S. Bureau of Labor Statistics. The proportion of the U.S. workforce that is "nonproduction or supervisory" increased from 12.6 in 1989 to 13.6 in 1992. So that while downsizing may have resulted in a decrease in employment in many companies, it did not lead to a decline in the ratio of supervisors to people actually producing, engineering, and designing products.

David Gordon had a long and distinguished career as a leading member of the Union of Radical Political Economists (URPE), which has made his conclusions suspect to many mainstream economists. Yet the numbers that he uses to make his case have proved persuasive to the few who have themselves looked at the numbers, such as Professor Samuel B. Hayes of the Harvard Business School.

Nowhere does Gordon suggest that those companies that have set out to cut employment have failed to get rid of people; instead he shows that among those who remain employed, the ratio of supervisory employees to total employees has risen. When confronted with this uncomfortable fact, devotees of the reengineering cult argue that many professional workers in the high-tech industries are classed as supervisors by the U.S. Census Bureau, when they are in fact mind workers rather than bureaucrats. We know of no surveys that either prove or disprove this point. What is revealing, however, is the growth in the number of business consultants in the wake of the reengineering movement. Consulting companies perform functions you would be more likely to see in the job description of a manager than of a regular worker. And when the number of business consultants is added to the total number of supervisory workers, the ratio of managers to workers sustained a truly amazing increase given all the talk of streamlined management. And there is no evidence, absolutely nothing, to lead anyone to believe that, in and of itself, an increase in the cadre of supervisors and cryptosupervisors will increase productivity.

MORALE AND PRODUCTIVITY

This is where the American economy stands in the mid-1990s: its workforce has been degraded by reengineering and roiled by the largest merger wave in history. A technological revolution no less but also no more impressive than earlier such revolutions in the history of capitalism is providing opportunities for rapid gains in efficiency. Yet there is no sign that the rate of productivity growth has increased in this decade, and, according to available projections, there is little prospect that it will accelerate over the next five years. Nor indeed is there any sign that the United States has emerged as a leader in productivity growth among the advanced industrial countries. As Table 4-3 shows, the U.S. productivity growth rate since the end of the cold war— 1.2%—is below that of five other advanced countries: Australia, Germany, Italy, Sweden, and Britain.

Mainstream economists profess much puzzlement over the failure of the rate of productivity growth to accelerate so far in this decade. Yet one question they have not yet asked is whether the failures of the reengineering and consolidation movements have combined with globalization to reduce, rather than to increase, the rate of productivity growth in the United States. Analysts have not tried to assess the

Table 4-3
Productivity Growth Rates: An International Comparison,
1960–1994

Country	1960–67	1967–73	1973–79	1979–89	1989–94*	Cumulative 1960–94**
Australia	n.a.	2.8%	1.8%	0.9%	1.6%	1.7%
Canada	2.4%	2.6	1.3	1.2	−0.2	1.5
West Germany	3.9	4.3	2.9	1.1	2.1	2.7
France	4.4	4.2	2.4	1.9	1.2	2.8
Italy	6.3	5.1	2.7	2.0	1.9	3.5
Japan	8.1	8.0	2.9	2.8	1.0	4.5
Netherlands	n.a.	n.a.	1.7	0.6	0.5	0.9
Sweden	4.1	2.9	0.5	1.2	2.3	2.1
United Kingdom	2.3	3.4	1.3	1.9	1.4	2.0
United States	2.7	0.9	−0.1	0.8	1.2	1.1

* Netherlands: 1989-93. Germany: 1989-92.
** Australia: 1967-94. Netherlands: 1973-93. Germany: 1960-92.
Data: Economic Policy Institute

strong likelihood that the loss in job security has affected morale in a way that has undermined job performance, and hence productivity. Anyone who has been through the terrors of downsizing knows that those who have escaped the axe work harder. But the real questions are: How do such workers really relate to each other? and How effective is their performance? Are they, in the end, more or less creative than they could have been without the reengineering?

As we mentioned earlier in the chapter, in *White Collar Blues,* Charles Heckscher, chair of the Labor Studies and Employment Relations Department at Rutgers University, reports on the results of interviews with over 250 middle managers from a wide array of firms, including Honeywell, General Motors, Pitney Bowes, Dow Chemical, Figgie International, du Pont, and AT&T. Managers who were interviewed were drawn from the ranks of those who were not fired during downsizings but managed to hold on to their jobs. Heckscher professes surprise at workers' reactions to the "trauma of downsizing." He expected, he says, "for people to turn against each other." This "scapegoating" phenomenon, he notes, "has been widely observed in many situations of social disintegration. But no such thing happened. On the whole," he says, "discord was a minor note in these companies. Rather than turning on each other, most people drifted apart, becoming more isolated and looking to be left alone." Among the survivors of reengineering, the feelings of isolation seemed to increase over time, eventually leading to what Heckscher calls "a full-scale retreat to autonomy." As a result, says Heckscher, managers did not "by any evidence I could find, work very well together."

Nothing could be more different from the results promised by reengineering and "teaming" than the feelings of isolation and autonomy Heckscher found in the course of interviewing over 250 executives. And it is certainly fair to ask, as traditional economists have not asked, whether a managerial cadre in the grip of feelings of isolation is in part responsible for the failure of acceleration in the rate of productivity growth. It is significant in this connection that unpublished research by Monitor, a consultant firm based in Cambridge, Massachusetts, found that nine out of ten firms that had outperformed other companies within their industries over a ten-year period had "stable" structures, with no more than one reorganization and no change (or an orderly change) in CEO.

The evidence strongly suggests, then, that those who earn their living from work have been traumatized by a kind of cultural revolution that has inflicted pain on millions of people while serving no socially useful purpose. The profitability of American business has certainly increased since the end of the cold war, not because companies have become more efficient, but rather because the spread of the market economy around the globe has prevented real wages in the United States from rising. What has been sauce for the goose has not been sauce for the gander. The increase in efficiency promised by the apostles of reengineering and the apologists for the great merger wave remains invisible.

Those who earn their living from work in the United States have been betrayed. Nor is their betrayal at an end. Pat Buchanan's 1996 run for the Republican presidential nomination did result in a political reaction to downsizing, as well as a hike in the minimum wage, which will, at best, have minor effects. The attention Buchanan brought to the issue led many companies to realize that they could no longer crow about the number of people they had forced out, in the hopes that Wall Street would reward them with a higher stock price.

Unfortunately the real effect of Buchanan's campaign rhetoric will not be on corporate practices but on corporate public relations.

Not very long after the Buchanan phenomenon appeared, the American Management Association scheduled a conference on the public relations aspects of downsizing. "But that," says an AMA official, "will not lead to changes in employment policies. The economic imperatives are too strong." Instead, we can expect companies to increase the size of the public relations screen used to hide what is going on. The strategy is to reassure those Americans who earn their living from work that their interests are still congruent with those of the great American corporations.

Yet companies will continue to shift their operations overseas so as to take more and more advantage of the leviathan labor pool of the post-cold war world. Productivity growth in the United States has been held back by still another factor that conventional economic analysts have downplayed, if not totally ignored: the transfer of production and technology to areas of the world where not only muscle workers but also mind workers are abundant and inexpensive. It is to an analysis of these workers and their world that we now turn. To do so, we must visit the Indian city of Bangalore, where formidable competition is emerging for the industry in which the United States still has the clearest lead—computer software.

CHAPTER 5

A Passage to India: The Case of Bangalore

I N HIS EXUBERANT, MUCH-CELEBRATED NOVEL *THE MOOR'S Last Sigh,* Salman Rushdie portrays the deep idiosyncracies of one family, the da Gama–Zogoiby clan, to illustrate the fate of modern India. Rushdie uses a canvas of surreal images—a stuffed bulldog containing the soul of Jawaharlal Nehru; a group of variously shaped Indian actors parroting Lenin's speeches in a dozen Indian dialects (comic opera efforts at importing the Russian Revolution); a torched spice grove in southern Kerala State strewn with the crucified bodies of those rumored to have belonged to India's Home Rule movement; a mysterious painting invested with the secrets of the past; and "Mother India" herself, the dazzling, brash, unsentimental artist, Aurora—to tell his story. Rushdie's saga is strewn with buffoons, fools, and seers, characters playing out the literature of magical realism who depict India's many follies and missed opportunities.

In some ways, the beautiful, chaotic, electricity-short city of Bangalore, sitting three thousand feet above the rest of southern India on a plateau deep in the interior, could almost be a page out of Rushdie's novel. But in contrast to the Moor's environs, it is very much a place where "the players" have somehow managed to win out, and the exuberance of quick fortunes being made through space-age megadeals are staged in spaces adjacent to noisy harangues over large sacks of grain being transferred from one bullock cart to another, as they have been for hundreds of years. It is in this often enchanted Indian city, still unknown to most of the Western world, that thousands upon thousands of Indian computer scientists work long days and nights in head-to-head competition with their American counterparts. Ironically, Robert Reich, secretary of labor in the first Clinton administration, has insisted that duplicating what he calls "symbolic-analytic" zones outside the United States is almost impossible. He has said,

> While specific inventions and insights emanating from them traverse the globe in seconds, the cumulative, shared learning on which such ideas are based is far less portable. Other nations may try, with varying degrees of success, to create a Hollywood, or . . . a Silicon Valley. But to do so requires more than money. Each of these symbolic-analytic zones represents a complex of institutions and skills which have evolved over time. To contrive exactly the right balance is no easy task.

Apparently Reich has not visited Bangalore, for although it will indeed take time to set up such an environment, that south Indian city does in fact contain a more than healthy embryo that exhibits the exact balance that Reich is talking about.

For in a kind of high-tech magical realism that defies all the odds, Bangalore has quietly put together all the ingredients of a broad frontal attack on American hegemony on the frontier of the information revolution, software. India's software industry, which barely existed ten years ago, notched up sales of more than $1.2 billion in 1995 and has been growing at over 40 percent a year. Unlike many other Indian industries, it is already highly competitive internationally.

It's easy to understand the progress Taiwan has made in computer hardware in the 1990s, which in the end, is a process industry in which Japan, two decades earlier, proved that America is vulnerable. In the competition between Bangalore and the United States in the software industry, it is not a battle of manufacturing process against manufacturing process but mind against mind, an arena where the United States has, up to this point, outwitted not only the emerging world but also Europe and Japan. It is frightening to remember how quickly American workers faced competition once our competitors got up to speed in process industries. Among the veterans at Toyota in Japan there is a famous story about their car being unable to climb the hills in San Francisco when it was first delivered to the United States in 1957. Yet a decade later America was already losing market share to Japan at an alarming pace. And Bangalore software is already way ahead of that 1957 Japanese clunker.

INDIA'S ELITE WORKERS HAVE ARRIVED

Workers in India, and particularly Bangalore, could easily give American workers stiff competition in the coming decade. India has managed to become a growing power in software maintenance even though no more than 150,000 computers were sold in the country in 1995. And Indian companies have already won awards for the excellence of the new software they have produced, even though in 1995 less than .5 percent of all the software sold in the world was produced in India. These are small numbers to be sure, but they point to the newness of Indian technology, rather than to its weakness. And enormous opportunities will exist as long as India retains its huge cost advantage and continues to graduate some twenty thousand software-literate engineers from its technical institutes each year. Ironically, the educational foundations for India's software industry takeoff were laid by decades of socialist government emphasis on free university education for Indians from all social classes. Although education was not mandatory, and unfortunately many poor Indians living in villages and large cities kept their children at home, through education the forty-four-year socialist-style government still managed to produce a middle class of about 120 million people, by far the largest educated class of Indians the country had ever known.

Middle-class Indians have begun to work with an army of formidable expatriate Indian professionals now hitting midlife who were of a generation that began leaving India in the late 1960s for the United States and Europe. For middle-class technology success stories, American journalists have concentrated mostly on the Japanese and Chinese. It has usually been India's spiritual emissaries, gurus in particular, who have garnered the most media attention in the United States. But it would be a mistake to ignore Indians, many of whom have worked as top mathematicians, technologists, doctors, and increasingly bankers not only in India but throughout the industrialized world. There were more than a quarter of a million Indian physicians, scientists, engineers, managers, administrators, and people in similar high-level occupations living in other countries in the 1990s.

More and more, both local and expatriate populations are working in tandem, bent on creating their own economic miracle, so as to move India alongside its counterparts in the rest of Asia. "The mid-1990s has been a time when most Indians I know believe very strongly that

India's time has finally come as a nation," says Vijay Kumar, a Wharton School graduate who helps oversee Coopers and Lybrand's operations in India. Over the last three years, Kumar has begun spending about half his time in India as a business adviser, helping businesses grow. "It is much more satisfying personally to be involved with helping people get jobs in India rather than watching the annihilation of reengineering going on in the American workplace," says Kumar.

"There is no doubt that Indians in the current generation have become more creative than they were twenty-five years ago when I was starting out," he says. "Indians have always had a reputation for being rather rigid in their thinking. That may have been true in the past because Indian teaching methods depended mainly on memorization instead of intellectual give-and-take. Now, however, as the Indian bureaucracy continues to be peeled back, schools are encouraging professors to be more freewheeling in terms of seminars and vigorous class discussions. For example, the Indian Institute of Technology and its various schools throughout India are currently turning out top-notch engineers and computer scientists who are also increasingly creative.

"The Indian software business has grown between 40 and 50 percent a year. But it is only in the last twelve months that there has been a large effort by this dynamic industry to actually *create* software products. It probably won't be long before several of these companies come up with some great innovative products. And there will, of course, be a built-in cost advantage for many years to come. Venture capitalists in the United States are just beginning to really understand this market and are beginning to pour real money into Indian software companies. One of these, a company called Mastek, recently went public on NASDAQ in early January 1997. In addition, large U.S. companies such as Northern Telecom and Motorola with subsidiaries in Bangalore are also involved in developing software, in addition to handling all of the software maintenance work that the Indian companies also do. General Electric currently produces medical equipment in Bangalore, taking advantage of the large population of Bangaloreans with engineering and scientific training to manage company projects."

Many like Kumar originally went abroad because there was no dynamic economic base in their own country. They often left home after getting first-rate undergraduate degrees in India for free. Once abroad they were supported by deep networks, or safety nets, of uncles, aunts, village relationships, university mates who automatically opened up their homes to any Indian "friend" in the United States who got off an airplane. These networks put a high premium on education and formed a strong protective shield for those who had gone far from home. Now this successful immigrant population has started to go back to India, putting its financial backing, knowledge, and networks on several continents to work not only in Bangalore but also in places like Hyderabad, Pune, and Delhi and teaming up with entrepreneurs who have stayed at home to put the infrastructure in place for the high-tech revolution.

FLOURISHING BANGALORE

The seeding for India to be a winner in the great software mind game is already visible in the yeasty capital of Karnataka State. Ranked by *Time* magazine in August 1995 as the fastest growing city in Asia, some say in the entire world, Bangalore is already inhabited by a first-class twenty-first-century scientific workforce of software engineers, research scientists, and medical workers. But it would be wrong to think of Bangalore as another Silicon Valley, or the equivalent of the Route 128 area outside Boston. You would come much closer if you imagined another emerging software center—Manhattan (minus its skyscrapers)—as a psychological metaphor for Bangalore. First of all, for Manhattan's hordes of pampered purebred dogs, substitute throngs of skinny, benevolent-looking sacred cows decked out with bright blue painted horns parading through the middle of Broadway traffic. Next mix in the insanity of New York traffic with zooming auto-rickshaws, motorbikes, and large platoons of new automobiles with newly licensed young drivers, creating a traffic free-for-all on potholed roads that would frighten even the most daredevil Manhattan cab driver.

For a long time some of India's most prolific writers, musicians, and artists have been Bangalore residents. But more recently, through the late 1980s and in the 1990s, the city has attracted a growing platoon of moviemakers, television producers, and graphic designers. Like Manhattan, Bangalore is also a major national center for medical research. Recently many southern Indian doctors trained in the United States and Europe have been lured back home, and they are equipping Bangalore's medical centers with some of the most sophisticated technology in the world.

All these talents live side by side in a moving kaleidoscope of heat, dust, pollution, sprawling high-tech industrial parks, an occasional squealing pig, the monumental three-hundred-year-old Mysore Palace up the road studded with sapphires, diamonds, and emeralds; women who carry cement mix in their proud headdresses at local construction sites; busy monkeys darting in and out of traffic a few miles from the center of town; mud and grass slums; a zany-looking violin-shaped music center; overworked electrical generators that produce spotty power; flickering phone connections; towering posters of movie-star lotharios; entrepreneurs with great technological vision.

On top of all this, a German horticulturist named Krumbigal, Bangalore's official gardener during the early part of the twentieth century, covered the city's broad avenues and rambling parks with lush blossoming trees—jacaranda, tabebuia, cassia, gulmohar, and acacia and lush cascades of bougainvillea. Bangalore became famous for its prosperous Indian contractors who first designed the large airy homes called bungalows for rich British officers, who liked to retire to the relatively cooler climate of this area. Indeed, a whole group of service workers—traders, tailors, shoemakers, tobacconists, and liquor vendors—grew up in the area, making Bangalore a Raj stronghold for more than a century and a half. It is still a great city for upscale shopping.

Jawaharlal Nehru, India's first prime minister (1947 – 1964), had a radically different vision for Bangalore. Calling Bangalore India's "city of the future," in the late 1940s Nehru sought to turn it into India's intellectual capital. It would be a place, said Nehru, where scientists could get away from India's overwhelming masses and produce ideas and programs that would guide the new democracy's ambitious plans to achieve economic and military self-reliance. The city had already established a group of engineering colleges as far back as 1860. Under Nehru, New Delhi lavishly subsidized Bangalore's civilian science and technology infrastructure as well as India's advanced military and space research facilities. As a result, Bangalore and its environs today boasts three universities, fourteen engineering colleges, forty-seven polytechnic schools, and a plethora of research institutes devoted to science, health, aeronautics and space, food and agriculture, and the environment. Public sector giants such as Hindustan Aeronautics, Bharat Electronics, Indian Telephone Industries, Hindustan Machine Tools, and the Indian Space Research Organization, which develops and launches satellites for civilian purposes, are all located in the Bangalore area.

Yet neither the Raj, Nehru, nor the early south Indian scientists themselves could possibly have imagined that their city would become a software capital of Asia, doing more software business than either Israel or Singapore. Recently the Bangalorean software industry has been aping what happened in Manhattan—moving some offices into the center of the city. But for the moment, the many major facilities are located a few miles outside of downtown Bangalore in a barren-looking area dotted with squatter camps and meandering cows. Electronics City, as it is called, houses software companies in what appear from the outside to be nondescript two- or three-storey buildings set not far away from one another.

Since there are no visible restaurants or stores near by, workers at Electronic City take all their breaks at the so-called office "campuses," which on the inside look very much indeed like their Silicon Valley, California, counterparts. At Infosys, for example, software engineers in their twenties and thirties obsess over their computer screens, chat by the coffee machine, or shoot baskets in the company gym to break up long, long work days. Often workers are picked up and delivered to and from their homes by company buses, fed company-subsidized meals, and in some cases provided with company housing. But they are not mere company drones used only to jack up corporate profits. Like many of his U.S. counterparts, their boss, N. R. Narayana Murthi, has instituted a comprehensive stock option system that has turned a handful of top staffers into millionaires and made most of the staff at Infosys at least financially comfortable.

It takes an intellectually open environment and an entrepreneurial edge to produce the kind of place that Bangalore is fast becoming. And it takes leadership, which the Bangalore software industry has in abundance. The industry has been nurtured and led by visionaries such as Murthi, who set up his own company, Infosys, more than a decade ago, and his friend and colleague, N. Varadan, a government technology expert who makes it his business to facilitate deals between Bangalore and the West. Murthi is sometimes thought of as India's Bill Gates, but he is somewhat older and more philosophical. Unlike most of India's bureaucracy, officials like Varadan are not bureaucrats' bureaucrats, but entrepreneurs' bureaucrats, totally committed to making the private sector go. Because of their deep commitment to an Indian technological nationalism, these remarkable leaders represent a huge psychological contrast to American CEOs, who don't much care about where their employees come from. Men like Varadan and Murthi care a lot about young Indian head workers and their role in the global economy, because these workers prefigure India's role in the twenty-first century.

THE SOFTWARE BUSINESS IN BANGALORE

Like Steve Jobs and Bill Gates, Murthi started his software company with a few hundred dollars and no big financial backers. His company came into existence in Pune, about 120 miles south of Bombay. But as the organization grew, Murthi decided to move to Bangalore, because, as he said, "This city offered better living conditions for professionals. And professionals are our most important raw material in the software business." The surrounding area also offered better opportunities for education.

Because of its tremendous cost advantage and professional reputation, Infosys is expected to grow over 50 percent during the next several years. But Murthi feels that he must move his company to the frontier of the information revolution. "Sometime very soon," he says,

> we would like 40 percent of our business to come from our own creative software. [Only about 10 percent comes from this source now.] This is where a large part of our future lies. We have about five or six years before the Chinese catch up to us and are able to do the same computer servicing for lower prices than we offer. Our industry will have to become more creative so our own products will grow in the global marketplace.

One of Murthi's many advantages is that his wife is a professor of computer science at a prestigious local university, so he can tap into some of the best new graduates in Bangalore. "Today, education is free," he says.

> India is the only country in the world which tries to transfer power from a very small section of the people—the Brahmans—to the larger mass. This is one of our major strengths. For example, in Karnataka, we [he is a Brahman] have only one minister out of twenty. That is all. It would never happen in any other country. Similarly, in the government, 90 percent of the jobs are for people who were formerly downtrodden. India is the only country in the world where over 70 percent of the places in the major universities are reserved for lower castes. It is an affirmative action program for 70 percent of jobs and university spots. We have many families working for us

who had no money at all several years ago. A man who is a cabdriver can easily have a son who ends up working at Infosys. Many Indians who study in the United States actually come from very modest families in India. This workforce is India's future. But we all have to work hard to make that future happen.

Murthi works very closely with Varadan, the veteran south Indian visionary who is in charge of the industrial park that houses many of Bangalore's largest firms, including Infosys. The government-owned, but autonomous, institution that Varadan represents helps export Indian software to other countries and helps to keep jobs flowing into his industrial park. Another of Varadan's major jobs is to communicate constantly with New Delhi ministers so that the problems encountered in the fast-moving software industry can be resolved quickly, a monumental job that Varadan has worked very hard at, considering the government's legendary glacial pace. By all accounts, the first hundred days of Prime Minister Rao's government brought the largest number of reforms. As one insider put it, "Many in the New Delhi bureaucracy had no idea how serious Rao's reforms were. Many things went through before the old establishment realized all that had happened." According to a number of Bangaloreans, the pace of change slowed down tremendously after the initial hundred days, and after the old bureaucracy bore down on the prime minister's reformers.

Varadan's job also includes helping out young entrepreneurs who want to set up small companies but don't have much capital. "The Software Technology Parks of India provide space and marketing support at bargain prices. They also do training and anticipate new areas that will make us continually competitive in the global market; it's a multifaceted society," says Varadan. "We are proud of what we are doing. We think we are going in the right direction. There are many Indian companies doing joint ventures."

The software business is spreading in India. Says Varadan:

In 1991 we tried to concentrate everything here in Bangalore. But now it doesn't matter where anyone is. The kind of communication we have set up permits an entrepreneur to be anywhere, a jungle, if that's where he wants to work from, a coffee plantation in Kerala. I'll give them a satellite dish, and they can work from there. Recently, I was in a place called Manipur, which is on the southwest coast of India and gave a presentation on the Internet. I never saw such a big crowd;

three hundred people flocking into the auditorium. And the entire population of Manipur is only 15,000. There has long been a feeling among young Indians that they had to go to the outside world to really learn what is going on. Today there is a reverse trend going on. Those who have been to the United States and Britain would now like to set up here. The majority of our software engineers are being trained in India today, rather than in the United States. Today's generation is different from that of twenty years ago.

As Varadan describes it, Bangalore is loaded with layers of new professionals.

The seventy-year-old Indian Institute of Science has produced a number of Ph.D.'s who now have top-level jobs in the United States. At the second level you have another ten or twelve institutions in and around Bangalore that are also well recognized; then you have the third level of institutions—about fifty or sixty of them, producing computer and electronics engineers. Today for the software industry, anyone who has a chemistry, physics, science background and engineering, train them for six or nine months, [and] they can easily go into software engineering. In Karnataka, the state produces about twenty thousand science and engineering graduates every year. [The total Indian pool is growing at about 20,000 a year as compared to 80,000 in the United States.] That's quite a potential pool. Technically we have the capacity to grow a lot. The medical field is also attracting a lot of growth. High-tech medicine is benefiting from local institutions, Indians who have worked in U.S. medical schools and hospitals are shipping back the latest equipment to us.

Indeed, the 1996 decision by Silicon Graphics, perhaps the most sophisticated major software company in the world, to erect a facility in Bangalore was governed by the company's belief that the city is ideally suited to develop computer applications in the field of high-tech medicine.

Recently, a new investment park called Information Technology Park, financed with money from Singapore and located not that far away from Electronics City, has attracted thousands of overseas inquiries about commercial space. Like most other parks growing up around Bangalore, it will have its own power, sewage, and satellite communications systems. One hundred and thirty other industrial parks have been started in other locations in India, but Bangalore is still considered the center of software activity.

Fortunately for Bangalore, it does not have to ship its wares to the developed world by way of India's antiquated transportation system, its abysmal roads, or even count on its erratic telephone system. The costs of ocean transport or of airfreight are largely irrelevant to Bangalore's software industry. Instead, companies commune with the developed world using the digitized satellite communications system run by Varadan's agency, which works in much the same way as do the international financial markets. And because moving the south Indian city's output to the rest of the world is so cheap, it represents a new threat to workers in the developed world, who, in the past, have been afforded protection by the high cost of transporting bulky goods into their markets, and the impossibility of swiftly moving the mountains of data needed to run businesses.

Bangalore's software gurus fret over the slow pace at which the New Delhi bureaucrats approve new projects. But Indian technologists like Varadan are well aware that two developments are on their side: the growing use of the Internet as a way of speeding the flow of information, and the corporate trend toward controlling the cost and production of information through outsourcing could create enormous benefits for facilities that can handle information at low cost. Indian businesspeople are aware that the recent development of new universal programming languages such as Java and the use of the Internet for internal communications within corporations—the so-called Intranet—will only serve to enhance India's competitive edge. And though they know that capital-starved India cannot readily replicate the expensive wired and cabled infrastructure of the developed world's information and communications industries, they realize that Indians can create a streamlined information highway of their own based on satellites and cellular phones.

It is the software industry more than any other that has started to free up and use Indian talent in a dynamic way. "There has been a very high frustration level for a long time," says Kumar. "People are bursting to do intelligent jobs." Some Americans coming to India for the first time are in awe of the energy level of the people they meet. "We came here to give demonstrations of a simple industrial cleaning machine used in hospitals and office buildings that we make back in Minnesota," says one recently converted Bangalore enthusiast from the Midwest. "We had two hundred people show up for our seminar. They asked every technical question they could. Some were so sophisticated we didn't know how to answer, and we stayed an hour longer than usual because the audience was so fascinated. It was kind of mind-boggling." Even something as simple as a cleaning machine catches fire. But software is obviously king in Bangalore.

THE POWER OF INDIA'S GROWING MIDDLE CLASS AND ELITE WORKERS

The strong positive impression that the Indian middle classes and elite workers make on businessmen from the industrialized world is new and important. An anecdote well known by many in India's emerging middle class is of a top executive of the Caterpillar Corporation who during a negotiation in the 1960s tossed a cigarette lighter across a conference table and said condescendingly, "When you guys can make one of these things, let me know about it." That kind of behavior, as middle-class Indians quickly point out, is unimaginable now.

Representative of the city's well-prepared elite is the couple we met for dinner our first night in Bangalore. Kumar's colleague in Bangalore, D. Ashok (everyone calls him Dash), who works as a software specialist, and his wife, Revathy Ashok, who is financial controller for AMP, India, an American electronics firm, took us to an elegant restaurant in a garden setting. Dash immediately began talking about his position in the world of information processing technology. "I spent a year in New York," he said, "which was one of the most important years of my professional life. I wanted to test myself against the Americans, and I found out that I came out very well indeed. It was a great boost to my confidence." Significantly, neither Dash nor his wife had been educated abroad. Both were products of India's homegrown elite universities.

Like most Bangaloreans, the Ashoks wanted to discuss the limits to growth imposed by the city's present infrastructure—bad roads; growing pollution from auto and truck exhausts; a telephone system that, although highly efficient in the middle of the city, reaches to the new industrial parks only with difficulty; the shortage of south Indian power and the resulting blackouts everyday in the morning and afternoon; a constant inflow from nearby villages in southern India of entire families who want to raise their own living standards by getting jobs in this new cyberspace capital.

But there is another infrastructure in Bangalore that the Bill Gateses and Andy Groves of the world are buying at an incredibly low price, and it partially explains why every big name, not just in software, but in the entire computer industry, is moving facilities into Bangalore. As our dinner conversation with the Ashoks proceeded, it gradually became apparent to us why Bangalore had become a magnet for high-tech firms trying to combine topflight work with low costs. For what American corporations are getting in India today is not only high-quality global professional talent, but also a family social network that supports workers at an extremely low cost. The Indian middle class can still rely on family to take care of elderly grandparents and children with working mothers. This built-in social infrastructure is an attraction for Western companies tired of the demands of family in the United States—demands that limit workers' availability and make U.S. workers more expensive to employ. Ironically, the very social fabric that draws multinational corporate employers like a magnet to the East has, to a large degree, been unravelled by these same companies through worker transfers and long working hours.

For instance, Dash and Revathy Ashok, the parents of two children, ages seven and thirteen, each has a driver supplied by their companies as well as a secretary. There is a governess, a family cook, a gardener, and more important, a set of intelligent, well-educated grandparents who live with their married children. Usually it is the paternal grandparents who look after the children during the many long hours that the professional pair work and travel. A dollar buys a lot in India. In round figures for the software industry, it currently costs about one third as much in India to do what is done in the United States—even with the thousands of miles of distance.

It's not just foreign corporations but Indian expatriates themselves who are becoming aware of these favorable economics. As Revathy says, "Many of our friends from graduate school who went abroad fifteen years ago are now coming home to India to work. They have found that they can maintain a much higher standard of living here, as we do, than they can by staying in the United States." Even families living on lower incomes can rely on Indian entrepreneurship to help them through their chores. Laundry men walk up and down the streets of Bangalore and other cities setting up ironing boards and pressing clothes on the sidewalk for a few rupees.

Low production costs and the low cost of good living are indeed attracting many Indian technologists back home. An MIT-educated software engineer in his late twenties on his way home to India says he now lives in Pune six months out of every year. "My company is set up in Cambridge, Massachusetts," he adds, "but we get a lot of the actual work done here in my old hometown." A fifty-two-year-old engineer from the Punjab who has worked at Hewlett-Packard among other hardware firms is involved in a start-up company with a handful of other Indians who have worked abroad. He says, "We crunched the numbers, and we have decided there is no other way but to set up our design operation in India. It is just so much cheaper and has the same kind of talent as the Silicon Valley. The only remaining question is where is the best place to locate in India?"

India's middle classes experience none of the job anxiety that has unhinged many of their American counterparts. "If you are well-educated, work hard, and know what you are doing, there is no chance in today's India that you will not have security in this exploding job market. There are so many opportunities to pursue." This is the assessment of Revathy Ashok. The thought of packaging and repackaging themselves as human portfolios, of never achieving real job permanence, is unthinkable among today's upper- and middle-class Bangaloreans. Instead they talk of the almost limitless opportunities that are now occurring. Kumar, who has spent thirty years straddled between the United States and India, sees a reversal of attitudes. "In the United States the anxiety level is higher than it's ever been, and in India, despite the many problems, people are extremely bullish, and they feel that the twenty-first century belongs to India. This," adds Kumar, "is without exception, whether you talk to professionals, or an average Indian on the street. And it was not so five or ten years ago. It's the way it was in the 1950s and 1960s in the United States."

The long-term impact of the emergence of a high-morale middle class in what will be the most populous country in the world early in the next millennium cannot be underestimated. Indian businessmen talk endlessly of the frustration they feel because of the huge successes achieved by their counterparts in less populous countries such as Singapore or Taiwan or Hong Kong or South Korea. And they seem highly motivated to eclipse the elites of those countries, whom they regard as fringe players in the long run.

The benefits of middle-class growth and prosperity to India are enormous. As Jane Jacobs has argued over and over again in her works, a sense of independence and of control over one's life is essential to satisfaction and productivity. The Indian middle class has achieved this sense of control, and though the politics of the country turned unstable after the May 1996 elections, a succession of weak coalition governments is unlikely to upset the country's basic reforms or, more important, to put huge roadblocks in the way of India's emerging middle class or its technological revolution.

The leading intellectual apostle and biographer of Indian reform lives not in New Delhi, or even Bangalore, but on the Upper West Side of New York City. "We lost a whole generation, perhaps two, to Fabian socialism," says Jagdish Bhagwati, the world-famous professor of economic development at Columbia University, and a longtime champion of deregulation and free markets. Bhagwati explains why by noting that the elites who ran the country after India gained independence in 1947 were almost all educated at Oxford and Cambridge. "We all became steeped in a kind of socialism that emphasized gradualism and, of course, a close ongoing relationship to bureaucracy," he says. "What India actually required, was in fact something quite different. If the Indian elites had, instead, been educated at the University of Chicago [the home of free-market economics]," he says only half facetiously, "then perhaps things may have been very different much earlier on."

Post–cold war reform in India was carried out by Prime Minister P. V. Narasimha Rao and his finance minister, Manmohan Singh, in 1991 when the pair began freeing business from the heavy weight of Indian bureaucracy. India's projected 6 percent economic growth rate in the fiscal year ending in March 1996, and the 5.6 percent growth rate for the three preceding years, is a stark contrast to its growth of only 0.6 percent in the year ending March 1992, the first year of economic reform, and the country's average growth rate of 3.5 percent for the preceding three decades.

Yet in some sense politics is almost beside the point in India, and the 1996 election results are not of great significance. To become familiar with Bangalore is to realize that much of the discussion of the city's future and therefore of the future of high-tech industry in India is completely misdirected. The Indian elite who live in the city talk of little other than the problems of New Delhi regulation or the city's overworked infrastructure, which are indeed legion. (There is no road leading in or out of the city that is more than one and a half lanes wide.) But it is also abundantly clear that the power and influence of the upper and middle classes is enormous. In Bangalore there is ferocious networking within the elites to assure that their needs are met. And they have been quite successful in furthering their interests.

On a trivial level, it was middle-class ridicule that helped end the attempt to shut down Bangalore's newly opened Kentucky Fried Chicken outlet in April 1996. A local court ruled that KFC, which had proven to be popular with many Bangaloreans, should stay open since it was not violating any local laws. On a more fundamental level, the power of the middle class in India is so great that its members can, in fact, have bumps put into the middle of the roads that pass by their houses so as to slow down traffic and preserve the safety of their children. In a practical sense, the Indian elite has more power to shape its surroundings than does the American middle class. And this, mind you, is in India, the last home of Fabian socialism.

Indeed, the power of the middle class to influence its work and living environment is far greater in Asia than in Europe or North America. In Taiwan, Indonesia, Malaysia, and even the Philippines society bends more swiftly and surely to the will of the technological elite. These are societies in the process of raising a new middle class to new highs, just as surely as during the Industrial Revolution, when steel managers, textile masters, and mine operators dominated industrialized societies. It is the world of the middle class on the move. And this is only the beginning.

THE IMPLICATIONS OF CORPORATE OUTSOURCING AND THE TRANSFER OF TECHNOLOGY

America's elite workforce in the data processing and software programming fields probably will face strong competition from Indian mind workers if we take the rapid growth of the software industry in Bangalore seriously. This elite workforce could soon easily face the same kind of competition that led to the decline of America's high-wage workforce in traditional industries such as steel and automaking. And it is to a realistic analysis of its impact on the prospects for the American worker elites that we now turn.

So far it's the move of global corporations into Bangalore that has caught the world's attention, particularly decisions in 1995 and 1996 of such leading-edge software companies as Silicon Graphics to open facilities there, focusing on medical applications. Bangalore became a software center very recently, and so far most of what is done there is relatively unsophisticated. Most of the work done in Bangalore currently is maintenance of software systems for major U.S. corporations, so Bangalore's software business is nestled toward the bottom of the world's high-tech information industry, for now. The facilities set up in Bangalore by U.S. corporations are meant to take advantage of low costs for software system maintenance, as well as the indigenous Indian software companies. There is another advantage. Bangalore also thrives on a clock that runs some ten hours ahead of America's eastern standard time. "When an American goes to sleep we wake up," says Murthi. "If AT&T has a computer snag at night with its system, our engineers try to get the problem solved by the time AT&T goes back to work at nine A.M. the next day. We e-mail them the work. This is the way we use this time difference to our advantage."

Murthi's clients include many American blue-chip companies including AT&T, Nordstrom, Citibank, and General Electric. Infosys does many "fixed-price projects"—tailoring software tasks to the needs of a particular company at a fixed price and setting up customized systems. At first there are usually on-site meetings with new clients and Infosys staff in the United States, but as the relationship becomes more long term, communications are often shifted exclusively to videoconferencing between Bangalore and New York, or any other location.

Infosys does a good job, according to clients. As one Citibank computer specialist puts it, "The only disadvantage with any of these Indian software companies is working with people who are so far away. But we lay out an incredible amount of detail so they can do the job, and they seem to thrive on this kind of orderliness and strong direction." Citibank also has about two hundred software engineers on its own internal staff, along with a core of Indians in the top ranks of management.

American workers are currently threatened by corporate out-sourcing and the globalization of work, and the more so since companies like Murthi's are so competent in performing the software maintenance work. There is no question that leading-edge work in the software business is still concentrated in the United States and the other industrialized countries and is likely to remain so for some time to come. But like almost every other industry, the software industry creates a chain of ancillary activities that are less intellectually demanding but closely related to the basic product. To take one obvious case, this kind of chain is present in the auto industry, where the production of a new vehicle automatically sets in motion huge requirements for secondary industries, maintaining cars, fixing them when they break down, servicing them with gasoline. It has frequently been estimated that one in every ten jobs in the United States has been created by the invention of the automobile. It is true, of course, that many of these jobs, mainly in parts production and in the production of cars themselves, have migrated abroad, but many of them are necessarily located in the United States. There is simply no way that a car can be transmitted to India for overnight repair.

Yet no such protections exist in an industry where the product, information, is digitized and moves between locations at almost the speed of light. That software and data processing problems can be solved anywhere and then transmitted almost instantly to a client company across the globe explains the breathtaking growth rate of Banglore's software industry. It is why Bangalore represents a template of what is to come in any era whose central feature is a stream of output that can be moved around at minimal cost. It is why Bangalore has caught the eye of those concerned with the future of the software industry. And it is why many experts in the software business believe that India will account for as much as 5 percent of the industry by the year 2000.

Bangalore also offers general insights into what is probably the most important threat posed by the spread of the free market to those who earn their living from work in the United States: outsourcing and the transfer of technology. In the days when the market economy was limited to the Eurocentric world and Japan, and when business only trusted ethnic Europeans with complex tasks, there were relatively limited opportunities for companies in any industry to transfer technology abroad. As a consequence, companies' ability to take advantage of low-cost workers to produce the supporting products and systems spawned by leading-edge technology was limited. So these less sophisticated products tended to be produced within the developed world. There was no way that Bangalore could have developed a software industry of any significance before India's trade liberalization. And the same is roughly true of the period before such countries as China, Malaysia, or Indonesia turned outward. But as these countries gradually, if fitfully, merge into the global market economy, fewer and fewer such barriers exist.

The effect of these changes in world geopolitics and economics are of critical importance. The migration of the textile industry from New England to the South to take advantage of cheap labor and right-to-work laws that limited the power of unions was tough on the Northeast, but it did no damage to, and probably helped promote growth in, the United States as a whole. Similar observations can be made about the migration of the garment industry out of New York, the spread of the auto industry out of Detroit, and the migration of the steel industry out of Pittsburgh, which may still be home to the Steelers football team but no longer contains any steel-making facilities within its municipal boundaries. Countries tend to thrive and general real-wage levels tend to grow in periods when leading-edge technology seeps into and is diffused throughout the general population, as surely happened in the past in the United States during periods of rapid growth.

The spread of the free market economy throughout the world has also limited the *internal* process of technological diffusion in industrialized nations which had long been their prescription for rapid productivity growth. To take a simple case, today there is less of an incentive for the textile industry to move to the South both because wages in that region have increased relative to wages in the Northeast and because the spread of the free market means that new facilities can be located in any number of locations all over the world. New textile plants can be located in Slovakia as easily as in Savannah, in Malaysia as easily as in Macon, in Cochin as easily as in Charleston.

Nor should it be imagined that the United States automatically does better in international competition in high-tech goods than it does in low-tech goods such as foods or medium-tech goods such as autos. Indeed, when it comes to the relative growth rates of imports and exports, the exact opposite is true. University of Toronto economist Sylvia Ostry and Columbia University economist Richard R. Nelson have calculated what they call trade ratios—a simple calculation of exports divided by imports—for the years 1978–1991. For the United States the ratio of imports to exports has been increasing far more rapidly for high-tech goods than for either low- or medium-tech goods. This may seem surprising, but it really shouldn't be. Wages have been rising more slowly in the United States than in many foreign countries, keeping the cost of labor to produce many low-tech goods relatively modest in the United States. At the same time, high-tech goods are more economical to ship than low-tech goods, simply because their value is high relative to their weight. It is cheaper and easier to ship a cargo plane loaded with computer chips across the ocean than to transport a load of coal by ship. Many workers in U.S. industries that produce goods whose value is low relative to their bulk are afforded some protection because it is expensive to transport bulky goods from country to country.

The Ostry-Nelson study covers goods rather than services, so the calculations cannot be applied automatically to all aspects of the software industry. The kinds of system maintenance jobs performed in Bangalore enter the U.S. balance of payments as services rather than as goods. Yet experience in Bangalore points to the probability that America's trade advantage in the data processing industry will erode even more quickly than in more traditional markets. That is simply because digitized output can move from continent to continent at extremely low cost. Bangalore is, of course, exporting the service of software maintenance. But what it is doing points the way to the handling of data of all kinds—banking, inventory levels, credit card information, and insurance claims. Indeed, it appears that the basic economic barriers to outsourcing are far weaker in many of the computer-related service industries than in the goods-producing industries. A recent study by the World Bank predicts that "trade" between the developed world and the developing world in data processing and the maintenance of data banks will grow far faster than trade in goods. The World Bank estimates that the value of this trade will be twenty times greater by 2005 than it was in 1994.

But India will not be content until its software industry moves firmly onto the leading edge, by producing products and programs of its own, rather than merely servicing programs and systems developed in the advanced countries. That is why the most serious long-term threat to U.S. software workers is the coming thrust by indigenous Indian companies, such as Murthi's Infosys. As these businesses succeed in introducing their own products, they will threaten not only the information revolution's lower-tier workers, but the information elite themselves.

CHAPTER 6

Have the Elite Workers Had It?

idiosyncrasy (ĭd′ē-ō-sĭng′krə-sē) *n., pl.* **-sies. 1.** A structural or behavioral characteristic peculiar to an individual or a group . . . **2.** A physiological or temperamental peculiarity.

—*The American Heritage Dictionary
of the English Language*

I N THE HARD WORLD OF LABOR MARKET COMPETITION, nothing is more comfortable, or felicitous, than to be blessed with a rare skill that is difficult to reproduce and is highly valued by the market. This simple fact lies at the basis of many supposedly original discussions of one of the most striking features of the post–cold war labor market: the appearance of huge earnings differentials between the leaders and the ordinary members of a particular line of work or profession. Books like *The Winner-Take-All Society* by Robert H. Frank and Philip J. Cook have arrived on the scene explaining why Michael Jordan makes so much more money as compared with the average professional basketball player than did Bob Cousy, why Boris Becker makes more money than Arthur Ashe did, why the relative income of Tom Cruise is so high as compared with that of Cary Grant, and so forth and so on. The development of a global market, combined with modern communications devices such as televisions and VCRs, enable those considered to be the very best to put their wares on display before wider and wider audiences. This increased exposure allows them to exploit their advantages over more ordinary mortals more easily than their predecessors could. The effect, of course, has been the celebration of the strength and power of the industrial world's stars and a devaluation of the work of their more run-of-the-mill competition.

107

Life being what it is, the world is always more ready to celebrate the triumphs of the more fortunate amongst us than it is to face up to the factors that are making life far more difficult for the average person who earns his or her living from work. But the hard facts are that the very trends that are elevating the incomes of a small number of the stars of the developed world are also working to undermine the income of more ordinary people. These processes are virtually certain to work with greater intensity as the global economy moves into the twenty-first century, and they will erode the position of the professional and white-collar elites—the middle classes of the developed world—over the next decade just as surely as they brought down the blue-collar elites in the last quarter of the twentieth century.

Our view of the future of elite workers differs radically from the conventional view. In that view, as we have seen, only about 20 percent of the workforce really has what it takes to succeed in the information age. Economists and other intellectuals of all political persuasions espouse the notion that the elite workers are insulated from the leveling effects of the spread of free market production and the growth of the world labor pool. Most economists argue that the bulk of the American workforce is afflicted by a "skills mismatch" between the job requirements of the new technology and the job capabilities of ordinary mortals. Liberals and conservatives disagree on the causes of this "mismatch," though neither group questions its existence. Conservative writers such as Richard J. Herrnstein and Charles Murray emphasize that most of the population lacks the mental firepower needed to succeed in our technologically sophisticated age. For their part, liberal writers are inclined to blame an inadequate educational system and a lack of spending by the large corporation and other businesses on job training. All this, of course, sounds like music to the ears of the elite workers. If a "skills mismatch" afflicts only the bottom four fifths of American workers, then surely the elite workers in the top 20 percent can confidently look forward to job security, rising salaries, and increasing wealth.

We, by contrast, argue that the relative good fortune of the elite workers of the developed world is the product of a phase of economic history that is showing signs of coming to a close. The economist Joan Robinson, who was a colleague of John Maynard Keynes at Cambridge University in the 1930s and early 1940s, pointed out that in a market economy, the highest rewards were likely to be earned by factors of production that she identified as "idiosyncratic," having, as *The American Heritage Dictionary* says, unique structural or psychological characteristics. It is easy to understand that it is this combination of unique characteristics that explains the incomes of a Jordan, a Becker, or a Cruise. Just as easy, in fact, as to understand that platinum, molybdenum, or gold derive their value from their scarcity.

What is slightly more difficult to grasp is that the educated elites of the developed world have been an idiosyncratic factor of production *as a class* for most of the four-hundred-year history of capitalism. Therefore they were able to lay claim to a large share of the world's income. It was the educated classes of ethnic West European countries, including the United States and some of the British Commonwealth countries, who were the repositories of virtually all knowledge needed to apply science to the production and distribution. They therefore had a monopoly on technological advances and the dynamics of capitalist production. And since access to this class and to its knowledge base was limited both by ethnic and racial prejudice among the captains of capital and by limited access to education during most of the history of capitalism, white ethnic Europeans, *as a class,* also had a monopoly on the vast majority of high-skill jobs.

There is little question that the *initial phase* of the triumph of capital has been an unmixed blessing for the elites of the industrial world. As the market spread throughout the developing world, so did the export of high-technology goods and of the popular culture of the industrial world, particularly that of America, which for a long time has been the beneficiary of the cultural dominance embodied—and exported—in popular music, movies, and television series. In economic terms, the appetite for these American goods shows up in the growing trade surplus that the U.S. has enjoyed in entertainment products. There has been a similar thirst for all kinds of American capital goods, including those used in industrial processes, chemical production, indeed in virtually all lines of manufacturing production.

Ever since the age of discovery, the history of capitalism has been a history of the globalization of production. The effects of the post–cold war spread of the market to what had been the Third World have been remarkably similar to those of earlier phases of the globalization of markets, until very recently. That globalization proceeded in waves. First there was the sixteenth-, seventeenth-, and eighteenth-century settlement of the New World that followed in the wake of the discoveries. Then there was the great nineteenth-century expansion of the market economy that resulted from the age of colonialism and the adoption of a gold standard as the basis for international currency exchange. These earlier waves of global expansion hardly presented a threat to the European middle class. On the contrary, during these periods the opportunities available to middle-class ethnic Europeans increased dramatically. In the time of the "white man's burden," middle-class citizens in the colonies had a lucrative "burden" indeed. For many years, ethnic West Europeans held most of the world's good jobs, in production, distribution, and trade. They also held positions of power in the administration of government, the dispensation of justice, and the defense of the colonial realms. That is not to deny, of course, that earlier ages of globalization did present some opportunities for education to the native people of the Third World. In general, however, there were substantial barriers to their ability to compete effectively with the white overclass. As Adam Smith observed in *The Wealth of Nations*, it was a world in which "[b]irth and fortune are evidently the two circumstances which principally set one man above another."

Colonialism essentially came to an end after World War II, and with the closing of that chapter of history a vast array of new jobs were suddenly available to the peoples of the Third World. This was only the first stage of liberation for the Third World's middle classes. Outside the industrial democracies, many people in the developing nations, including those in the middle classes, were held back by socialist and communist governments that foreclosed foreign investment and, in the end, hindered economic growth. Yet, at the same time, countries modeled on the Soviet system, including India, "seeded" large parts of their populations for future middle-class and elite expansion by investing heavily in education.

Nevertheless, it was the triumph of capitalism over communism that created the potential for true economic liberation. The Third World was conveniently transformed into the emerging world by Wall Street, and its people, particularly its stifled, newly educated vast middle classes, now have more opportunities than ever before to seize hold of their own economic destinies. So far the industrial world's elite workers retain the vast proportion of the good jobs that the world has to offer. But a host of factors are at work that will make the skills of the ethnic European elites less and less unique and will threaten the livelihoods of many among them.

There is, to begin with, the reality of numbers. Population, as we have seen, is increasing far faster in the developing world than in the industrial world, and the difference in growth rates is bigger for the middle classes than for populations as a whole. In Chapter 3 we saw that the emerging world's middle class will grow far faster over the next quarter of a century than the middle class of the First World. Rapid economic growth in some of the smallest countries of East Asia—Taiwan, Hong Kong, and South Korea—has already provided formidable competition to American elite workers. The jockeying will only become more intense as middle-class life becomes a realistic prospect for the hundreds of millions in the two truly populous countries of the emerging world, China and India. In and of itself, the growth in the developing world's middle class does not spell doom for citizens of the white ethnic European world, but it does strongly portend that their unique talents will become far less scarce, and what has been the world's most idiosyncratic factor of production will become a far more common coin.

Trends in education paint an analogous picture. The Western, and especially the American, system of higher education retains superiority in the world. But it is a stark fact that the Western industrial world's lock on scientific and technical education began to fall apart after World War II, when Taiwan, South Korea, Singapore, and Hong Kong all eventually followed Japan's lead in offering cutting-edge science and technological education to those who possessed a talent for numbers. The industrial world's dominance in the technical fields has since been dwindling, as has its proportion of the world's supply of scientists and engineers. As is well known, and as Table 6-1 shows, many countries, including China and India, are now graduating far more engineers and scientists than the United States is. By common consent, the quality of scientific education is still higher in American institutions of higher learning than in all but a few schools in Europe and Japan, but it is also true that indigenous technical education in many countries of the emerging world is improving with dazzling speed. And it is also well known that the products of these institutions of learning can be hired at a far lower price than can American graduates, and this situation is likely to prevail for a long period of time, even though salaries for elite workers are rising more rapidly in the emerging world than in the United States.

Attitudes often count for as much as education. And in this regard there is no doubt that the middle classes of the emerging world have an edge. Their morale is high in comparison to that of America's middle class, for whom, as we saw in Chapter 4, the degradation of work has become a serious problem. Rutgers University labor expert Charles Heckscher, author of *White Collar Blues,* reports on a basic

Table 6-1
The Growing Professional Challenge to the U.S.

Country	Annual Graduates in	
	Engineering	Natural Sciences
China	113,000	40,000
Japan	81,000	25,000
United States	80,000	105,000
Germany	38,000	26,000
Mexico	30,000	9,600
India	20,000	147,000
South Korea	26,000	23,000
Czech Republic	9,400	3,000
Taiwan	8,900	6,500

Data: Economic Policy Institute

shift in expectations among the 250 middle managers he interviewed from downsized blue-chip companies. "This plan involves not only the obvious loss of income and standard of living but also the moral upheaval of losing a community, of trust betrayed. While other studies have documented it among the laid-off, I found it as strongly among those who remained employed." In an analysis of an actual company that he renames "Glover," Heckscher finds that among the people who stayed on after the downsizing, the changes were "deeper, both harder to see and more profound. Along with cost and waste, the transformation also eliminated, or at least damaged, the links among people. It did not make them selfish or bitter, but it did make them more isolated, more cautious, less able to enter into informal and spontaneous agreements. The organization therefore became more rigid and 'bureaucratic' than ever before."

Stresses and insecurities like the ones Heckscher describes have contributed to unprecedented behavior among anxious middle-class workers, such as middle-aged men undergoing cosmetic surgery so that they will look younger. Surgery to remove wrinkles, big stomachs, jowls, and anything else workers believe makes them vulnerable in today's job market is at an all-time high. Family therapist Ann Miller reports,

> Increasingly, many of the families I come into contact with— with houses that cost over $400,000 —can no longer meet their financial obligations. There is a quiet desperation around the

whole area. If the major wage earner becomes sick or falls out of the workforce, as is happening more and more, there's just a slow death in these communities. It's all very quiet. Very private. But the agony is widespread.

The changing attitude of the great multinational corporations toward executives, engineers, and scientists in the developing world is another reason the developed world's cognitive elites cannot feel secure. Managers and professionals are told that the exploding economic growth in the developing world will draw in U.S. exports to these countries, which will result in massive job growth. What is true enough is that U.S. and European companies are spending vast sums to build new markets in places that they viewed until recently only as sources of cheap labor. According to UN estimates, for example, direct investment in foreign plant, equipment, and service operations worldwide hit $325 billion in 1995, up 46 percent from 1994. American companies accounted for the biggest chunk of that investment, pouring a record $95 billion into overseas affiliates, according to the U.S. Department of Commerce.

News reports usually center on export trade to these countries. What goes largely unnoticed, however, is the fact that the total annual receipts of U.S.-owned companies operating in the developing world are already double the total value of U.S. exports of goods and services to those developing countries, and that gap is expected to widen sharply over the next decade. The reason? It is cheaper to staff research facilities with local personnel in the developing world than to use staff located in the developed world. Local management and marketing staffs also tend to be more productive because they instinctively know the terrain. In contrast to their earlier 1950s "Ugly American" image, U.S. companies such as Citibank now are often viewed as flexible and intelligent in dealing with Asians and others from different cultures. Ironically, this ability was probably developed and fostered in response to the enactment of affirmative-action regulations by the federal government in the 1970s. Now U.S. businesspeople have taken that expanded corporate sensibility—which the Japanese still have a lot of trouble duplicating—and are hiring the best and the brightest abroad to manage and create growth in the biggest markets with the most long term potential. Citibank, Procter and Gamble, General Electric, and others are offering tremendous opportunities to local members of the cognitive elite, and they trust these workers because often they have been trained at America's top universities.

The existence of a rapidly growing elite labor force around the world has led a whole new cohort of companies to seek the new paradigm of the "virtual corporation." To become virtual, a company seeks to shed all its permanent employees, get rid of its production facilities, and farm out work to other companies around the world that function as subcontractors. Following the virtual route to its logical conclusions, a virtual corporation is stripped down to a point where its only employees are its top managers; every other function is performed by subcontractors. Few companies have yet attained this status, but many are well along the way.

The virtual corporation first appeared among companies that sell products that are basically easy to produce and whose success or failure depends on shrewd and sophisticated marketing. The Reebok Corporation specializes in the sale of sneakers of all types and descriptions, from basketball shoes to volleyball shoes. At Reebok the marketing function is carried on by U.S. employees, and all the production is contracted out to manufacturing subcontractors in the emerging world.

But there are many signs that other companies with far more sophisticated products are going virtual, seeking to subcontract as much as possible routine data handling and record keeping to low-cost producers using workers for whom they need not pay high wages or provide benefits. Not all the subcontracting goes abroad. In some cases data handling firms, such as Ross Perot's former company EDS, are hired to do the work. There are even cases where the employees rendered redundant by the subcontracting of work actually remain in their jobs, sitting at the very desks they occupied before the subcontractors were hired. The difference is that they lose their jobs with their original employers and are hired, in a new management structure with a new wage and benefit scale, by the companies that become the subcontractors.

In many emerging countries, for example in India (see Chapter 5), the social structure that supports elite workers still remains far more traditional and far less expensive to maintain than that of the United States. The East Asian economic miracle has been fueled, in large part, by capital that in the United States would have been used to make transfer payments such as Social Security and Medicare. In many parts of Asia these expenses are still being carried by families rather than government programs. With minimal transfer payments to be made, government spending in Hong Kong and Singapore particularly has been heavily weighted toward investment in both nations' infrastructures. Even in bureaucracy-heavy India working people often still rely on family members to take care of elderly grandparents and small children. This built-in social infrastructure, which is already eroding to a certain extent, is nonetheless still an attraction for Western conglomerates tired of the demands of the family in the United States, demands that limit workers' availability and make U.S. workers more expensive to employ.

The growth in the sheer numbers of middle-class citizens, their educational achievement, coupled with the strong family underpinnings of many of the middle classes of Latin America, Eastern Europe, and Asia strongly suggest that the process of wage convergence which, as we have seen, is the principal force at work in the global market economy, will continue strongly over the next quarter of a century. Thirty-one-year-old Radek A. Gronet, a Pole who has returned to Poland after working briefly in a Chicago law office and getting a master of arts at the University of Illinois, has more than quintupled his salary back home in Poland. His new salary does not equal in dollar terms what his American counterparts would get, yet his style of living has certainly improved. Soon he will be vacationing in Italy, and he has recently bought a fancy duplex apartment. The well-educated Pole also has a law degree from Warsaw University and is perfectly positioned to take advantage of the economic expansion currently taking place in Poland. "When I did the calculus, it was obvious to me I'd have more advantage in Poland than staying in the United States," said Gronet, who is settling into his new position as a lawyer at Pepsico in Warsaw after completing two years as an associate at another American law firm with offices in Poland. According to the Polish State Agency for Foreign Investment, the number of foreign-owned business ventures in Poland has jumped from 1,100 in 1990 to 27,000 in mid-1996. Although most of these companies still import chief operating officers from headquarters in the United States or Western Europe, increasingly middle-management positions, particularly in finance, law, and marketing, are being filled by Poles. Headhunting firms—unknown in Communist days—have multiplied.

Jobs in which middle-class professionals such as Radek Gronet already have strong qualifications will continue to migrate from the old industrialized nations to the newly industrializing countries as long as the wages and social costs of maintaining a middle-class existence abroad remain lower than in the industrial world. In this brave new global free market, there is little doubt that the process of convergence will shift what are currently viewed as elite jobs from the industrial countries to the emerging world.

CENTERS OF CREATIVITY

Under these circumstances, one ingredient of production can be expected to work to the advantage of the industrial world. It is *creativity*—the most difficult of all the ingredients of production to analyze. A subtle and mysterious force, it explains the ability of the industrial countries to retain an edge along the frontiers of invention and innovation. Even though the wellsprings of creative work are difficult to pinpoint, it is clear that a country, region, laboratory, or university that turns out to be the source of a major invention or innovation must ordinarily be located in an area where workers and researchers are operating at the frontier of knowledge. The silicon semiconductors that evolved into the sophisticated computer chips and microprocessors that formed the basis of the information revolution were invented at Bell Labs in the United States in the 1950s. At that time AT&T was at the cutting edge of telephone technology, and it needed a new system to shift the information contained in telephone calls.

The San Francisco Bay Area's Silicon Valley and the Boston area's Route 128—and not Biloxi, Mississippi—had the right blend of elements required to create path-breaking new information technologies in the late 1950s and early 1960s. And they have been joined as fertile areas for invention and innovation by North Carolina's Research Triangle, by Seattle, New York City, and southern California. All of these areas have contained the right blend of idiosyncratic factors of production.

Production at the creative edge of the new technology becomes expensive as the demand for engineers, scientists, houses, and living expenses in the focal area rises. After a time, the companies at the leading edge begin a hunt to locate the less advanced substratum of productive facilities in new areas where wages and prices have not been driven up by economic success. These factors, as we have seen, explain the migration of the more routine applications of software technology to cheaper, though remote centers like Bangalore in India.

So far we have drawn our examples of the hot spots for invention and innovation from the exciting world of information technology, but in many other industries innovation also tends to be centralized in specific areas. For instance, the notion of continued small improvements in production technology was applied most creatively in Japan. In the vicinity of Nagoya, and what became Toyota City in central Japan, Toyota began the transformation of the automobile industry, and that same area is still the focal point of innovation in the production of the types of ceramics that are used in high-tech applications. As well, the revolution in the steel industry that led to the replacement of cumbersome methods of open-hearth process by small, flexible production runs developed in the Ruhr Valley, of what was then West Germany. Finally the revolution in retailing that was embodied in Wal-Mart was invented in the suburbs of southern cities in the United States.

But there is absolutely no reason to believe that the fertile centers of the information revolution will in the future be confined to what is now the industrial world. As production of routine products shifts to countries in the developing world, it appears likely that these nations will begin to develop centers of creativity of their own. Just as the entrepreneurs of Bangalore are obsessed with developing products and processes that are on the frontier of software technology, it is highly likely that similar high-morale middle-class elites in other parts of the emerging world will soon offer stiff competition to the developed world in other industries.

As that happens, the probability that the next breakthroughs in technology will occur in what we now know as the developed world drops, and drops sharply. Ethnic West Europeans have been the inheritors of several centuries of scientific culture and startling technological innovation. But there is absolutely no reason to believe that they have any sort of advantage when it comes to raw intelligence. Given the increase in education and training in the developing world, as well as the transfer of technology, it is only a matter of time until what is now the emerging world begins to develop its own share of innovative products. Middle-class populations in these countries are certain to develop felicitous idiosyncrasies of their own.

Indeed, the emergence of centers of creativity will become a numbers game, and the industrialized countries are certain to lose their advantage. Since economic and population growth is happening so much faster in the developing world, the odds for innovation are simply there. Already the most powerful companies in the information world are setting up shop nearby the most powerful universities in India and China—those developing countries with the most potential for explosive growth. For example, Microsoft has undertaken to train thousands of computer technicians at the Chinese Academy of Social Sciences and seventy other centers around China; this investment is bound to trigger innovation there. In addition, Microsoft has joined up with Chinese researchers to develop technology in such areas as interactive television and Chinese handwriting and speech recognition—areas many experts consider crucial to the popularization of PCs in China. (Currently there is difficulty in entering Chinese characters onto a keyboard.) IBM is also collaborating with the Chinese in developing software, setting up some joint universities to teach object-oriented software design. As a result, great breakthroughs become equally as likely in Guangdong Province as in California, as likely in Karnataka or Kerala in India as they are in Massachusetts or North Carolina. Bangalore, as we have seen, has an intellectual climate similar to that of New York, because its "high-morale" middle class contains the same mix of computer jocks, medics, artists, and writers.

One may argue that the developed countries often retain the ownership of new technologies and thus control them. But who owns the technologies is likely to make little difference these days, since the captains of capital in the developed world are, in effect, equal opportunity employers of elite workers, and they will tend to invest in the hot spots, the new centers of innovation. As a result, knowledge and development of these technologies will inevitably spread to the new nations.

SHIFTING TASTES IN ENTERTAINMENT AND POP CULTURE

American elites like to point to their exports in entertainment and pop culture as a major economic strength. But how long American entertainment companies and American singers, actors, and designers will continue to dominate the world's popular culture is an open question. In the original flush of victory in the cold war, nothing was more desired than the products of American pop culture. But as the middle classes of the countries that had been under communist and socialist sway have been drawn into the orbit of the market economy, their taste for purely American pop culture has waned.

It is probably in the popular music business that economists can find their own version of the drosophila, the fruit fly that is so central to certain kinds of research because its reproductive cycle is so rapid. Just as the emergence of rock and roll set the stage for total dominance of the youth culture by American music for more than three decades, the more recent fragmentation of the popular music market offers a glimpse of the likely future of American pop culture, which, including movies, records, and television programs, generated a significant balance of payments surplus for the United States.

Experts on the music business hold that New York and London are well on their way out as the world music towns. They contend that the standards of what is hip on the global scene ceased to be determined by U.S. megastars in the latter half of the mid-1990s. The action is shifting to such spots as South Africa, where Johannesburg's "pulse jive" sound—a mix of traditional African beats, jazz, and rhythm and blues—is gaining popularity worldwide; and Hong Kong, where superstar Jacky Cheung is creating hits that sell like gangbusters as far away as Amsterdam. Says Ken Berry, president of EMI music international: "The demand for American music is starting to recede. Now the big growth is in local artists."

The $40 billion a year U.S. music industry is in the midst of a dramatic transformation. Formerly the business relied heavily on U.S. sales and exports, but now it is becoming more decentralized and geared to local tastes. Many experts think that the U.S. portion of the worldwide music market will decline to just 20 percent by 2000, down from 33 percent in 1996 and 50 percent in 1987, just before the cold war ended. After years of selling the songs of Michael Jackson and Mariah Carey to mass markets throughout the United States and overseas, the five large companies that control some 80 percent of the music industry—PolyGram, Warner, Sony EMI, and Bertelsmann—are pouring billions of dollars into regional studios, plants, and distribution centers.

The national pride that drives the work efforts of the developing world's middle classes is also influencing the musical tastes of its younger generation. An engineering student in Beijing says he prefers rock singer Dou Wei to stars like Madonna because "her lifestyle is too far from our own." The move away from American music has been particularly strong in Asia. As the political winds shifted in the early 1990s, newly liberated music fans went for Western idols such as Whitney Houston. A little later a "Cantopop" genre developed, named after the Chinese city of Canton, consisting mostly of music lip-synched by film and soap-opera stars. Now fans seem to want to rediscover a common heritage and sing in their own language. The result is that the big five music publishers of the industrial world are battling tough new regional independents, such as Taiwan's Rock Records and Brazil's Sigla.

Books and movies appear to be undergoing the same kind of metamorphosis worldwide that is transforming the music business. The switch in tastes away from America and the other industrial nations has gone the farthest in popular music, the cultural dominion of the young. But the vitality of Latin America's literature of magical realism, India's eye-popping, larger-than-life "Bollywood" films, (made mainly in Bombay), and China's emergence as a new center of filmmaking and artistic life, all signal an ongoing surge of fresh, original insights in the arts that make the American literary, film, and music world sometimes seem tired. As these many evolving artforms go worldwide, they could easily limit the appeal of American products, just as surely as this trend is already occurring in the music business.

WILL THE VITALITY OF SMALL BUSINESS SAVE THE ELITES?

As worldwide popular tastes redefine markets and corporations continue to hire in the developing world and lay off in the developed world, an influential group of futurists, writers, and consultants have been arguing that those workers seeking secure employment in America's corporate sector are on the wrong track. They argue that elite workers who have become dissatisfied with, or dismissed by, the corporate sector can find a comfortable refuge in small business or independent practice. An embodiment of this belief is an endless parade of how-to books and articles that exhort and instruct people to reinvent their lives in the new, exciting, decentralized "Third Wave" economy. In 1995 the *New York Times* ran a glowing piece on how independent businesspeople who left the city for offices in places like Hoboken and Hasbrouck Heights, New Jersey, could impress their clients by arranging back-to-back meetings in the tearooms of New York's most expensive hotels. This was not to be a one-shot arrangement, but a standing weekly, deskless, rentless, secretaryless "power" meeting at a tiny tea table—because office space in the New York area costs too much. The *Times* made it sound exciting and trendy, but the reality was that most of the independent "power players" featured in the article were so broke they could no longer afford to work in New York City.

Someone should have tipped these people off before they opted for the independent life. There have always been those who have been smart enough, talented enough, or hooked into enough networks to make it as independents in any age. But there is nothing going on right now—not the home computer, not the cellular phone, not the megabaud modem, not even the Internet—that is boosting the ability of those who work alone or in small groups to compete effectively. On the contrary, every trend that has emerged since the end of the cold war has increased the power of the giant multinational corporations, especially American ones. Thus even if we don't like it, the fate of elite workers continues to be linked to the great transnational corporations, despite the preachments of countless self-help books, inspirational speeches, and seminars that argue to the contrary.

The idea that transnational corporations are becoming more powerful than ever may come as a surprise, given that the dynamism of entrepreneurial small business is being so widely extolled. But while Alvin and Heidi Toffler make big money writing about a "Third Wave" in which mass production and mass consumption are replaced by "customized production, micro markets, infinite channels of communication," they neglect to inform their public that this devo-lutionized system of production continues to be dominated by the great multinationals. The Tofflers are correct to notice the technologi-cal trends that are transforming business organizations from what were essentially hierarchies into what are, increasingly, decentralized networks. Certain parts of companies have become more autono-mous in their operations and decision making, but that does not mean, as the Tofflers maintain, that small business is growing at the expense of the transnational corporation.

The myth that small business is the prime generator of new jobs in the United States is so pervasive that to clearly understand the post–cold war world one needs to subject the interpretation of current trends to a good dose of debunking. "For more than a decade," writes Bennett Harrison, a Carnegie-Mellon professor in his book *Lean and Mean,* "the public has been told repeatedly that small companies are now the engines of economic growth and development. According to this new conventional wisdom, the large corporation was in many respects be-coming something of a dinosaur, increasingly unable to compete in a post-industrial world." But Harrison's research clearly demonstrates that "the importance of small businesses as job generators and as engines of technological dynamism has been greatly exaggerated."

David L. Birch, a business consultant, popularized the idea that very small firms were responsible for a whopping 88 percent of all

Table 6-2

The Small Business Job Growth Myth:
Percentage of Employment in Small Business,
1976-1986

Year	Firms with Fewer than 100 Employees	Firms with Fewer than 500 Employees
1976	36.3	50.4
1978	36.5	50.8
1980	35.0	49.5
1982	35.6	50.2
1984	36.2	50.9
1986	35.0	49.7

Data: *Employers Large and Small,* Charles Brown, James Hamilton, and James Medoff (Cambridge, Mass.: Harvard University Press, 1990), 25.

net jobs created in the years from 1981 to 1985. By contrast, Birch argued, the large corporations were depleted and becoming powerless. This scenario was adopted and broadly publicized by the political Right, which was eager to demonstrate that monoliths (either in government or business) no longer work and that small is both beautiful and profitable. Birch's view was also not discouraged by big business, whose lobbyists quickly realized that any legislation designed to free small business of the burdens of government regulation would also work to the benefit of the largest companies, in the end making it far easier for them to dominate the U.S. economy. Because the public was well aware that big companies have been downsizing, there was a ready acceptance of the twin mythologies that the corporation is enfeebled and small business is empowered.

But Birch's analysis is deeply flawed. Small businesses did *not* create a growing share of permanent jobs in the United States in the period that was analyzed by David Birch. That is the conclusion reached by the University of Michigan's Charles Brown and Harvard University's James Hamilton and James Medoff, as Table 6-2 shows.

Not only are Birch and his followers wrong; they are dead, 180 degrees, wrong. It is a testament to the vitality of the corporate sector that its share of job creation in the United States has not declined, even though, as we have already shown earlier in this chapter, the developing world is claiming a larger and larger share of the investment capital generated in America.

THE NEW NETWORKED ORGANIZATION

The wave that the Tofflers should have been observing and writing about is the linked series of technological innovations that have allowed the corporation to transform itself into a global network by enabling people in widely dispersed locations to work together on the same projects. One such innovation, called "groupware" is a collection of computer and communications hardware and software. There are LANs (local area networks) and WANs (wide area networks), routers and brouters. There's SONET and ISDN and TCP/IP, each representing a huge advance in the ability to move information via computer within corporate networks. The Electronic Industries Association estimates that U.S. manufacturers shipped $64 billion in communications gear in 1995. IBM is betting that its customers so badly want groupware technology for networks that it spent $3.5 billion to buy up Lotus Development Corporation. Lotus's main products, Notes and CC:Mail, are geared to enabling widely dispersed people employed by the same organization to work together.

The development of software for corporate networking is still in its early stages; it has been held back by regulatory restraints that telephone companies say restrict their ability to offer the most advanced services. Partly as a consequence, most of the world's phone companies have yet to deploy modern digital transmission systems. Within a building, a local area network can transfer data at broadband speeds—10 megabytes per second or more. When the data hits local and long-distance telephone networks, the speed drops quickly to 2 megabytes. But that telephone bottleneck is likely to disappear, at least in the United States, because of the new telecommunications bill passed by Congress in 1996. The full development of groupware combined with the new regulatory atmosphere will generate a quantum leap in the capacities of the networked corporation. Yet even before the needed technical substructure is in place, companies are beginning to take advantage of networking to allow skilled workers around the world to work together. By 1995 the Swedish electronics firm L. M. Ericsson had some 17,000 engineers in forty research centers situated in twenty countries around the world, all linked into one network. The company's development teams in India and Australia worked together on the same design then sent off a final blueprint to a factory in Portugal.

In the history of capitalism, the close link between the rise of technology and the development of the modern corporation is an oft-told tale. In their classic work *The Modern Corporation and Private Property,* Adolf Berle and Gardiner Means carefully traced the growth of corporate power in the nineteenth and early twentieth centuries. John Kenneth Galbraith brought the story through World War II and then on through the 1970s. *But, powerful as the corporation has been throughout the history of modern capitalism, it has achieved virtually total economic hegemony only since the end of the cold war.* The new information technology, coupled with the decline in the power of the state, has opened the entire world to the unprecedented reach of corporate power. Each giant corporation has, in effect, become the center of a global network, ideally suited to take advantage of the new trends in telecommunications and software.

Insofar as small and medium-sized business survives, it will be as part of an increasingly entrenched "web," a complex network of contractors and subcontractors, that surrounds and depends on the major transnational players. This web, as Bennett Harrison, author of *Lean and Mean,* describes it, is far from independent. Transnational corporations have moved increasingly toward growth strategies that weave information technologies into the fabric of everyday work. According to Harrison, each of these new networked organizations is an integrated complex to which each unit

> brings its own specialty—technology, financial power, access to government regulators—and its own constellation of small-firm suppliers. As their name suggests, the networked corporations tend to be somewhat less formal, less rigidly contractual versions of the market-sharing, joint venturing, licensing, equity partnering, R&D consorting, coproduction and even bartering arrangements that have been linking the big firms both within and across national borders since at least the 1960s.

But to mistake a reduction in formality for a loss of power would be an error. Indeed, the greater flexibility inherent in the networked corporation may make it possible for a single management team to more efficiently operate ever larger corporations. If it materializes, that increased efficiency may in the end produce at least a sliver of the productivity increases that have so far proven elusive in the great corporate merger wave of the mid-1990s.

THE DISPLACEMENT OF ELITE WORKERS AND THE U.S. CORPORATE COMEBACK

These increasingly decentralized corporations are also made stronger by the global spread of the free market over the last nine years. As government regulation wanes worldwide, corporations are freer than ever to seek low-cost production, compliant workers, friendly regulation, and subsidies for locating at any point on the globe. If a corporation feels badgered by government officials, hounded by social agendas such as day care or flextime, or hemmed in by requirements to fund pensions and health care, it is freer than ever to pick up and leave. For most of the 1980s that international mobility undermined mostly blue-collar workers. But now the threat is moving in on the elite workers.

Neat, clean statistics on the fate of elite workers in the labor market are scarce. Yet the data that do exist strongly suggest that, *as a class,* the position of elite workers in the workforce is beginning to deteriorate. The U.S. Bureau of Labor Statistics conducts a regular survey of displaced workers, and the most recent published data reflects February of 1994. Table 6-3 summarizes the displacement rates (defined as the number of workers displaced per 100 employed) for the 1981–1982 period and the 1991–1992 period. *Displacement* is newspeak for "being fired." The numbers in the table reflect the percent of workers with three or more years of tenure who were fired during the given periods.

The table shows that the forces destroying jobs in the American economy were still at work in the early 1990s. Both 1981–1982 and 1991–1992 were recession years. But even though the 1981–1982 recession was far more severe than the more recent slump, the overall number of workers displaced (fired) was roughly the same proportion of the workforce. Thus the propensity of employers to get rid of workers was stronger in the early 1990s than in the early 1980s.

What is relevant to the worker elites, however, is the fundamental change in the *incidence* of displacement. Table 6-3 shows that older white-collar (probably higher paid), workers were considerably more at risk of displacement in the 1991–1992 recession than during the

Table 6-3

The Rise in Displaced White-Collar Workers:
Changing Incidence of Worker Displacement*

	Displacement Rates	
	1981–2	1991–2
Total	3.9%	3.8%
Occupations		
White-collar	2.6	3.6
Blue-collar	7.3	5.2
Age		
24–34 years of age	5.0	3.8
35–44 years of age	3.8	3.9
45–54 years of age	3.0	3.8
55+	3.6	4.3

*Expressed as a percent of workers with three or more years of tenure on their current job.

Data: U.S. Bureau of Labor Statistics, *News,* USDL, 92-530, 94-434.

previous recession. A similar conclusion was reached in a special report prepared by the President's Council of Economic Advisers (CEA). The report says that "further analysis shows that job displacement rates rose for more educated workers. So that while blue collar and less educated workers remain more likely to be displaced than others, displacement rates have clearly risen among those workers who had been previously immune from the threat of job dislocation." It also demonstrates, of course, that while certain elite occupations continue in strong demand, elite workers as a class have come under significant job market pressure in the 1990s.

Nor should it necessarily be assumed that the elite workers who have been fired have found shelter in the new Tofflerian world of the independent self-employed. Men are far more likely to be elite workers than are women. Labor force participation rates measure the proportion of the population of working age that is either employed or seeking a job. The data, which include the self-employed, show that the labor force participation rate for men aged twenty-five to fifty-four has been falling since 1971. For men in the prime working age bracket, thirty-five to forty-four, the participation rate fell from 96.5 percent in 1971 to 93.5 percent in 1993. Government data show that in 1995 alone, a prosperous year for the American economy by the standards of the post–cold war era, 838,000 men lost their jobs and wanted to go back to work but weren't actively pursuing employment.

This "mass disappearance" of male workers in the prime of life has unnerving implications for the future of elite workers in the American economy. It occurred in the fifth year of a business cycle upswing, a period during which job opportunities for prime-age workers have, in the past, characteristically tended not merely to rise, but to explode. And, more important, the shrinkage of the male workforce occurred in an era when American transnational corporations were relatively strong as compared to those of Germany and Japan. A strong U.S. corporate sector did not save many elite workers.

In a strong comeback, the years since the end of the cold war have seen an increase in the power of American corporations compared to those of Germany and Japan. For much of the past two decades, it appeared that U.S. companies would no longer be competitive with foreign rivals and that America would follow Spain, Austria-Hungary, and Britain into economic decline. Japan seemed poised to become the world's hegemonic economy, eclipsing the United States in everything from economic policy to industrial organization. This perception was mirrored in changed valuations in the world's stock markets. In 1980 the U.S. stock market was 50 percent of world market capitalization; Japan's was 17 percent. By 1988 Japan was 44 percent of world market capitalization, and the United States was only 29 percent.

Today American business revels in a substantial competitive rebound. Its return on capital has more than doubled since 1980, and investment in capital equipment in this country has revived somewhat. The United States at the end of 1995 was 39 percent of world market capitalization, and Japan is up 25 percent. The consulting community has taken the opportunity to trumpet the change. "In a truly competitive global economy, the U.S. performance has been outstanding," says Grady E. Means of Coopers and Lybrand. William Lewis, director of the McKinsey Global Institute, says, "The United States has the highest productivity and the best job performance in the world."

The United States's competitors admit this. Kuniyoshi Sasaki, executive director at the Japan Productivity Center for Socio-Economic Development, says, "Overall, Japan's competitiveness against the United States is weakening." Nariman Baverish, an international economist at DRI/McGraw Hill, agrees: "The Japanese are world class in autos, consumer electronics and a few other high-tech areas. Once you get beyond those industries, Japan is not very competitive or productive." In fact, the United States is ahead of everyone in most high-tech industries, from software to biotech.

America's corporate revival can be explained in part by the magnificent success of the innovating companies on the cutting edge of technological change. Many remarkable American companies specializing in telecommunications, computer software, and microprocessors have been, and will remain, at the forefront of international competition. The United States is also assured of a strong presence in the industries that promise to profit from the breakthrough technologies of the next decade: genetic engineering, where the United States is a clear leader, and superconductivity, where America is at least tied with Japan. This technological leadership is based on the strength of graduate education at America's leading universities, and, as we shall see later in Chapter 9, represents its great hope for the future.

But a good part of the American revival has come about as the result of a darker achievement—a dubious victory in First World downsizing and wage competition. Wage gains in Germany and Japan have been greater than those in the United States ever since the early 1950s, when those countries began their serious post–World War II economic reconstruction.

In some significant respects, then, the years since the end of the cold war have turned U.S. economic history on its head. Americans traditionally believed that, as the competitive strength of American business improved, corresponding benefits would accrue to American workers. This sentiment was often expressed by American businessmen, who believed in the ideal that a high-wage policy was essential to creating the purchasing power among the masses that was necessary to build bigger markets for the products of American factories. (Henry Ford's willingness to pay workers $5 a day during the 1920s to produce the Model T so that they could afford to buy a car themselves is part of American business folklore.)

The recent change has been dramatic. Corporations no longer brag about their generous benefits; instead they take pride in offering stingy benefits and low wages. In fact, this is a major explanation for the revival of American corporations.

For all these reasons, the startling improvement (relative to Germany and Japan) in the competitiveness of U.S. corporations does not offer the elite workers, or the average American, the comfort they are looking for. Nor should anyone assume that because the United States has caught up in competitiveness, the era of paltry compensation gains is at an end. In the global economy, competitiveness is a race with no finish line, and gains in competitiveness are fleeting. Corporate rivals in Europe and Japan recognize that they have been slipping, and the severe squeeze on profits they are experiencing in this decade is forcing those countries into vast corporate restructurings that will renew their ability to compete with the United States. This round of downsizing and reengineering will set in motion an ominous international wage and benefit competition that will hurt American workers, and hurt them badly, putting a lid on any income gains American workers might have been expecting.

Indeed, there is reason to believe that U.S. corporations will continue to be less solicitous of the welfare of their employees than their multinational rivals are. Nor is there any assurance that American businesses, as they gird for the next decade's competition against Japan and Germany, against the established "tigers of Asia," and against such newer competitors as India and China, will use American workers or managers. In 1994, a strong year during which corporate profits rose by 40 percent, American corporations cut 516,000 jobs, as compared to 316,000 jobs that were cut in 1990, during a recession.

So despite American leadership in many areas of technology, there is little guarantee that the elite workers whose fortunes are directly tied to global competition will fare well in the future. The bitter disappointment of corporate employees who managed to survive the layoffs of the 1990–1991 recession only to be fired in the boom years of 1994 and 1995 points to a new reality: the paternalism that characterized successful American corporations in the past has given way to a new transnational competitive dynamic; American corporations have become dispassionate and emotionally distanced from their employees, even those elite workers on whom they have placed great value in the past.

THE MARKET'S ASSAULT ON THE TRADITIONAL PROFESSIONS

Town and gown. Anyone who has lived in a small college town in the United States is aware that there are two separate elites in America. One is composed of those who have mastered the advanced technological, organizational, and administrative knowledge that lies at the base of the global power of the American economy, the wearers of the gown. The other is the tight community of professionals who earn their living in the traditional professions—lawyers, physicians, dentists, accountants, and members of other occupations that are linked to one another by custom and country club, the insurance agents, real estate brokers, optometrists, and the like, occupants of the town.

The second elite has always had enormous power in America. Many Americans are obsessed by the power of labor unions and the special legal rights granted to unions by the National Labor Relations Act of 1935. The special power of unions has been analyzed to death by many labor economists and lawyers. But the special power of unions is trivial as compared with the safeguards that have been built up to protect the special interests of members of the traditional professions. Their strength, of course, lies in the licensing requirements for practicing such professions—licensing power that is guaranteed by every state legislature in the United States and also, in some cases, by the federal legislature. There have been penetrating analyses of this power by critics on both the Right, Milton and Rose Friedman in *Capitalism and Freedom,* and the Left, C. Wright Mills in *White Collar.* The Friedmans analyzed the role played by the special regulations that limit entry into these professions and protect the incomes of their practitioners. For his part, Mills analyzed the role of networking among the members of the Rotary, Lions, and Elks clubs of small-town and suburban America, the back-scratching that serves to expand the incomes of these professionals. These groups have often been satirized and ridiculed. They are, after all, the class that Sinclair Lewis wrote about in *Babbitt.* But knowing that American government, particularly at the state level, is a virtually unchallenged province of Rotarians, neither the Friedmans nor Mills, and certainly not Sinclair Lewis underestimated their power.

But the analyses by both Mills and the Friedmans were completed before the forces attendant upon the end of the cold war and the coming of the information revolution were unleashed. These powerful forces are showing the initial signs of breaking down professional monopolies just as surely as they have already broken down the power of the unions. The professionals will experience the same kind of downward pressure on their incomes that has already been experienced by those in less fortunately positioned occupations.

In economics the tail wags the dog. What happens to the incomes of the marginal members of each occupational group eventually begins to affect the incomes of all members of the group. And each of the distinctive features of the current period—global competition, the information revolution, slow growth, and the spread of the free market ideology—is combining with the others to deal heavy blows even to the professional groups whose privileged positions have heretofore been protected by special and unique guarantees. Indeed, there are strong parallels between the likely fate of today's learned professions and the decline of the medieval guilds in the early phases of the development of modern capitalism. Just as new methods of organization devastated the guilds in the sixteenth and seventeenth centuries, the new global economy will end up by attacking local professional monopolies. One way or another, lawyers, doctors, insurance brokers, and real estate agents are almost certain to be gradually absorbed by giant companies. And, given America's history, when that happens it will indeed represent what is almost the final phase of the triumph of capital in this hemisphere!

The new power of the market has already had profound effects on the lives of America's doctors. America's resistance to "socialized" medicine (the government-provided single-payer health insurance system, which has long been in place in virtually every other industrialized country including Germany, Japan, Canada, France, and Italy), high-tech medicine, and the power of the private insurance industry have driven health care costs up to the point where they now absorb some 13 percent of the nation's gross domestic product, a far higher proportion than what is spent in the other advanced industrial countries, whose citizens already enjoy greater life expectancy than do Americans.

The effect of this costly entrenched, independent medical care system has been profound. Once upon a time the physician was a small businessman who ran his own practice. Under the lash of foreign competition, the great American corporations have already turned to health care organizations and other forms of managed care to provide health care to their employees at reduced costs. The high costs and "inefficiency" involved in running traditionally financed public hospitals and the legal requirements that force these institutions to treat the 30 million uninsured Americans have led many public hospitals into bad financial straits, and a new wave of corporations that run for-profit hospitals have been only too willing to capitalize on their own opportunities to reap a gain.

At the same time, the slow economic growth that is the standout characteristic of the post–cold war era has placed relentless pressure

Table 6-4

The Growth Slowdown in Physicians' Incomes
(Mean Net Income, in Thousands of Dollars)

Year	All Physicians		General/Family Practice	
	Amount	Percent Change	Amount	Percent Change
1985	112.2		77.9	
1989	155.8		95.9	
1985 – 1989		8.55*		5.33*
1990	164.3	5.00	102.7	7.0
1991	170.6	4.00	111.5	9.0
1992	181.7	7.00	114.4	3.0
1993	189.3	4.00	116.8	2.0
1994	182.3	−3.70	120.3	2.9
1995	195.5	7.20	131.2	8.3
1990 – 1995		3.54*		5.00*

*Annual rate of change

Data: American Medical Association, Chicago, Ill., *Characteristics of Medical Practice,* annual.

on the two government programs that underwrite the health care expenses of the three groups whose medical insurance is underwritten by the government, the elderly protected by Medicare, the poor protected by Medicaid, and the disabled, who get a little of both programs. Serious analysis of these programs shows that in an era of slow growth, the payroll taxes that finance Medicare will not provide nearly enough money to finance the system into the next century, and the slow growth of general revenues also limits the financial capacity of government to finance Medicaid.

These pressures on the financing of health care point not only to a possible deterioration in the quality of medical care we can expect, but also to limitations on income growth among health care professionals. What has already happened to the incomes of physicians is a striking example of the impending assault on the professions. Table 6-4 compares the growth rates of the incomes of all physicians, including specialists, with the growth rates of the incomes of those engaged in general or family practice. As can be seen from the table, when the incomes of specialists are included, doctors' incomes have been growing far more slowly in the 1990s than in the 1980s. In sharp contrast, growth in the incomes of those in general or family practice has barely declined. Two aspects of the assault by capital on the professions are visible here: the rise of corporate medicine, the HMO, has put a squeeze on doctors' incomes in general. At the same time, the managements of the HMOs have substituted the cheaper factor of production, the GP, for the more expensive factor, the specialist. This of course benefits the income of the less expensive factor of production, as is inevitable when capital holds sway.

The new assault on the professions is most visible in health care. But the first signs are also appearing for practitioners of other professions. Under the same pressure that provides incentives to cut the cost of medical care, the corporate sector is hell-bent on reducing its legal costs. In a rare exception to the rule that costs can be cut by outsourcing, companies in almost all fields have expanded their in-house legal staffs to reduce the horrendous bills that they had been paying giant law firms for services. Reports of savings have come from companies ranging from IBM to Steelcase. At the same time, routine legal tasks have become increasingly computerized, allowing companies to substitute paralegals for actual lawyers. In addition, the relentless legislative drive, often generously financed by business interests, to limit the size of the awards granted in product liability, medical malpractice, employment discrimination, and other kinds of cases that can be brought against businesses can at least in part be explained by the pressures that global competition is putting on business costs. Legislatures are, of course, dominated by lawyers, and the attempt to limit settlements meets stiff legislative resistance. Nevertheless the drive to limit these kinds of claims has been relentless and is certain to become more intense as the reviving corporate sectors of Europe and Japan begin their next assault on the currently preeminent position of the American corporation in the world market.

As capital has become more powerful, it has also sought to dissolve other local monopolies that have hitherto been immune. Large corporations have sought, and are achieving, entry into the insurance business. Banks such as Citicorp and giant brokerage houses such as Merrill Lynch and Charles Schwab have sought and achieved the right to sell insurance, thus undermining the power of local insurance agents. A similar assault can be observed in real estate as companies such as Century 21 gobble up local real estate agencies. And as in the field of law, the new dominance of capital over work is being aided and abetted by the computer and the Internet. The sale of real estate is now being conducted, at least in part, with computer programs that actually allow prospective buyers to examine new homes on computers rather than make on-site inspections in the company of real estate agents. In virtually every field, those who have argued that the information revolution empowers small business at the expense of the large corporation are missing the essential nature and ramifications of current information trends.

Back to the town and gown. Just as the market is dissolving the power of local monopolies, it is also beginning to affect the special privileges that have been vested in members of the academic community. In the same way that the rising cost of medical care is causing the health care industry to stress efficiency, the rising cost of education is beginning to bring about radical change on campus. So far the strikes at Yale University by teaching assistants and other low-paid workers of the academic community have received the greatest attention. But there are also signs that the most treasured possession of the academic elites, tenure, is under assault. The experiment being conducted at the University of Minnesota to do away with tenure is being closely watched throughout the United States. Marginalized academic departments that don't produce revenue are under constant pressure, as are the academics who run them, in spite of their tenured positions. Although a handful of acknowledged academic stars are reaping huge salary gains and are provided with instant job security, data gathered by the American Association of University Professors show that a smaller and smaller proportion of college teachers are covered by tenure, and once again, outsourcing has become a key model for cost-cutting. Academics, often working at more than one college with no benefits and no prospects at all for tenure are routinely yanked in and out of teaching assignments based on departments' needs to meet administrative financial goals. An internationally known Ivy League economics professor says sadly, "I recently took my very best student to a mediocre Pennsylvania college and practically got down on my hands and knees so they would offer him a job. He did get a job, even though there were four hundred applicants. None of the others in his group have gotten an offer. In my thirty years of teaching I've never seen anything like this before!"

The fortunes of the young are always the most affected by radical economic change. As in music, the surest signs of what is occurring in the professions can be seen in the lives of young people. The high incomes of a few leading lawyers, such as Melvin Belli and Johnny Cochran, and a few physicians, such as Dr. Michael DeBakey, may attract the most attention. But as data provided by the National Association of College placement officers show, the growth rate in the first-job salaries of virtually every aspirant to the traditional professions, including those in the groves of academe, has slowed in the past five years.

THE PRESSURE ON ELITE INCOMES

Income inequality unquestionably increased in the 1980s and 1990s, so most people had the impression that those who held the elite positions in the workforce have been doing extremely well, an impression that has been reinforced by writers on both the Left and the Right who have drawn a sharp distinction between the top 20 percent of income earners—the managerial and professional classes—and everyone else. But just because inequality has increased we should not automatically assume that the workplace earnings of professional and managerial workers have been increasing rapidly.

The evidence points in exactly the opposite direction. The increase in the incomes of elite workers is only relative; it does not result from their own stellar economic gains. Instead the real (inflation-adjusted) incomes of the top 20 percent of workers have managed to hold up relatively well in a period when the real incomes of the remaining 80 percent stagnated, and in many cases actually fell.

That is the story told by the overall data on the performance of income from work. And as Tables 6-5 and 6-6 show, the statistics tell basically the same tale whether workplace status is measured by occupation or whether it is measured by levels of educational attainment. Measured in constant dollars in terms of 1994 purchasing power, the median earnings of those in what the U.S. Census Bureau calls "management-related occupations" fell from $34,398 in 1987 to $32,608 in 1994. When measured by the change in mean income— which reflects the huge increase in the salaries paid to the captains of capital whose salaries have soared in the past decade—the picture for those in management-related occupations get a bit better. The mean salary increased from $40,313 in 1987 to $41,887 in 1994, a hardly princely compound annual growth rate of less than .5 percent per year.

Table 6-5

Income and Education: Change in Real Hourly Wage by Education,
1973-1975 (1994 Dollars)

Year	Less Than High School	High School	Some College	College	Advanced Degree	Non-College Graduates**
Hourly Wage						
1973	$ 10.65	$ 12.17	$13.45	$17.66	$21.52	$ 11.89
1979	10.59	11.86	12.92	16.55	20.34	11.80
1989	8.91	10.79	12.53	16.98	22.07	10.96
1995	8.16	10.46	11.64	17.26	22.81	10.39
Percent Change						
1973-79	−0.6%	−2.6%	−3.9%	−6.3%	−5.5%	−0.8%
1979-89	−15.9	−9.0	−3.1	2.6	8.5	−7.1
1989-95	−8.4	−3.0	−7.1	1.6	3.3	−5.2
1979-95	−23.0	−11.8	−9.9	4.3	12.1	−11.9
Share of Employment*						
1973	28.5%	41.7%	15.1%	8.8%	3.6%	85.4%
1979	20.1	42.1	19.2	11.0%	5.0	81.3
1989	13.7	40.5	22.3	14.0%	6.9	76.5

* Since the shares of those with one year of schooling beyond college are not shown,
the presented shares do not sum to 100. There are no reliable data for 1995 using same
definitions.
** Includes high school graduates and some college.
Data: Economic Policy Institute

Professional specialty occupations are the other workplace haven
of the elites. The average member of this group has fared somewhat
better than the average manager. Again, the measurement is in dollars
based on 1994 purchasing power. Between 1987 and 1994, the
median income of this group rose from $39,122 to $39,151, a barely
detectable amount. But the group's mean income rose by a meaningful amount, from $44,468 to $49,075, a respectable annual growth
rate of almost 1.4 percent per year in real income. But remember that
this group includes such truly idiosyncratic factors of production as
Michael Jackson and Michael Jordan, Tom Cruise and Julia Roberts.

Data that classifies the workforce overall by educational attainment tells approximately the same story about the elites as do the
occupational figures, so we need not go into this data in detail. What
is fascinating, however, is recent data on how age is affecting earnings

Table 6-6

Dry Years for Managers: Median Earnings (Constant 1994 Dollars)

Year	Administrators and Officials	Self-employed Administrators and Officials	Management-Related Occupations	Professional Specialty Occupations
1982	$42,043	$23,084	$33,660	$35,432
1983	41,681	24,606	33,863	35,467
1984	42,741	24,100	34,003	36,819
1985	42,791	22,595	34,130	36,837
1986	42,302	26,276	35,346	38,635
1987	40,883	27,821	34,398	39,122
1988	40,772	24,605	33,893	39,300
1989	42,954	26,519	36,007	39,741
1990	41,626	24,533	34,174	39,258
1991	40,500	23,672	33,974	39,097
1992	41,145	23,453	33,013	38,866
1993	41,313	24,796	32,827	39,208
1994	41,592	22,461	32,608	39,151

Data: MGB Information Services. See *Trading Away U.S. High Wages and Good Jobs* (Washington, D.C.: MGB Information Services, May 1996), 37, for complete definitions of categories.

growth at each level of educational attainment (Table 6-7). So far in the 1990s, the incomes of those with lower levels of educational attainment (through high school) have been growing at about the same rate among younger workers as among older workers. But at the higher levels of educational achievement, earnings growth for the older members of the workforce far exceeds income growth for the younger members of the workforce. As Table 6-7 shows, for example, the median income of workers between the ages of forty-five and fifty-four holding a bachelor's degree increased from $55,183 in 1991 to $62,326 in 1994. But for workers aged twenty-five to thirty-four, income fell from $39,387 to $36,194. For those holding professional degrees, income increased for workers between the ages of forty-five and fifty-four from $94,056 to $110,602. In sharp contrast, the incomes of those professionals age twenty-five to thirty-four fell from $66,416 to $55,203. But we need to keep in mind that the figures for those in the older age brackets are obviously for survivors only. Many in this age group were probably fired or lost their jobs during the period covered.

Table 6-7

Younger Workers Fall Behind

Education/ Experience 1979–95	Hourly Wage				Percent Change			
	1973	1979	1989	1995	1973–79	1979–89	1989–95	1979–95
High School								
Men								
1–5 yrs.	$10.54	$10.43	$8.15	$7.58	–1.0%	–21.8%	–6.9%	–27.3%
6–20	15.96	15.99	13.55	12.63	0.1	–15.2	–6.8	–21.0
21–35	16.92	17.20	15.52	14.41	1.6	–9.8	–7.2	–16.2
Women								
1–5 yrs.	$7.93	$7.92	$6.89	$6.42	–0.2%	–13.0%	–6.7%	–18.9
6–20	9.64	9.69	9.46	9.30	0.5	–2.4	–1.6	–4.0
21–35	10.03	9.90	9.97	9.92	–1.3	0.7	–0.6	0.1
College								
Men								
1–5 yrs.	$14.08	$14.04	$13.86	$12.54	–0.2%	–1.3%	–9.5%	–10.7%
6–20	24.85	22.58	21.54	21.99	–9.2	–4.6	2.1	–2.6
21–35	25.22	25.56	24.64	24.89	1.3	–3.6	1.0	–2.6
Women								
1–5 yrs.	$12.30	$11.24	$12.51	$11.55	–8.6%	11.2%	–7.7%	2.7%
6–20	15.62	13.44	14.77	16.31	–14.0	9.8	10.4	21.3
21–35	14.87	13.45	14.51	16.05	–9.6	7.9	10.6	19.4

Data: Economic Policy Institute

While the data do not cover a long enough period of time to be decisive, they are broadly consistent with the view that the elites are approaching a time of troubles that will be equivalent to that experienced by blue-collar workers in the 1970s and 1980s. The competitive storm that will engulf the industrial world's elites has already appeared on the horizon.

PART 3

SAVING CAPITALISM FROM ITSELF

CHAPTER 7

Can We Depend on Wall Street?

The banks are made of marble
With a guard at every door
And the vaults are filled with silver
That the workers struggled for.
  —"Old Wobbly Song"

The Great Depression in the United States . . . is a testament to
how much damage can be done by missteps on the part of a few
men [the leaders of the Federal Reserve system] when they
wield vast power over the monetary system of a country.
  —Milton and Rose Friedman,
  Capitalism and Freedom

I used to think if there was reincarnation, I wanted to come back
as the president or the pope or a .400 baseball hitter, but now I
want to come back as the bond market. You can intimidate
everybody.

  —James Carville

IF THE ECONOMIES OF THE INDUSTRIAL WORLD SHOULD GO
into permanent decline, history will show that the road to disaster
was paved by their great central banks, the Federal Reserve Bank in
Washington, the Bundesbank in Frankfurt, the Bank of Japan in
Tokyo, and the Bank of England in London. By bowing to the dictates
of the financial markets, which decree an all-out fight against inflation
at any cost, these financial institutions have become the deadly
enemies of those who earn their living from work. Instead of seeking
an appropriate balance between growth and price stability, the
central banks have put the entire industrial world on a course that

141

makes it painfully difficult for their citizens to achieve even minimal gains in their standard of living. Central banks have produced an industrial world economy that is growing so slowly that in the end it will undermine capital just as it has already debased work.

Central bankers are allowing global capital to run wild. They have, as a consequence, decreed that in the post–cold war globalized environment industrial world workers, capitalism's natural heirs, should live the lives of underachievers. Their analysts are quite willing to tolerate growth rates of over 5 percent per year in emerging countries while refusing to condone fast growth in the industrial world if the perceived threat of even the slightest whiff of inflation is a consequence. Instead of balancing the interests of those who owe money and those who are owed money, they have consented to run the economy of the industrial world in such a way that the interests of debtors—most young working families, no matter how high their income from work may be—are sacrificed to the interests of creditors—the bankers and people who live, and have lived for a long time off capital invested in the bond and equity markets.

The United States has been thrown into a phase of history where finance rules all. Mutual funds and the stock exchange, rather than the research lab and the factory floor, have become central to the culture. The graduating classes of the nation's great business schools, from Harvard to Stanford, now flock in droves to investment banking rather than to jobs in the real economy. Historically, the financialization of society has always been a symbol that a nation's economic position has entered a phase of deterioration. By the mid-eighteenth century, the Dutch elite, already on the road to decline, had become little more than speculators and rentiers who lived on unearned income, lending their money to any foreign prince or company able to pay the interest. Britain was at a somewhat similar stage by the first decade of the twentieth century. Although its manufacturing industry was losing ground, its financial services had never been stronger— and its elite of investors, bankers, and rentiers, who controlled nearly half of the world's movable investment capital, were confident that finance and investment would make up for any ebb in textiles, steel, and shipbuilding. They were proved wrong, and those who now proclaim the wonderful wisdom of Wall Street will likewise be shown to be in error.

By creating an economic environment in which inflation-adjusted interest rates have been stubbornly high, central bankers in the developed world have presided over a huge transfer of income from both households and ordinary businesses to banks and other financial institutions. They have turned the world of industrial capitalism into a world of finance capitalism. And the financially shortchanged workers have been transformed into a strange new twenty-first-century class of indentured capitalists—rooting for the interests of capital because work itself no longer pays the bills; while stock market investment (no matter how marginal) gives some hope of a bright future.

We all now live in a world of weak government and strong central banks. That is the consequence of the latest era of finance capitalism that has been created by the emergence of the new global economy and the failure of economic policy. No economic sector has moved more swiftly to turn the potent combination of globalization and new technology into a moneymaking machine than has the financial sector. The central bankers of the world have been entrusted with responsibility for keeping finance under control, but instead of becoming the masters of the new world of finance, they have been turned into its abject slaves.

It's almost as though the economy was caught up in Hollywood-style "special effects" technology, inside a megawhirlwind that whooshes through and overwhelms the audience—but never blows over. Back in the early 1970s, before the global economy was hooked up to supercomputers and before we changed to the megabyte standard, the total financial trades conducted by American firms on American exchanges over an entire year came to a dollar amount less than the gross national product. By the mid-1990s, however, through a cascade of electronic trading, the total trades of the financial sector have soared to an annual volume thirty or forty times greater than the turnover of the "real economy," although it is obviously in the real economy that most Americans earn their living. It has been estimated that the annual trading volume of CS First Boston, a leading financial house, by itself exceeded the dollar value of gross domestic product, about $6.5 trillion in 1995. So did that of Goldman, Sachs, Morgan Stanley, Citicorp, and several other top financial firms. And the volume of trading continues to grow each year as financial mathematicians, Wall Street's famed "rocket scientists," invent ever newer and more exotic computer programs and derivatives, hybrid financial instruments with a peculiar twist.

The globalization of the world financial markets has raised a new class to power: those who trade in the global currency and bond markets. This new powerful class of workers is unlike the small businesspeople, manufacturers, or soldiers, all of whom have put their complex sociological stamps on the United States at one time or another. The bond market traders, like the products they manage, have no identifiable personal presence anywhere. But even vaporized as the bond market is, it holds tremendous sway over our times. The iron rule of the market has been much less obvious than was the rule of the military during the cold war. But to an increasing degree, interest rates, the speed at which economies will grow, how rapidly prices will rise, and who will get and hold a job appear to be decided by thousands of young people in their twenties who spend their days staring at computer screens and trading currencies and bonds in great banking and brokerage centers in New York, London, Frankfurt, Hong Kong, and Tokyo.

With the waning of the cold war and the emergence of the new global economy, the leaders of the financial world have replaced the hierarchy of the military industrial complex as the major movers and shakers in the American economy. Whatever its failures and vices may have been, the old military industrial complex recognized that a strong industrial sector was important for defense purposes. It was in the heyday of the cold war that the Pentagon founded DARPA (Defense Department's Advanced Research Projects Agency), which funded the research that, among other things, made the Internet possible and financed the Mantech (manufacturing technology) program, which subsidized projects needed to keep American industrial technology up-to-date. But industrial might is no longer a defense requirement—at least as compared to during the old cold war days—and American industry and American workers receive support only from the financial community. That support for American work is forthcoming only when domestic costs have been driven low enough to ensure industry's ability to compete in the new global economy.

Since the end of the cold war the efforts of Washington have been devoted to satisfying the needs of the financial sector. Financial deregulation has freed banks and other financial institutions to greatly expand their activities, and among other things to profit as much as they can from their ability to make high-interest loans. It was to protect the financial sector that the U.S. Congress instituted the famous bailout of the savings and loan industry, at an initial cost to the taxpayer of $240 billion, an amount that could easily have covered the budget of such scorned welfare programs for the poor as Aid to Families with Dependent Children (AFDC) for many years. It is, indeed, the interest of the financial community that explains much of the thrust of economic policy thinking in the mid-1990s. The reluctance of government regulatory agencies to halt huge mergers and acquisitions despite the damaging effects these deals may have on competitiveness in individual markets means that little stands in the way of Wall Street's continuing to profit from the huge investment banking fees that are generated each time a new merger is consummated. The fascination of Congress with schemes to establish medical savings accounts and to privatize Social Security also represents a willingness to hand over a huge bonanza of management fees to financial institutions. To the financial institutions of America these schemes, if enacted, look like the promised land did to Israelites wandering in the desert.

As power has shifted to the financial sector, policy has had to learn to dance to Wall Street's tunes. When he was battling for his economic program in 1993, President Clinton asked, "You mean to tell me that the success of the program and my reelection hinges on the Federal Reserve and a bunch of f——ing bond traders?" The answer was yes, and it was given by the man who was then Clinton's chief economic policy adviser, Robert Rubin, who made his reputation and his fortune as chief trader for Goldman Sachs. Not long after that exchange with President Clinton, Rubin was promoted to secretary of the treasury. In that post his trader mentality acts as a brake on the more liberal tendencies of other Clinton advisers and makes him advocate within the administration to make sure that policy responds to what's happening on Wall Street.

And the signals that Wall Street and all other financial capital centers send to policy makers around the world are unambiguous: impose highly orthodox policies; maintain tight money, a balanced budget, and a balanced international trade account or else! In this new world, any departure from the narrowest fiscal path is hazardous to the health of the offending country. The markets mete out severe punishment to any country whose inflation rate is seen to be accelerating, whose government deficit is rising, and whose international trade account is deteriorating. In recent years, this fate has befallen the Canadian dollar, the Italian lira, the Swedish krona, the Mexican peso, and the American dollar. At various times in recent years the markets judged that the central bankers of these countries were not stern enough in fighting inflation. Former Soviet bloc countries, specifically Hungary, Poland, and Russia, have paid dearly for the market's perception that they were guilty of financial mismanagement. Among the less-developed countries, the punishees are legion, including Argentina, Brazil, and, most recently, Mexico. As a result, most of these countries have switched to orthodox fiscal and monetary policies to curb inflation. There may be hundreds of thousands of Mexicans in unemployment lines, but Mexico's central bankers are now following the new "party line" (slashing the value of the peso and sending interest rates to the sky).

THE WICKED LAND OF OZ

The constraints placed on monetary policy by the global financial markets have worked their way into the very heart and soul of the Federal Reserve—the U.S. central bank, the Atlas of the financial world. The effect has been to strengthen the antigrowth, anti-worker stance this little-understood organization has always taken. Somehow for us, the figure of Frank Morgan, the talented actor who played a tippling carnival operator transformed into the Wizard of Oz in the wonderful movie based on Frank Baum's tale, comes to mind when we think about central banking. We are constantly aware of a remark made to one of us by G. William Miller during his brief, disastrous stint as chairman of the Federal Reserve under President Jimmy Carter. "Most people," said Miller, "still think that Federal Reserve is a brand of whiskey."

For that, the men who have served as chairmen of the Federal Reserve are due the "thanks." Often called up by Congress to testify, and by the trade associations of the financial community to lend an aura of importance to their deadly conventions, the chairmen of this powerful institution have conformed to the ancient traditions of central banking: dissemble; tell the public as little as possible about what you are really up to lest someone find out that any reasonably intelligent person could do the job as well as you can, provided of course, that he can act.

What the Federal Reserve chairman has to hide is the stunning simplicity with which he can work his magic—to create money. The basic process is the same everywhere. Central banks create money by buying something. It could be shoes or ships or sealing wax, but in most countries it is securities; in the United States these days it is usually Treasury bills or bonds. Though there are arcane aspects to the money creation process (depending on the peculiar banking conditions of individual countries at specific points in time), these need not concern the chairman of the U.S. central bank himself, having at his disposal the services of a giant Washington research staff, including many economists and bankers. If that is not enough, he can call on the research staffs of the twelve regional Federal Reserve banks spread across the country from Boston to Chicago to San Francisco.

The chairman of the Federal Reserve is, then, America's Wizard of Oz appearing now and then out of a cloud, just like the other "special effects" being manufactured in today's market. He appears in special productions, especially at meetings of the central banker's own central bank, the Bank for International Settlements in Basel, Switzerland, out of a cloud created by the smoke of expensive cigars. (Could that have been a Havana in Paul Volcker's hand?) Indeed, Miller's rapid downfall may well have occurred because he conformed too closely to the description of the fictional wizard in Frank Baum's story—"A good man but a bad wizard."

No other Federal Reserve chairman has played the wizard's role with the same fidelity. Most have, instead, been bad chairmen but good wizards. Not bad in any mercenary sense. One real and truly admirable characteristic of America's central bankers is their exemplary record of fiscal rectitude. Throughout its history, the Federal Reserve has handled billions of dollars a day, cleanly and without a major scandal. Its record is truly amazing and a real source of the institution's strength, and of the admiration in which it is held by those, especially journalists, who know how sharply the Fed's spotless reputation contrasts with the rap sheet of the financial sector on Wall Street, which has been riddled with larceny, the misappropriation of funds, and many variants of the original Ponzi scheme.

But there is more than one way in which a public official can be bad. An official fails when he or she identifies the national interest too closely with the interests of his or her own constituency. The Federal Reserve is a public institution deriving its powers over money from an act of Congress, which gives the Fed the power to create money "and regulate the value thereof," a power that was vested in Congress itself by the U.S. Constitution. But the Federal Reserve is formally owned by the commercial banks who hold the stock in the system—not by the citizens of the United States. The seven members of the Fed's board of governors are appointed by the president and are subject to confirmation by Congress. The power over money creation is exercised by the Federal Open Market Committee, which, in addition to the members of the board of governors, includes five of the twelve presidents of the regional Federal Reserve banks, who serve on a rotating basis. These regional bank presidents have normally been anti-inflation hawks and have been single-minded in protecting the interests of the commercial banks that pay their salaries.

THE LEADING INTERESTS OF THE CENTRAL BANKS

Like other regulatory institutions, the Federal Reserve has been subject to "capture" by the industry that it regulates. It is in this sense that the Federal Reserve and many of its chairmen are bad. Apart from Miller, the Federal Reserve chairmen of recent memory—William McChesney Martin, Arthur F. Burns, Paul A. Volcker, and Alan Greenspan—have shown few inhibitions about closely identifying with the interests of the industry that they are supposed to regulate.

To observe that the Federal Reserve single-mindedly protects the industry that it is supposed to regulate is not to totally condemn its activities. A country that maintains a strong banking system and a strong, stable currency reaps real rewards. The Federal Reserve Act of 1913, which set up the U.S. system of central banking as we know it, did lay a foundation for the growth and success of the American financial sector. And it is certainly true that the other great economic success stories of the post–World War II world, Germany and Japan, are nothing if not sound currency countries.

But recognizing the need for the maintenance of sound money is not the same as giving the Federal Reserve and other central banks the right to use their blank checks, as it were, to dominate policy. Yet this is what has happened. A trend toward vesting central banks with increasing authority first emerged in the mid-1960s as a result of inflation caused by President Johnson's "guns and butter" approach to financing the Vietnam War. It intensified after the OPEC oil embargo in 1973, and after the end of the cold war central banks began to totally dominate economic policy. We now live in a world of weak government and strong central banks. No other trend has worked more surely to betray those who earn their living from work.

The domination of economic policy by the Federal Reserve and other central banks is new. In the well-ordered world of the 1950s and 1960s the Federal Reserve did play an important role, but its influence on policy was offset by presidents who did not fear criticizing the Federal Reserve or putting pressure on the Fed to promote growth. Progrowth pressure was a steady drum beat during the Democratic administrations of the 1950s, 1960s, and the early 1970s, and it even played a role in the Eisenhower and Nixon administrations. Congress also acted in ways that put limits on the power of the Federal Reserve. The ability of Congressman Wright Patman, the Texan who was chairman of the House banking committee in most of those years, to call Federal Reserve chairmen to account was legendary, as was that of Senator Paul H. Douglass of Illinois, who then served as chairman or vice chairman of the Joint Economic Committee of Congress.

None of this is to say that the pro–high employment forces were always right and the Federal Reserve was always wrong. But the system of checks and balances, in which the United States rightly takes pride, did work as rigidly to limit the Federal Reserve. And inflation was not a problem during these years. Between 1948 and the outbreak of the Vietnam War in the mid-1960s, the U.S. inflation rate was a modest 1.7 percent.

The Federal Reserve's anti-inflation hysteria is, pure and simple, special interest politics, practiced by an institution almost totally free of effective oversight. As a class, bankers are creditors who have a strong interest in making sure that the money they lend out—ranging from revolving credit such as Visa or MasterCard to thirty-year mortgages—is paid back in money that does not lose value through time. The central bank is most concerned to limit inflation because inflation depreciates the value of the assets held by the commercial banks.

The incentive of central banks to protect the interest of creditors has been increased by the globalization of the financial markets. Owners of liquid capital hate inflation. So in a world where capital can flow freely, and where it is scarce as compared with an oversupply of willing workers, there has been a power shift toward *all* institutions with a vested interest in avoiding inflation. Like the banks, the bond market, which is an open market for loans, is dominated by creditors and tends to serve their interests. When prices are rising (inflation), debtors can repay their loans to creditors in cheaper currency; for this reason creditors hate inflation. But when prices are falling, debtors are forced to repay their debts with expensive (harder to earn) currency. Thus creditors benefit at the expense of workers, and the result in a world of capital triumphant is continued downward pressure on prices. That is the kind of world that the bond market, dominated by lenders, loves.

There are many other reasons besides the power of the central banks' financial constituency why economic policy power has migrated to the central banks. One is the great post–World War II success of the German economy. That nation's central bank, the Bundesbank, is rightfully given credit for slaying the dragon of inflation in a country that was haunted by inflationary episodes after both World War I and World War II. In the 1970s and 1980s the Bundesbank achieved enormous influence by demonstrating that tight money and a strong currency need not interfere with economic success, particularly in an economy where productivity is growing rapidly. German growth has sagged in the 1990s, but the reputation of its central bank has remained intact.

MARKET-DETERMINED ECONOMIC POLICY: ANTI-INFLATION, ANTI-GROWTH, PRO–TIGHT MONEY

The notion that it is good fiscal policy to vest the fierce enemies of inflation with extraordinary powers is a lesson that has been drawn from the experience of many countries in the developing world. The emerging world is full of stories about countries, such as Chile, Portugal, and Indonesia, that have sharply boosted their growth rates by cutting their inflation rates.

But it is the *globalization* of the world's financial markets that has turned central bankers into despots. It is these markets that lend the behavior of even the most restrictive central banks an aura of unquestioned virtue. Globalization started well before the end of the cold war, of course. It traces back to decisions made in the early 1950s to abandon exchange controls and make all the currencies of the leading countries freely convertible one into the other. Globalization gathered momentum in the 1960s when countries finally stopped pegging their currencies to the price of gold—Japan, Britain, Germany, France, and the United States after the Plaza accords of 1971. The depth and range of the global financial markets increased with the emergence of the "tigers" of the Pacific Rim, whose currencies became more important in international financial markets. The voracious appetite of global markets for policies that fight inflation is both reinforcing the Federal Reserve's natural deflationary tendencies and giving the Fed the power to impose them on a society whose real interests are betrayed by slow growth.

The antigrowth story really starts with the unfortunate Mr. Miller himself, an industrialist rather than a banker; he rose to chairman of Textron, a large textile company. A Democrat rather than a Republican, he was appointed chairman of the Federal Reserve to replace Arthur F. Burns, a Columbia University professor who was appointed chairman of the Federal Reserve after long service to President Richard M. Nixon.

Miller took over the Fed in the aftermath of the inflation caused by OPEC. Because the American inflation rate had not fallen, because Miller was not a banker, and because he was a Democrat, he was widely mistrusted by the financial markets. The Miller regime at the Fed was so shaky that it contributed to a "dollar" crisis in the fall of 1979. Faced with the possibility of severe political troubles, President Carter, who inherited Miller, was forced to change his Federal Reserve chairman. His White House instituted a search for a new man. The name that kept turning up was Paul A. Volcker, then the president of the Federal Reserve Bank of New York, and a politically androgynous economist who worked in the economics department at the Chase Manhattan Bank and had served in the Treasury during the Johnson and Nixon administrations.

It was the cigar-smoking Volcker who proved to be the very model of the kind of central banker who would be deemed acceptable by Wall Street in an era when financial markets dictate economic policy. As soon as he took over, Volcker instituted a reign of monetary restraint that has lasted to the mid-1990s, into the regime of his successor, Alan Greenspan. Volcker's devotion to price stability was unswerving, and his psychological makeup was such that he could virtually ignore the problems associated with slow growth and unemployment. At a lunch at *Business Week* magazine's headquarters in New York in the fall of 1980, Volcker argued with conviction that the economy was still growing, although later data showed that the United States was well into the severe 1980–1981 recession at the time of this luncheon speech. No economist is a perfect forecaster, of course, but the point is that Volcker is the kind of man to whom the dangers of inflation always seem much clearer and more present than the dangers of slow economic growth and high unemployment.

Volcker may have had exalted credentials as a central banker, but he was not deemed politically safe enough by Ronald Reagan. Soon after being elected president, Reagan replaced Volcker with Alan Greenspan, an economic consultant who had been appointed as chairman of the Council of Economic Advisers by President Gerald

Ford. Though not a banker, Greenspan had established his credentials as an inflation fighter and a man unwilling to assume the risks of growth during his stint in the Ford administration. In fact, he counselled policies of restraint so severe that he probably cost his boss the 1976 election. His total dedication to price stability and his unwillingness to take the risks inherent in encouraging growth made Greenspan an acceptable chairman of the U.S. Federal Reserve as far as the markets were concerned.

The ability of the market to dictate who should and who should not have influence at the Federal Reserve continues. President Clinton reappointed Greenspan to the chairmanship of the Fed in February of 1996, even though the president's close economic advisers had severe doubts about the ability of the United States to avoid a recession if Greenspan continued in his job. President Clinton was not successful in his efforts to broaden the Federal Reserve's horizons to the extent that it would rank growth as a goal equal in importance to price stability. Early in 1996 Alan Blinder, who had been appointed vice chairman of the Federal Reserve by President Clinton and given the duty of encouraging growth at the Fed, resigned in frustration, explaining in an article in the *New Yorker* that he could exercise no leverage at the Federal Reserve. When Clinton floated the name of the Lazard Frères investment banker Felix Rohatyn as Blinder's replacement, cries of anguish could be heard on Wall Street and among conservatives in Congress, because Rohatyn had been critical of the Fed's antigrowth policies in the 1990s. The chorus of criticism grew so loud that Rohatyn asked that his name be withdrawn from consideration, a request that President Clinton was forced to honor. Clinton instead nominated his Office of Management and Budget director, Alice M. Rivlin, a woman who had spent twenty years inveighing against large federal deficits. She is the kind of Federal Reserve vice chairman that the markets can live with (even if she is a lifelong Democrat). President Clinton, Chairman Greenspan, and Vice Chairman Rivlin are the kind of ménage à trois that does not offend the sensibilities of Wall Street.

The power of the markets to push central banks toward restraint shows up clearly in every statistic that measures the thrust of monetary policy. One such measure is the rate of growth of a nation's money supply.

Figure 7-1 shows the monetary growth rate for the United States measured in two ways. The dashed line shows the growth rate of the most conventional and widely accepted definition of money, a monetary aggregate that includes currency, basic demand deposits, and

Figure 7-1
Growth of the U.S. Money Supply, 1972–1996

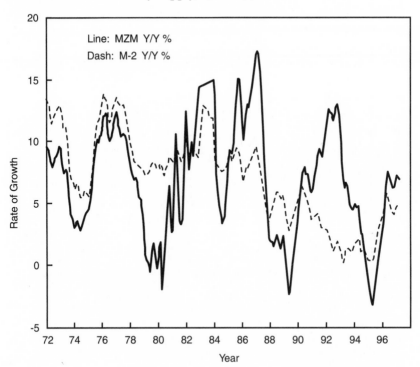

Data: ISI Group

time deposits in the commercial banking system. Because of the growth of money market mutual funds and other kinds of accounts whose differences from conventional money cannot be easily discerned, some have argued that the conventional M-2 definition of money is an inaccurate measure of what has happened to the ready purchasing power available to business and consumers. We have therefore added another measure of money, MZM (money of zero maturity), measuring the total supply of money and near monies available to the American public. As Figure 7-1 shows, the growth rates of both measures of money have decelerated since the mid-1980s, although the growth rates of MZM swing up and down more from year to year.

A similar constraint is visible in the monetary growth rates of *all* the advanced industrial countries. Edward Hyman, Jr., president of ISI Corp., keeps a set of statistics that combines the monetary growth rates of all the leading industrial countries, including the United

Figure 7-2

The Global Squeeze on Money Growth*

*Combined year-to-year percentage change in monthly money growth data for five
industrialized countries (U.S., Germany, Japan, Britain, Canada).

Data: ISI Group

States, Japan, Germany, Britain, and Canada. As Figure 7-2 shows, the
combined monetary growth rates of these five key countries have
decelerated even more sharply than that of the United States alone.
This is a stark indicator of the fall in monetary growth since the end
of the cold war. And that fall has had its intended effect—one near
and dear to the hearts of central bankers. Figure 7-3 shows the
combined rate of increase in the consumer price index for five
advanced countries: the United States, Japan, Germany, Britain, and
Canada. There is of course some cyclicality in these numbers, but the
trend of inflation is down for these five important countries dominated by the imperatives of their central banks.

This decrease in inflation has not been achieved without a price.
Figure 7-4 shows the combined real economic growth rate of these
countries. Again, a downward trend is evident. All-out war against
inflation cannot be waged without claiming victims, and those who
earn their living from work are the prime hostages to slow growth.

Figure 7-3

The Global Decline in Inflation*

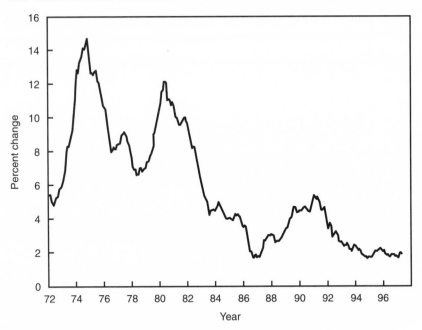

*Combined year-to-year percentage change in monthly consumer price data for five industrialized countries (U.S., Germany, Britain, Japan, Canada).

Data: ISI Group

We can also see the full extent of monetary restraint when we add in an analysis of the trend of real interest rates. Real interest rates are simply market interest rates minus the inflation rate; they represent the "real cost of money to borrowers." It is true that market interest rates have come down as inflation has decelerated in recent years. But real interest rates stayed high.

The real rate of interest is simply the difference between the market rate of interest and the inflation rate. It is derived by subtracting the inflation rate from the market rate of interest. So the real rate will go up in any period when the market rate either rises when the inflation rate falls or, in the more usual case, when the market rate of interest falls by less than the inflation rate. Here is a simple example of the more usual scenario. If the market rate of interest on a long-term Treasury bond should fall from 8 percent to 6 percent in a year when the inflation rate falls from 5 percent to 2 percent, the real rate of interest would increase by 1 percentage point

Figure 7-4

The Post–Cold War Growth Slowdown*

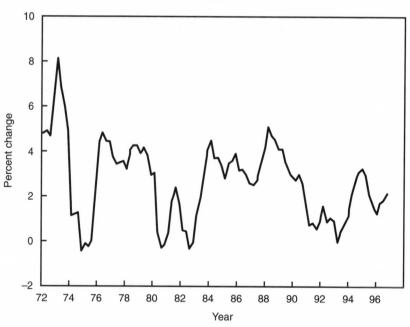

*Combined year-to-year change in quarterly real GDP for five industrial countries (U.S., Japan, Germany, Britain, Canada).

Data: ISI Group

from a real rate of 2 percent (8 – 6) to a real rate of 3 percent (5 – 2). Creditors and the owners of capital benefit when real rates rise since the effect is to transfer real, inflation-adjusted, purchasing power from debtors to creditors and from those of average income to the rich.

The moral of this story is that the ultimate paradise for a bondholder would be a period when the inflation rate is zero and the market rate rises. In that case, for example, a 6 percent market rate on bonds would be sheer gravy because the creditors would have lost nothing to inflation, and the purchasing power of the interest payments they receive would remain totally intact. No wonder creditors hate inflation! And as Figure 7-5 shows, real inflation-adjusted rates have actually stayed high in the same period, even as economic growth has slowed down. In this kind of an economy, consumers and business must pay more "real dollars" for loans, and as a result they have less money left over either to invest or to consume. Particularly since the end of the cold war we have been living in a

Figure 7-5

U.S. Real Interest Rates Stay High: Spread Between Long Bond* Yield and Inflation Rate

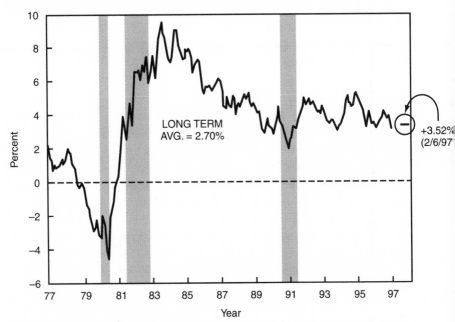

Data: Bureau of Labor Statistics; Federal Reserve Board
*30-Year Treasury; 20-Year Treasury used prior to 1978

world where the true cost of borrowing has stayed high even though market interest rates have declined.

There is one, and only one, conclusion that can be drawn from these data on monetary growth and real interest rates: the industrial world is living through a period of exceptionally tight money. And that translates into slow growth and high unemployment in Europe and Japan, and stagnant wages in the United States.

Economic growth is slow because the tyranny of the financial markets has imposed an exceptionally constrictive new paradigm on Federal Reserve policy making. When deciding on how tight or easy to make money, recent Federal Reserve doctrine focuses on a concept called the *natural rate of employment,* or, in the lingo of economists, NRE (which economists, significantly, pronounce as though it rhymes with *eerie*). NRE is defined as that rate of employment that is consistent with price stability. Recent Federal Reserve doctrine holds this natural rate to be about 94 or 95 percent, meaning that unemployment must be kept somewhere between 5 percent and 6 percent to ensure that inflation isn't reignited. In this view, moreover, the Federal Reserve has the backing of most members of the economics profession, from liberals such as Paul Krugman to virtually every mainstream conservative economist such as Martin Feldstein, the chairman of the Council of Economic Advisers in the early days of the Reagan administration.

Conventional wisdom also holds that under current economic conditions, the economy cannot grow at more than about 2.5 percent per year without pushing the unemployment rate below 5 or 6 percent, and therefore risking inflation. Indeed, virtually every government document that was produced during the mid-1990s decreed that the appropriate growth rate for the United States is somewhere at or a little below 2.5 percent. The idea is not only enshrined in all the official work of the Federal Reserve; it has appeared in the *Economic Report of the President,* and in virtually every prediction of noninflationary growth that has been issued by the Congressional Budget Office (which does the technical economic work for Congress).

There is, of course, a fatal flaw in all this: the economic growth rate that produces an unemployment rate that seems "natural" in the mid-1990s is in fact highly unnatural by the standards of U.S. economic history. For as we have already seen, the long-term growth rate of the United States has historically been well over 3 percent.

As long as Washington remains fixed in its conviction that real growth should not exceed 2.5 percent, the future of work in the United States will be bitter. Unfortunately, it appears certain that the Federal Reserve will not take the risk of seeking higher growth. *Business Week* in early 1995 published an article arguing that productivity in the United States was showing signs of growing faster in the 1990s than it had been in the preceding two decades. Given such economic momentum, said the story, the Federal Reserve could run a more stimulative monetary policy without risking inflation.

The reaction the article provoked makes for a very revealing story. Soon after the story appeared in the magazine, Bill Wolman received an interesting phone call from Fed chairman Greenspan. Calls to journalists from the Federal Reserve chairman are rare, so one can only imagine that Greenspan must have regarded the argument as cogent enough to pose some danger to the general complacent focus on keeping growth low to avoid inflation. In the course of the conversation, Greenspan granted that there was some evidence that productivity growth has accelerated in the 1990s, but he said that he could not take the risk of encouraging faster growth because the international markets would punish the United States by pushing the value of the dollar down in the foreign exchange markets, and forcing the Fed to raise interest rates to prevent an outright raid on the dollar. Greenspan's message was that he could not act on his belief that productivity growth had accelerated—an economic Catch-22 if there ever was one.

The policy paralysis imposed by the tyranny of the financial markets will doom the United States to slow growth and the betrayal of work into the twenty-first century. There will be no relief for those who earn their living from work unless not only the United States but also all the industrial nations undertake a radical rethinking of policy and devise some method of insulating faster-growth policies from attack by the global financial markets. We will look at the means of accomplishing this goal in the final chapter of this book, Chapter 9.

WHAT INFLATION?

America is in the thrall of a frightful myth: that the United States is an inflation-prone country. This myth survives even though there is not a lot of evidence to suggest that it is true. That is not to say that inflation has not been a problem in the post–World War II years, for clearly it has been. The critical point is that the inflationary episodes of the years since World War II did not result from the normal processes by which economic policy was made. Rather they were the result of abnormal events: Federal Reserve behavior during Richard Nixon's presidential campaign of 1972 and the OPEC oil embargo of 1973.

A study of the behavior of prices since the end of World War II clearly shows that the inflation problem of the 1970s can be explained by the toxic impact of these two events. The overall U.S. annual inflation rate, compounded from 1950 to 1994, is 4.1 percent. But there is one period of rapid inflation that stands out, and it explains most of the price increases since World War II: the years from 1972 to 1982, when the compound inflation rate was 9.1 percent. Omitting that period, the U.S. inflation rate since World War II is hardly frightening. It averaged 2.5 percent between 1950 and 1972, and 3.9 percent between 1983 and 1995.

The idea that the United States is an inflation-prone country is obviously influenced by the 9.1 percent inflation rate of the years between 1972 and 1982. But the statistics are heavily distorted by abnormal economic policies. The inflation spurt that began in 1973 was caused partly by the highly inflationary policies pursued by the

Federal Reserve board under Arthur F. Burns, a close Nixon adviser, in order to pump up the economy by Election Day. It received further impetus from the four-month oil embargo imposed by the Organization of Petroleum Exporting Countries (OPEC) following the hostility that broke out in October of 1973. Indeed, it was the oil cartel, and not domestic policy, that fanned the inflationary spark of Nixon's electoral drive into an inflationary fire. This episode of inflation is not evidence that the United States is prone to inflation.

The decision to wage an all-out war against inflation in a country that is not prone to inflation risks disaster. It resembles the kind of thinking that led World War I generals to send millions of men over the top to a certain death by barbed wire and machine-gun fire.

If pursued with an appropriate sense of balance, price stability is a worthy goal, yet there is a vast difference between encouraging price stability and encouraging deflation. One of our fundamental theses is that countries in the developed world are being forced into economic policies that are not merely consistent with price stability but are in fact deflationary. This argument may seem to fly in the face of the conventional wisdom of the financially orthodox, but what the orthodox refuse to see is that the industrial world seems already embarked on a deflationary course. All the evidence shows that throughout the industrial world the years since the end of the cold war have been characterized by extremely slow growth and concealed deflation.

Our current economic policy has the makings of disaster. Holding monetary growth so low virtually dooms the United States to stagnant wages and social tensions. Such low growth also virtually guarantees that social programs designed to put people on welfare to work are certain either to fail or to succeed only in throwing the already working poor out of a job. By pounding away at the nonexistent inflationary forces that supposedly hound the international markets daily, the central bank agenda has contributed to creating an environment in which work is betrayed and workers are degraded.

If history demonstrates anything, it is that rapid economic growth is the best friend, the surest friend, that work ever had. Since the age of discovery, the rapid economic growth that has been the hallmark of the modern capitalist world has lent dignity and respect to work. It is the rapid growth since the Industrial Revolution that has created a broad middle class in the United States and that accounts for much of what is great about American society today.

THE CASE FOR RAPID GROWTH

The story of the world economy since the end of World War II can be viewed as a model for explaining why work needs a strong economic growth rate to flourish. In their race to bow to the dictates of the global financial system and its twenty-five-year-old currency and bond traders, central bankers seem to have forgotten the magic worked by fast growth in the early postwar years. The years between the end of World War II and the beginning of the fight against inflation in the mid-1970s were, for the developed world, one of the most successful periods in history. Angus Maddison, the British historian whose books are bibles to students of economic growth, calls this period "the golden age" because during this time the standard of living in the developed world as a whole increased at a pace *never* before seen in peacetime.

Actually, the roots of this prosperity really date back farther than that. To understand the bitter economic disappointment of the American middle class in recent years, it is important to realize that the "golden age" of the postwar years was a continuation of a period of even more spectacular progress during World War II itself. The war's impact on the average American's standard of living was described vividly by Doris Kearns Goodwin in her Pulitzer Prize-winning book *No Ordinary Time,* about the presidency of Franklin Delano Roosevelt during World War II. By the end of the war, Kearns Goodwin writes,

> No segment of American society had been left untouched. More than seventeen million new jobs had been created, industrial production had gone up 100 percent, corporate profits doubled, and the GNP had jumped from $100 billion to $215 billion. The war had radically changed the shape of the American economy, exerting a profound impact on the everyday lives and expectations of people in all parts of the country. In 1940, only 7.8 million Americans out of 132 million made enough money to pay taxes; in 1945, that figure had risen to nearly 50 million in a population of 140 million. The wartime economy allowed millions of Americans who had been on relief to get back on their feet and start over again. Miners had enjoyed steady employment for the first time in twenty years. Automobile workers had doubled their incomes and expanded their skills. Black sharecroppers had left the rural South for the cities of the North, where despite terrible racial tensions and a hard destiny, they

would find a more abundant life than the one they had left behind.

The society of a few haves and a multitude of havenots had been transformed. Because of the greatest—indeed, the only—redistribution of income downward in the nation's history, a middle-class country had emerged. Half of the American people—those at the lower end of the compensation scale—had doubled their income, while those in the top 20 percent had risen by little more than 50 percent. Those in the bottom half of earners had seen their share of the country's income increase by 16 percent, while those at the top had lost 6 percent. As a result, social historian Geoffrey Perrett observed, "[B]arriers to social economic equality which had stood for decades were either much reduced or entirely overthrown."

Nothing describes the power of rapid economic growth more surely than the social and economic transformation that occurred during World War II. Of course, there is no way that the United States could replicate the forced draft economy of those war years. But the growth rates of the "golden years" from 1950 to 1973 were remarkable in themselves. Between 1950 and 1973, the American economy grew at an annual rate of 3.6 percent, compared to 2.6 percent between 1973 and 1988, and the even more disappointing 2.1 percent of the post-cold war years.

Indeed, the economic policies that have been in place since the end of the cold war have not only ignored the great success story of the years since World War II, but actually represent a reversion to policies that were in place in the 1920s, one of the most disastrous periods in world history. Our analysis of the differences in economic policy in the 1920s versus that of two decades immediately following World War II, Angus Maddison's "golden age," applies in varying degree to the entire developed world, but for the sake of this book we will focus on the United States.

Just as in the aftermath of World War I, politicians since the end of the cold war have put their trust in the markets to yield solutions to economic problems. The 1920s were, outside of the Soviet Union, of course, the last time when the free market was as dominant as it is now. Then, as now, the economic policy was to "leave it to the free market." Indeed, the free market was trumpeted so much that it assumed an almost mythic quality. During the 1920s and up to the catastrophe of the Great Depression, the White House was occupied by three free market presidents: Warren G. Harding, a corrupt captive of the corporate classes, especially the oil industry (the Teapot Dome scandal); Calvin Coolidge, who felt that government could remain inert because the nation's business was, after all, business; and Herbert Hoover, an ethical but dogmatic engineer who believed that any departure from the free market would only make things worse for the American worker. The 1920s were also characterized by a contempt for securities regulation, a faith in the gold standard as a means of regulating trade between nations, and a feeble trade union movement.

The policies of central banks in the post-cold war years bear an uncanny resemblance to those of the 1920s. The same financial folly that now invests central bankers with an undeserved monopoly on financial wisdom also prevailed then, as does what then turned out to be highly deflationary monetary policies. In Britain Winston Churchill, chancellor of the exchequer from 1924 to 1929, kept his country on the gold standard; the accompanying unemployment rate averaged 10 percent. The United States, benefiting from innovations in the auto industry, electric utilities, and the construction of national highways, prospered during the 1920s, despite short recessions in 1921–1922 and in 1926–1927. But as a whole the 1920s was a period of tight money, especially after a well-known (in those days) financial hero, Benjamin Strong, president of the Federal Reserve Bank of New York, engineered what many economists now believe was a fatal tightening of the money supply in the late 1920s. The parallels with the years since 1988, also characterized by strong deflationary pressure and tight money, are apparent.

In other key ways, too, the current era resembles the 1920s. In the 1920s, H. L. Mencken characterized Samuel Gompers, the cigar roller who became head of the American Federation of Labor, as "tame as a tabby cat." The years since 1988 have similarly been a time of weak unions. As in the 1920s, income from capital is rising compared with income earned from work. Just as the distribution of income has become more unequal since the end of the cold war, the 1920s also witnessed progressive income inequality. And one must add, of course, the parallel stock market booms.

The economic policy debate today ignores the lessons of "the golden age"—the most successful economic peacetime in American history. The economic policy of that era featured virtually every policy and trend that is today declared the enemy of growth. The post-World War II era saw a still strong trade union movement, an expanding social safety net, a growing welfare state, and diminishing income inequality. All these conditions are anathema to the antigovernment spirit of today. There was considerable government intervention in business during this period. Who now remembers John F. Kennedy's famed "all businessmen are sons of bitches" quote when he faced down steel industry price rises in 1962? During this era the government also imposed wage–price controls at several times and launched major government initiatives such as the space missions, the war on poverty, and Medicare and Medicaid.

The willingness of government to steer economic policy in these years was not confined to Democratic administrations. Eisenhower began one of the most important, far-reaching, and expensive public works programs in the nation's history: the federal interstate highway system. President Nixon also was quick to intervene in the economy—witness the wage–price controls he imposed in 1971 to slow inflation. Both of these Republican presidents undertook aggressive antitrust actions, and both strongly supported, and expanded, federal housing programs.

There was also an attempt during those Republican years to return power to state and local government, but for the most part, the relative power of the federal government grew. The Supreme Court's decision in *Brown vs. Board of Education* in 1954 increased federal power in education. Civil rights, equal opportunity, and Great Society legislation in the 1960s also vested more power in the federal government. The point is that none of these government programs hampered the accompanying unprecedented economic growth. The GI Bill and special federal mortgages for war veterans gave the average American the opportunity to receive a college education, own a home for the first time, earn a white-collar living, and last but not least, join the ranks of multicar families.

These extraordinary accomplishments occurred primarily because of one basic fact: the U.S. economy grew extremely rapidly in the 1950s and 1960s. Nor was the growth an accident. Emerging from World War II, the Allies were determined not to let the world slip back into recession. In the founding meeting of the United Nations in San Francisco in June 1945 the Allies committed themselves to and carried out policies aimed at achieving full employment.

This commitment continued through the 1950s and 1960s. Though President Eisenhower regularly denounced profligate spending, his administration was committed to the reforms introduced by the New Deal, trying perhaps to slow down the growth of the welfare state, but never to end it. With John F. Kennedy the

Democrats returned to power in 1960 with a commitment to growth, expressed in a slogan from his presidential campaign: "Let's get the country moving again." When Lyndon B. Johnson became president, the commitment to growth became if anything more real. There was a shift toward restraint after a flare-up of inflation in 1967-1968 that resulted from the guns and butter policies of the U.S. military buildup in Vietnam, but in the early 1970s Richard Nixon, first elected president in 1968, again returned the country to a policy of full employment. After all, it was Nixon who said, "We are all Keynesians now," to underscore his commitment to a policy of high economic growth and full employment.

International economic cooperation was the second, even more important, policy that promoted rapid growth in the years after World War II. In the 1920s, in contrast, an essential mistake of the United States was its refusal to join the League of Nations or to cooperate strongly with the market democracies in Europe to achieve the common good. In other ways, too, the contrast between the 1920s and the years following World War II are sharp. Instead of turning its back on Europe, the United States instituted the Marshall Plan; instead of punishing its defeated enemy, Germany, as it did following World War I with the Treaty of Versailles and the exaction of impossible reparations that ruined the German economy, the United States and Britain treated both Germany and Japan with "magnanimity," as Winston Churchill put it. Instead of continuing to rely on the gold standard, Washington was instrumental in founding and supporting the International Monetary Fund and the World Bank. Indeed, it was the strength of international cooperation that allowed the world to return to convertibility of currencies and to lay the foundation of an expansion in world trade unprecedented in history.

Today it is a growing possibility that international cooperation will stall. The industrial countries have proved less than magnanimous in providing economic aid to the former Soviet Union and (more narrowly, but no less importantly) may prove unable to prevent recurring currency crises that threaten the world trading system. A breakdown in international cooperation must be avoided, because working together and helping each other are the only ways to achieve faster economic growth.

The cost of slow economic growth will, if anything, be higher in the coming years than at any time in this century, and this is one of the more critical implications of the triumph of capital. If the United States resigns itself to becoming a slow-growth country, it will be deserted by those who control the global flow of capital. The United States will almost certainly suffer a severe drop in investment as capital moves to those countries that are growing far faster than the United States, especially the fast-growing countries of Asia. Once firmly embarked on the slow-growth road, the United States cannot avoid the ominous spectre of social and economic decay.

Though not out of the range of historic experience, absolute economic decline is, of course, an extreme scenario. If American prosperity dies, it is more likely to be with a whimper, not a bang. Unless the chairman of the Fed gives up all attempts to play the wizard and turns into a good man, the most plausible scenario is that those who earn their living from work in the United States will slowly be ground down by deflationary economic policies, which are totally inappropriate in a global economy in which emerging countries are growing rapidly. We now turn to an analysis of the crisis of capitalism that could result should this sustained attack on work continue unabated.

CHAPTER 8

A New Crisis of Capitalism?

T HE GREAT SLOWDOWN IN INCOME GROWTH SINCE 1989 strongly suggests that the market democracies of the developed world snatched defeat from the jaws of victory in the cold war.

This is an age that extols the virtues of the private sector and is highly skeptical of the power of government to serve the public interest. The great economic policy debate is still anchored by a liberal progovernment ideology on the Left and a conservative antigovernment ideology on the Right. But in most countries of the industrial world, the left-wing parties are far more willing than in the past to embrace promarket ideas. Symbolic of the shift in the United States was a statement President Clinton made in his 1996 State of the Union speech: "The age of big government is over."

Ironically, as faith in government has waned in the United States and Europe, governments in many developing nations have spurred prosperity. In the last quarter of the twentieth century, government had a major role in creating the Asian miracle—not by playing the part of social benefactor but by serving as a dynamic actor helping, at every step, to propel Asian industry onto the world scene. From its role in technical, mathematical, and scientific education, to its institutions that financed business, to its economic planning, the government in each of the four "tigers" of East Asia seeded growth in such a way that the economic miracle, originally inspired by Japan, occurred in other East Asian countries, one after another.

The economic pathology of communist and socialist states does not by itself prove the case against government. The state has done enough good and the unfettered free market enough harm in the industrial countries of the West during the twentieth century to raise serious concerns about the ultimate impact of the rightward drift of economic policy throughout the industrial world. Indeed, plenty of signs already exist that the total victory of capital and capitalism in the cold war is creating a series of economic imbalances serious enough to eventually provoke a new crisis of capitalism. A world where the free market is allowed to run wild is an environment where the kinds of catastrophes that followed the age of high imperialism— the years before the outbreak of World War I—and the roaring twenties are not the exception but the rule. There are at least three powerful trends at work in the post-cold war economy that threaten a new crisis of capitalism.

CAPITAL'S NEW POWER AND HOW IT AFFECTS THE DISTRIBUTION OF INCOME AND WEALTH

Few of us have had breakfast at Tiffany's, but a good number of us have gazed in wonderment at the jewelry displays in that elegant store's windows and those of its major competitors, Cartier's and van Cleef & Arpels. Each expensive piece is carefully displayed, set out on velvet cushions, set off by expensive floral arrangements or pieces of exquisite sculpture, and protected by security systems. Most of us have also walked in shopping districts that cater to the poor, passing by huge piles of cheap merchandise set out in jumbled heaps in the open air.

Behold the market. Its power is unparalleled. It cherishes that which it deems valuable and cheapens what it deems close to worthless. Therefore, as workers have become more abundant, the value of their labor has plunged—with devastating effects. The value of work in a world where each American competes with 15 workers globally is far lower than it was when he or she was but one in five in the industrialized West. As we have seen, both the market and public policy have turned against work. Wages are under pressure, pensions are being scaled back, rules to protect health and safety are attenuated, workers are being forced into early retirement. And most symbolic of the change, those supposedly "cherished" programs that were woven carefully into the fabric of society in a happier age for work, Social Security and Medicare, have come under attack.

The contrast between the treatment of work and the treatment of capital since the end of the cold war has had an impact on virtually all aspects of economic life. Begin with one of the two fundamental measures of economic well-being—income. One fact stands out about the years since 1989: There has been a sharp increase in the return to

Table 8-1
More Hours, Smaller Wage Gains:
Trends in Average Wages and Average Hours, 1967 – 1994
(1995)

Year	Productivity per Hour (1992=100)	Wage Levels			Hours Worked		
		Annual Wages	Weekly Wages	Hourly Wages	Annual Hours	Weeks per Year	Hours per Week
1967	69.2	$19,511	$459.59	$11.96	1,633	42.4	38.4
1973	80.7	22,694	536.01	14.22	1,598	42.3	37.7
1979	86.4	22,862	534.92	14.11	1,620	42.7	37.9
1983	89.9	22,334	519.45	13.88	1,609	43.0	37.4
1989	95.8	24,600	552.42	14.35	1,714	44.5	38.5
1994	100.7	25,070	558.96	14.40	1,740	44.9	38.8
Annual Growth Rate*							
1967 – 73	2.6%	2.5%	2.6%	2.9%	0.4%	0.0%	0.3%
1973 – 79	1.1	0.1	0.0	−0.1	0.2	0.2	0.1
1979 – 89	1.0	0.7	0.3	0.2	0.6	0.4	0.2
1989 – 94	1.0	0.4	0.2	0.1	0.3	0.1	0.2

* Log growth rates
Data: Economic Policy Institute

capital, compared to the earnings from work. There are many ways to measure the return on these two basic factors of production, all of them controversial. Yet the basic facts concerning how the division of income between work and capital has changed are fundamental— and incontrovertible.

For those who earn their living from work, real wages (money wages corrected for inflation) have been stagnant since 1973, as Table 8-1 shows. The trend was particularly painful between 1973 and 1979, the years that followed the OPEC oil embargoes. And though there was some recovery between 1979 and 1989, the rate of real wage gain fell back in the years following the cold war. As can be seen from Table 8-1, annual wages held up better than did hourly wages, only because there was rapid growth in the number of hours each worker put in, as the growth rate in the amount of capital supplied to each worker declined, and production became more labor intensive.

It should not be imagined that a lengthened work week and an increase in the number of working people in each family have totally

Table 8-2

The Squeeze on America's Families:
Real Family Income Growth, 1947–1995
(1995 Dollars)

Year	Lowest Fifth	Second Fifth	Middle Fifth	Fourth Fifth	Top 5%	Average
1947	$9,975	$16,096	$21,827	$30,971	$50,834	$22,331
1967	17,251	28,318	37,974	52,060	83,648	37,865
1973	19,634	32,398	45,203	62,164	96,913	43,983
1979	20,183	33,287	47,141	64,889	103,484	45,959
1989	19,668	34,413	50,145	73,189	121,629	51,012
1995	19,070	32,985	48,985	72,260	123,656	51,353
Annual Growth Rate						
1947–67	2.8%	2.9%	2.8%	2.6%	2.5%	2.7%
1967–73	2.2	2.3	2.9	3.0	2.5	2.5
1973–79	0.5	0.5	0.7	0.7	1.1	0.7
1979–89	−0.3	0.3	0.6	1.2	1.6	1.0
1989–95	−0.5	−0.7	−0.4	−0.2	0.3	0.1

Data: Unpublished census data, Economic Policy Institute

sheltered family income from the impact of wage stagnation. As Table 8-2 shows, the growth in real family income virtually screeched to a halt between 1989, the year after the cold war ended, and 1995. There is, moreover, scant comfort in this family income data even for the "super elite" workers who form the top 5 percent of the workforce. Their income held up only relatively well. For as Table 8-3 shows, the actual improvement in the real family income of the top 5 percent was a scant .3 percent per year between 1989 and 1995, a growth rate that looks good only because the real incomes of the less well-positioned members of the workforce declined during this period. There is as well a strong suggestion in the data that most of the gains scored by the top 20 percent were concentrated in the relatively few workers at the very top of the income ladder, as Table 8-3 again shows. The numbers on real income show that the big gains were scored by the top 5 percent of the workforce, whose real incomes grew at a 7.1 percent annual rate between 1989 and 1994. The other members of the elite either suffered falling income (the 80–90th percentile of income earners) or achieved modest gains (the 95–99th percentile). The vast majority of those who earn their living from work are in trouble.

Table 8-3

Only the Truly Rich Have Flourished:
Income Growth among the Top Fifth
(1994 Dollars)

Fifth Quintile	Average Family Income			Percent Change	
	1979	1989	1994	1979–89	1989–94
Top 80-90%	$72,210	$81,055	$79,386	12.2%	–2.1%
Top 90-95%	91,816	105,674	107,504	15.1	1.7
Top 95-99%	138,301	171,465	n.a.	24.0	n.a.
Top 1%	279,122	523,449	n.a.	87.5	n.a.
Top 5%	166,465	241,862	259,093	45.3	7.1

Data: Economic Policy Institute

Table 8-4

An Era of High Profits:
Profit Rates* at Business Cycle Peaks, 1959–1995

Profit Rate	1959	1973	1979	1989	1995
Before-Tax	10.4%	7.6%	7.7%	7.5%	10.8%
After-Tax	5.6	4.7	5.1	5.1	7.0
Capital/Output Ratio	1.73	1.78	2.01	1.83	1.39

* Profit rate is the ratio of all capital income (profits, rent, and interest) to the capital stock.

Data: Economic Policy Institute

The opposite is true for those who earn their living from capital. Table 8-4 represents a calculation of the rate of profit on the employment of capital, including rent and interest as well as "pure" profit. Because profits tend to swing more sharply than wages over the business cycle, the data are presented for those comparable years that represent peaks in the economy. And as the table shows, the rate of profit in 1995 was high, having increased by some 44 percent between 1989 and 1995, the period when both wages and family incomes were essentially stagnant. After-tax profits did not grow quite as quickly, but even here the increase was some 37 percent. It is also worth noting, as we have shown earlier (Figure 4-1 on page 78), that despite the increase in the profitability of capital, the capital/output ratio, which shows how much capital is employed for an equal amount of output, declined over the critical six-year period from 1989 to 1995. This is decisive evidence that the existence of relatively cheap labor around the globe reduced the incentive of companies to equip American workers with new capital goods, economic behavior

Table 8-5

The Longer-Term Fortunes of the Top One Percent:
Share of Total Household Wealth Held by Richest
One Percent of Individuals, 1922–1981

Year	% of Wealth Excluding Retirement	% of Wealth Including Retirement
1922	38.3	37.9
1929	37.2	36.7
1933	28.9	28.2
1939	38.1	33.4
1945	28.9	22.4
1949	25.7	20.5
1953	28.1	21.6
1958	27.0	20.7
1962	30.1	22.5
1965	31.9	23.4
1969	29.0	21.0
1972	28.6	20.5
1976	18.9	13.8
1981	23.6	n.a.

Data: Edward N. Wolff, "Change Inequality of Wealth," paper presented at the January 1992 meeting of the American Economic Assoc.

that is fully consistent with Adam Smith's observation that it is only the scarce factors of production that are treated relatively well and that earn a high rate of return.

The increase in the inequality of income is minor compared to what is happening to the distribution of wealth. To the frustration of economists, data on changes in wealth distribution are scarce and usually become available for analysis long after the periods to which they apply. Nevertheless, the data that is available does make possible penetrating insights into what has been happening in the 1990s.

As a background to recent trends in the distribution of wealth, it is important to realize that the insights of Simon Kuznets and other students of the long-term impact of economic growth on income distribution apply to an even greater degree to trends in the distribution of wealth. To begin with, there has been a long-term trend in the United States toward more equal wealth distribution—a trend that worked with particular intensity in the years between the Great Depression and the mid-1970s. Table 8-5 tracks the share of total household wealth held by the richest 1 percent of households between

Table 8-6
Who Owns What: Percent of Total Assets
Held by Wealth Class, 1992

Asset Type	Top 1%	Next 9%	Bottom 90%
A. Assets Held Primarily by the Wealthy			
Stocks	49.6%	36.7%	13.6%
Bonds	62.4	28.9	8.7
Trusts	52.9	35.1	12.0
Business Equity	61.6	29.5	8.9
Non-Home Real Estate	45.9	37.1	17.0
Total for Group	54.4	33.3	12.3
B. Assets and Liabilities Held Primarily by the Nonwealthy			
Principal Residence	9.0%	27.1%	63.9%
Deposits*	22.4	37.3	40.3
Life Insurance	10.0	35.1	54.9
Pension Accounts**	16.4	45.9	37.7
Total for Group	12.9	32.2	54.8
Total Debt	13.8	23.8	62.5

* Includes demand deposits, savings, time deposits, money-market funds, and certificates of deposit
**IRAs, Keogh plans, 401(k) plans, the accumulated value of defined contribution plans, and other retirement accounts
Data: Economic Policy Institute

1922 and 1981. It shows that the share of wealth held by the top 1 percent of households declined fairly sharply between the end of the great stock market boom of the late 1920s to the mid-1970s. When retirement wealth is included, that share declines sharply from over 36 percent in 1929 to under 14 percent in 1976. Excluding retirement wealth, the share of total household wealth held by the richest 1 percent declines from over 37 percent in 1929 to under 24 percent in 1981. The decline in the concentration of wealth that Americans had become accustomed to both during the New Deal years and the golden age of economic growth after World War II ended steadily decreased in this economy and had given hope that the American economy was producing not only more prosperity but also more equality.

This economy no longer exists. Data comparable to that presented in Table 8-5 is not available for more recent years and is downright nonexistent for the years since 1992, missing the great stock market boom, as well as the rise in the prices of long-term bonds, both of which would only exaggerate the concentration of wealth described in the charts. For as Table 8-6 shows, it has been the

Table 8-7
The Rich Get Richer: Change in Wealth
by Wealth Class, 1983-1992
(1992 Dollars)

Wealth Class	Wealth* (000)			Percent Change**		
	1983	1989	1992	1983–89	1989–92	1983–92
Top Fifth	$744.1	$950.8	$893.6	27.8%	−6.0%	20.1%
Top 1%	6,176.0	8,777.0	7,925.0	42.0	−9.7	28.3
Next 4%	1,022.0	1,228.0	1,218.0	20.2	−0.8	19.2
Next 5%	444.3	516.1	503.9	16.2	−2.4	13.4
Next 10%	239.9	275.2	255.8	14.7	−7.0	6.6
Bottom Four-Fifths	$42.7	$45.7	$43.2	7.1%	−5.5%	1.2%
Fourth	115.0	129.0	122.2	12.2	−5.3	6.3
Middle	47.8	51.1	46.7	7.1	−8.6	−2.2
Bottom 40%	4.0	1.4	2.0	−65.2	44.8	−49.7
Average	$183.0	$224.8	$213.3	22.9%	−5.1%	16.6%
Median	47.0	50.8	43.2	8.1	−15.0	−8.1

* Wealth defined as net worth, equal to a household's assets less its debt.
**Change calculated from underlying unrounded data.

Data: Economic Policy Institute

class of large stock- and bondholders that has been the great beneficiary of the huge appreciation in the value of the financial assets that
represent claims on the income of capital. Taken by themselves, the
top 1 percent of the population held over 49 percent of stocks, over
62 percent of bonds, and 61 percent of business equity in 1992. By
contrast, the share held by the entire bottom 90 percent of the
population was under 14 percent of all stocks and under 9 percent of
all bonds. The impact on wealth distribution was already visible by
the end of 1992, as Table 8-7 shows. Between 1983 and 1992, the net
worth of the top 1 percent of the population increased by 28.3
percent and that of the top 20 percent by 20.1 percent. Over the
same period, in the meantime, the net worth of half of the population
actually declined. In the 1990s, we witnessed a concentration of
wealth that is probably without historical precedent in the United
States, one to which the wealth concentration that occurred in the
decade that ended with the great 1929 crash was only a pallid
prelude. And our data do not even cover the effects of the great stock
market boom of 1995 and 1996.

Nor should there be any mistake about the major reason for larger portions of the economic pie going to people in the top brackets of income and wealth. The discrepancy has, as we have seen, little to do with the purported skills mismatch of the information age. Instead, the real explanation lies in certain people having access to the preferred position relative to the scarce factor of production in the new global economy: mobile capital. The star of the wealth inequality show is obviously the stock market itself. Between the end of the 1990–1991 recession and 1996, the stock market put on a pyrotechnical display, while the real wages of workers languished.

A rise in the share of national wealth owned by the average American has been held back not only by the slow growth of wages as compared to stock prices but also by the slow growth in the value of the assets held by the average American household as compared to the value of the kinds of assets that are held by the rich, as Table 8-7 shows. This is particularly true when the behavior of home prices is compared to the behavior of stock prices.

Since the end of the cold war there has been a sharp relative decline in the value of the asset that the average working American prizes most highly, that which forms the basis of any claim that he or she may have on wealth: the family home. When average income is rising slowly and the real cost of debt stays quite high, it stands to reason that the demand for housing will turn weak. In contrast, financial wealth, particularly the ownership of an equity in business through stocks, is far more important. Since 1988, stock prices have been rising far faster than housing prices. The Standard and Poor's 500 Composite Stock Price Index covers the five hundred U.S. companies with the largest capitalization and therefore measures the stock prices of the American companies with the greatest global reach. From the beginning of 1988 to the end of the third quarter of 1995, the S&P 500 rose at an annual rate of 12.75 percent. The rate of growth of house prices was 2.6 percent per year over the same period.

The policies and conditions that have driven down the value of work have had an impact on workers' benefits as well as their wages. Pension coverage, as Harvard economists David Bloom and Richard Freeman have demonstrated, has also fallen sharply during the post-cold war period. Among all employees, the percentage of workers enrolled in company-sponsored pension plans dropped from 75 percent in 1988 to 42 percent in 1994. The decline in the proportion of employees covered by privately provided health insurance has been equally dramatic, dipping from 57 percent in 1988 to 45 percent in 1994.

The shrinkage in wage growth, pension coverage, and health insurance coverage is far from the most sinister manifestation of the deterioration of the workplace. The post-cold war years have also seen a startling decline in what are perhaps even more basic measures of employee welfare, health and safety. U.S. Bureau of Labor Statistics data on the incidence of injury and illness in the workplace are perhaps even more disturbing than the wage data itself. The data show that total injury rates and days lost to illness, which had generally shown a declining trend since the data first began to be collected, started to stabilize in the early 1980s, and then, in a critical and surprising reversal of the trend, started to rise as the cold war ended. A study by Robert Smith shows that the percentage of manufacturing workers experiencing lost workdays because of injuries was 6.1 percent in 1993–1994, up from 5.3 percent in 1972. This is true even though the proportion of the population engaged in the heavy, dangerous work of manufacturing had declined and despite the creation of the Occupational Safety and Health Administration (OSHA) in 1970, which has been responsible for over 1.5 million safety and health inspections. Based on the statistics, it appears that the basic economic forces now at work in the world economy have provided incentives to business to circumvent health and safety laws, ignoring the rules established through legislation to reduce the dangers that lurk in the workplace.

The pressure that the new global economy is exerting on those who earn their living from work does not end in the workplace itself. As workers have become more abundant and capital scarcer, workers have been forced to assume a larger and larger proportion of the cost of government. In an era that cherishes the free and unhampered flow of money, the federal tax code has been changed so that income derived from work is penalized as compared with income earned by accumulated capital.

There have also been major tax cuts on the return to the investment of capital including accelerated depreciation of capital equipment and a cap on capital gains taxes, which stood at 28.6 percent in 1996; in comparison the combined tax rate on income from work was some 49 percent. At the same time, taxes on work have relentlessly increased. The Social Security tax is a pure payroll tax, whose burden is shared equally between those who work and those who provide jobs, the latter paying the tax once a hiring decision is made. During a period when the capital gains tax has been reduced, the Social Security tax has increased: since the "reform" enacted on the basis of the recommendation of a bipartisan commission headed by now Federal Reserve Board Chairman Alan Greenspan in 1981, the combined Social Security tax rate has risen from 12.26 percent to over 15 percent. Since then, the share of the total federal tax burden paid for with corporate and individual income taxes has decreased from .59 percent to .57 percent. In 1995 more was paid into the Social Security system on behalf of the average family than that family paid in federal income tax.

The effect of the reform has been to greatly increase the burden for covering federal expenditures carried by those who earn their living from work. The notion that there is a firewall between the Social Security trust fund, which finances Social Security benefits, and the financing of the rest of the government is a gigantic myth. Between 1988 and 1994 some $326 billion of receipts from Social Security taxes have been used to meet the general expense of running the government, including covering the trillion dollars in interest payments due to the holders of government bonds, who tend to be wealthy, and to foreign holders of American government securities. The notion that the Social Security system is facing a severe crisis is a vast and cynical overstatement. The truth of the matter is that the federal government, including the Social Security trust fund, is running out of money partly because monies that have been paid into the Social Security system by those on whose behalf it was created—those who earn their living from work—have been used to pay for ordinary government expenditures and to finance tax breaks for capital gains.

Average workers' basic sense of security has been undermined by repeated warnings that the system that they rely on for supporting them in old age and for protection in the case of disability is going broke. Indeed, the legislation for Social Security makes it abundantly clear that the system is designed to replace the income earned from work. The cost of these programs places a heavy burden on those who work. For those businesses that are considering increasing output, the knowledge that they will have to pay Social Security taxes for each new worker they hire may be enough to tilt their decision about the amount of wages they can afford to pay. The direct cost of Social Security and Medicare to employees stood at $464 billion in

1994. Payroll deductions for Social Security and Medicare were by far the largest federal tax paid by the bottom four-fifths of the income distribution in 1995. Payments to support these two systems absorbed some 9.5 percent of their incomes, taking $4,470 out of the income of the median American family that earned $47,062 in that year. It is hardly as if the average Social Security check mailed out, $674 a month in 1994, represented a huge gift by society to workers. Rather it was an unprincely stipend paid out to those who had put in a life of hard work. And though the Medicare program is generally regarded as effective by both physicians and patients, it hardly represents a lavish level of medical benefits. These programs may indeed be "entitlements," but they are modest entitlements, bought and paid for by heavy taxation imposed during a life of work.

The statistics leave no doubt that the triumph of capital has lead to more and more unequal distribution of income and wealth. If this increase in inequality had occurred in an era of satisfactory economic growth, it could be argued that the increased opulence of the classes lucky enough or smart enough to own the bulk of the nation's financial assets is an essentially harmless phenomenon. But the other chief characteristic of the post-cold war economy—slow economic growth in the industrial world accompanied by stagnant or declining incomes for the majority of workers—has created a pileup of income and wealth in the hands of the few at the expense of the many, leaving both average workers and the government without the means of financing necessary expenses out of ordinary income. Rising inequality is also a symptom of another trend that could also be a trigger for the new crisis of capitalism: an unsustainable increase in debt for all but the very rich.

DEBT VERSUS INCOME

There is no greater paradox in the economies of the industrial world than the role of debt. The image of the flinty-eyed banker denying a loan to anyone who lacks impeccable financial credentials is a strong one in the financial culture of the modern industrial world. Yet at the same time the financial history of this century, particularly in the United States, has been a story of a series of vicious financial cycles in which the banks have overextended credit to shaky sectors of the world economy, a history that includes excessive lending to Greek shipping magnates such as Styros Nicharos and Aristotle Onassis in the 1950s, the extension of credit to companies particularly in the defense business, such as the old Lockheed Corporation and Chrysler in the early 1970s, to the overextension of credit to Third World countries to buy oil after the OPEC embargoes of the mid- and late 1970s, to the financing of fanciful leveraged buyouts in the days of Michael Milken and Ivan Boesky in the early 1980s, to the fiasco of excess lending by savings and loan institutions in the late 1980s and early 1990s that resulted in the gigantic savings and loan bailout. Each of these episodes brought on periods of financial instability. But in each case, the Federal Reserve and other public institutions such as the Federal Deposit Insurance Corporation (FDIC) moved to provide money to rescue the banks from their own errors.

Because the damages were relatively limited in scope, the costs of rescuing the financial system from its own mistakes were relatively limited in the 1970s and early 1980s. But when the savings and loan crisis occurred, the damage was so severe that, first, the American public was burdened with a tax liability of $240 billion, the potential cost of the savings and loan bailout; second, the crisis changed forever the attitude of bank regulators about what profit margins are acceptable in the dealings between the banks and ordinary consumers and small businessmen. Since the end of the savings and loan crisis, banks have been permitted to sharply increase the margin between what they pay for money and the interest rate at which they lend it out.

As a result the banking system is putting increasing pressure on the standard of living of ordinary consumers. On the one hand, the exceptionally tight money policy that has been imposed on the industrial world by its central banks has resulted in stagnant incomes. And on the other, ordinary consumers, already under pressure because of slow income growth, have been faced with high real interest rates. As a consequence the amount they pay for mortgages, credit card payments, car loans, and other loans cuts into their disposable income. The effect, of course, is to dampen the growth of disposable income. In the 1990s the slow growth in disposable income places a lid on the ability of the consumer sector to absorb the goods that the economy is capable of producing. That is the real danger in the painfully slow growth of the years since the end of the cold war. And it is fertile soil for a severe economic downturn in the post-cold war world economy.

In effect the highly visible financial problems associated with excessive lending to shipping magnates, defense contractors, and leveraged buyout artists have been replaced by a slow burn crisis with overextended consumers. And there is a vast difference between businessmen in financial trouble and consumers in financial trouble. There is an old saying that if you owe a bank $10 million, you have the bank where you want it; if you own the bank $10,000, the bank has you where it wants you. The financial system moved to relieve the problem of debtors (shipping magnates and the like) in the earlier debt crises of the post–World War II years because the troubled debtors had access to huge sums of money and tons of political influence. The system will move much more slowly to relieve the crisis of the 1990s, because the people in trouble are, after all, mere consumers with little bargaining power.

More than that, they are also the reason that debt collection has become a huge growth industry. According to a Nielson study, average consumer debt per household will grow from $50,529 in 1995 to $65,796 by the year 2000. By 1994 there were already 2.4 debt collectors for each 1,000 families in the United States. And according to the Small Business Administration (SBA), employment in the debt collection business will soar by 68 percent by 2004, to nearly 3 million from 1.7 million in 1994. If the Small Business Administration forecasts are correct and the number of debt collectors almost doubles, there will be about 3.7 debt collectors for each 1,000 families—a sorry sign of the times.

Though not much thought has been given to the subject, the high cost of debt has hurt workers just as surely as they have been hurt in the labor market. As a class, those who earn their living from work tend to be debtors, and therefore they suffer when interest rates rise. The owners of capital are, in contrast, creditors, so by definition they are helped when interest rates rise. The effect of rising interest rates is therefore to transfer wealth from those who earn their living from work to those who earn their living from capital.

And just as real, inflation-adjusted wages are the right measure of what is happening in the workplace, real interest rates (market interest rates minus the inflation rate) are the correct measure of the most significant trends in the economy. Even though market interest rates, not adjusted for inflation, have fallen between the 1970s and the mid-1990s, the real interest rate on long-term government bonds, often and rightly considered the purest measure of the interest rate, has averaged 3.8 percent since 1988, 2.7 percent between 1970 and

Table 8-8
How Debt Weighs on Families:
Household Debt Burden, 1949–1995

Year	Debt as Percent of:	
	Personal Income	Assets*
1949	29.7%	6.3%
1967	60.4	12.2
1973	58.6	13.1
1979	64.0	13.5
1989	77.9	15.5
1994	83.9	16.9

* Financial assets (including pension funds and insurance), real estate, and consumer durables.
Data: Economic Policy Institute

1987, 2.53 percent in the 1960s, and 2.64 percent in the second half of the 1950s. Once we make the adjustment for inflation, the widely advertised fall in interest rates in the 1990s is revealed to be a sham. The real rate as measured by the rate on long-term government bonds has actually risen since the end of the cold war. Though the numbers seem small, the rise in real interest rates is hardly insignificant: since the end of the cold war it had, by 1995, cut the amount of spending consumers could have financed out of their real incomes by some $50 billion.

The rise in real interest rates has combined with stagnant real wages to put severe financial pressure on most Americans. And in a desperate attempt to maintain their standard of living most American families have been forced to take on more and more debt. Table 8-8 shows the ratio of personal debt to disposable personal income. There are, of course, cycles in this ratio, partly because consumer spending binges are inevitably followed by retrenchment, either voluntarily or under the lash of the collection departments of banks and other financial institutions that lend to the consumer sector. Nevertheless, as the chart shows, the trend is headed toward a higher and higher ratio of consumer debt to disposable personal income.

Part of the reason for increased personal debt is consumers' desire to maintain comfortable levels of consumption and the need to borrow for such long-term investments as education. But part is also explained by the deliberate effort by the Federal Reserve to ensure that inflation-adjusted interest rates, or real interest rates, remain high, for reasons we have already discussed.

As might be expected, the rise in real interest rates has benefited the creditor class at the expense of the debtor class. To most people, a spread is something that you put on your bread or something that appears in the waistline as you approach middle age. But in banking "the spread" is a great moneymaking machine—the gross profit banks earn on the simplest kind of no-brainer transactions. It is the revenue that banks earn simply because they pay less for money than the interest rate they charge their customers.

There are many ways to measure this spread. But one good way is to take the difference between what banks pay each other for loans—the famous federal funds rate that is tightly controlled by the Federal Reserve—and what they charge ordinary mortals for accessing the same money. That spread has been levitating in the stratosphere since the end of the cold war. The average spread between the prime interest rate—the benchmark for many consumer loans—and the federal funds rate has been about 2.6 percentage points since 1988, as compared with a spread of 1.9 percent earlier in the 1980s, 1.17 percent in the 1970s, and 1.1 percent in the 1960s. Indeed, the post-cold war "spread" exacted by the banks has been the plumpest since the federal funds market was invented in the early 1950s.

The size of the spread is a measure of the most fundamental transfer of income to the financial sector from other parts of the economy. From the vantage point of those who earn their living from work, the spread represents that part of their income that must be transferred from their pocket to banks, mortgage companies, and credit card companies in order to finance debt. As the spread has increased, so have the real costs of carrying a mortgage, buying a car, or paying off a student loan.

And when it comes to pure revolving credit, the kind of financing that lies behind the average consumer's Visa or MasterCard, the spread has become downright obese. The fall in market interest rates that has occurred in the 1990s has hardly been matched by a decline in the interest rates on revolving credit, as anyone who has just paid his or her credit card bills well knows. Since 1990 the rate on credit cards, including variable rate cards, has averaged 16.9 percentage points, as compared to the 3.36 rate the banks pay each other for money. The net effect has been a shift of income from consumers to the financial sector, from those whose principal source of income is work to those whose principal source of income is capital.

The significance of this massive shift of income between debtors and creditors is usually overlooked in public discussion of the financial pressure on consumers. And the willingness of the Federal Reserve to tolerate, indeed, even to promote, large spreads represents complicity in a quiet but deadly attack on the ability of the American economy to grow. Our stagnant real economy is fertile ground for financial crises; it virtually guarantees that consumer debt will grow faster than the capacity to pay it off.

THE EXPLOSION IN U.S. FOREIGN DEBT

No aspect of America's economic performance in the 1990s has drawn more praise, or has been the cause for more celebration, than the rapid growth of exports. Commentators have often commended the business community on having sufficiently reengineered and slimmed down so as to make American goods more and more competitive in world markets. It is also true that the fall in U.S. wages relative to those of other industrialized countries has played a role in enhancing our competitiveness, but that unquestioned fact has not been ballyhooed. Less celebrated has been a companion event: the even more spectacular growth of imports. Since the end of the cold war, U.S. imports of foreign goods have grown at a rate of 7.7 percent per year, some one and a half times the rate of growth of exports. So that although the United States has unquestionably increased its efficiency since the end of the cold war, foreign countries have apparently done even better.

Debt and trade deficits are linked as the shoulder is to the arm. There is one way, and only one way, in which a country can import more than it exports. That is if the other countries involved in trade with this country are willing to provide it with the capital that it needs to finance the difference between what the country spends on imports and what it earns from its own exports. Insofar as the margin is covered by flows of capital voluntarily absorbed in the private sector there may be no great problem. Indeed, foreigners who are investing in projects in developing countries often allow those countries to import more capital goods so as to increase their productivity; this has been a characteristic of the relationships between many industrial countries and developing countries throughout the history of capitalism.

But the United States has not been in that position in this decade. It is perfectly true that foreign countries such as Germany, Japan, and others have made large investments in the United States, to take advantage of low U.S. labor costs, to exploit the special tax breaks given to foreign investors by many state governments, particularly in the South, and to take advantage of the research work done in the excellent American university system. The Japanese have also invested in the United States to reduce the political heat over its huge trade surpluses with the United States.

But large as these private inflows of capital have been, they have fallen far short of what was needed to maintain America's position in international finance. Throughout most of this century the United States has been a net creditor in foreign dealings, but its international balances began deteriorating in the 1960s, and since the early 1980s the United States has become a net foreign debtor. In 1996, foreign governments and central banks held $722 billion in U.S. securities and bank deposits.

Nor is the total size of America's foreign debt the best measure of the potential trouble the trade imbalance could cause. Insofar as the external debt is held by private institutions, it represents the result of an economic decision that investing in the United States offers rates of return in excess of what can be earned elsewhere. But the gap between what America has earned on its foreign transactions and what it has spent on foreign goods and services is partly financed by a buildup in foreign holdings of U.S. government securities, and American taxpayers have to make the interest payments. In October of 1996, the holdings of U.S. bank deposits and treasury bills, certificates, and bonds by foreigners stood at $722.7 billion, up from $520.9 billion at the end of 1994. And in late 1996, as Table 8-9 shows, the holdings of Asian countries stood at $371.2 billion, up from $236.8 billion at the end of 1994, and the holdings of Europeans were at 246.5 billion. At mid-1996, Japan alone held $249 billion in U.S. Treasury bills, Britain $131 billion, and Germany $60 billion. More surprising are the holdings of such countries as China ($41 billion) and the Netherlands Antilles ($37 billion).

The transformation of the United States from a major international creditor to an international debtor has major implications for future United States economic growth. It is no accident that back in the 1950s and 1960s, when the United States was a creditor nation, interest rates were lower here than they were abroad, and the dollar was a strong currency. But since the United States has become a debtor nation, U.S. interest rates are higher than those in the other

Table 8-9
The Burden of Foreign Debt:
U.S. Liabilities to Foreign Official Institutions

Foreign Debt	Million of Dollars, End of Period		
	1994	1995	1996*
Total	$520,934	$630,867	$722,708
By Type			
Liabilities of Banks in the U.S.	73,386	107,343	109,942
U.S. Treasury Bills and Certificates	139,571	168,534	186,180
Marketable U.S. Treasury Bonds	254,059	293,691	363,063
Nonmarketable	6,109	6,491	5,890
By Area			
Europe	215,374	222,406	246,543
Canada	17,235	19,473	21,764
Latin America and the Caribbean	41,492	66,720	70,477
Asia	236,824	310,966	371,218
Africa	4,180	6,296	6,587
Other Countries	5,827	5,004	6,117

*End of Oct. figures
Data: Federal Reserve Bulletin, Feb. 1997, A52.

industrial countries, and the dollar, despite its revival in 1996, has become a weak currency. The effect is, of course, to squeeze the average American's standard of living both because Americans are forced to pay high real interest rates for what they borrow and because a weak dollar means that America must produce and export more goods to earn foreign currencies than it had to when the dollar was a stronger currency. Debtor status has the same effect on a country as on the citizens of that country: what is, in effect, the disposable income of the United States is under downward pressure just as surely as is the disposable income of its highly indebted citizens.

The growth of both personal debt and national foreign debt therefore places a heavy weight on the shoulders of the American economy. It forces real interest rates into the stratosphere and makes rapid growth extremely difficult. And because the burden of high interest rates relative to income has continued to escalate, the possibility of a full-scale financial crisis, like the great crash of 1929, has been elevated to the status of clear and present danger.

FINANCE VERSUS INDUSTRY

To most Americans, the outstanding characteristic of the past decade has been the rise of high-tech industry and the service economy. These are indeed important trends. But they must take a backseat to another, less well recognized aspect of the new global economy: the rise of the financial sector and its increasing dominance over those parts of the economy that produce real goods and services.

Although historical analogies must be drawn with caution, it is true, and the best economic historians have noticed, that in each major phase of the development of capitalism the leading country of the capitalist world goes through a period of financialization, wherein the most important economic dynamic is the creation and trading of abstract financial instruments rather than the production of genuine goods and services. The work of these historians raises a powerful caution about the implications of the kinds of trends we are now seeing vis-à-vis the position of the United States in the world economy: the growth of sophisticated high finance is not necessarily a sign of nirvana, but rather an ill omen that the country has entered the late stages of greatness and is heading into trouble.

The Netherlands and Britain were, as we have seen, decisively the leading economic powers in the emergence of modern capitalism. And each of these countries, as it passed its peak, entered a period during which finance found itself riding high, feeding on trading and speculation as manufacturing lost its importance. As Kevin Phillips has said, "In Holland, as the mid-eighteenth century spread decay across much of the country, observers compared the plight of the old manufacturing towns with the splendid residences of the stockbrokers." Instead of putting money into new technology in their own nation as they had done a century earlier, the Dutch financiers had become mere investors, living off the British financial markets in many cases. The great economic historian Ferdinand Braudel cites the following observation of a Dutchman circa 1766 to underscore the great power of the major European financial houses during that period:

> If ten or twelve businessmen of Amsterdam of the first rank meet for a banking (i.e. credit) operation, they can in a moment send circulating throughout Europe over two hundred millions of florins of paper money which is preferred to cash. There is no sovereign who can do as much. . . . This credit is a power which the ten or twelve businessmen will be able to exert over all the states of Europe, in complete independence of any authority.

The next great capitalist power, Britain, found itself in a similar stage at the beginning of the twentieth century. Like Holland, its lead as a strong technological innovator had deeply eroded, while its financial sector had never been stronger. British financiers were confident that finance would replace manufacturing and technology as Britain's textile, steel, and shipbuilding businesses decreased in importance. Yet as Kevin Phillips again points out, "A prominent critic, Colonial Secretary Joseph Chamberlain, put his doubts before a meeting of bankers in 1904:

> Granted you are the clearing house of the world, are you entirely beyond anxiety as to the permanence of your great position. . . . [B]anking is not the creator of our prosperity, but is the creation of it. It is not the cause of our wealth, but is the consequence of our wealth; and if the industrial energy and development which has been going on for so many years in the country were to be hindered and relaxed, then finance, and all that finance means, will follow trade to the countries which are more successful than ourselves.

His warning proved prophetic. By 1946 what had been the world's leading capitalist dynamo in 1914 was a chronic international debtor, its once proud finances in shambles: by the 1990s this decline in circumstances would push Britain's GDP below that of Italy." The lesson is obvious: each of the great economic powers of the past four hundred years has gone through an era in which earlier reliance on seafaring, manufacturing, and commerce yielded to a cocksure faith in finance and a financial services economy. Are we to be next?

There are, of course, enormous differences between the position of these earlier leaders of capitalism in their periods of economic hegemony and what is now occurring in the United States. But there are also substantial similarities.

It is useful in this respect to give some thought to what is happening to the global position of America's manufacturing economy. Please refer to the five figures covering the balance between U.S. exports and U.S. imports (Figures 8-1 – 8-5). Taken together they demonstrate clearly that even though the growth of U.S. exports is justly celebrated, the growth of imports has been even greater. Figure 8-1 shows the size of the merchandise trade deficit. Notice how it has soared as production has become more global, particularly since the end of the cold war. Figure 8-2 shows the size of the trade deficit by industry group. Notice that although the size of

Figure 8-1

The Growing Trade Deficit*

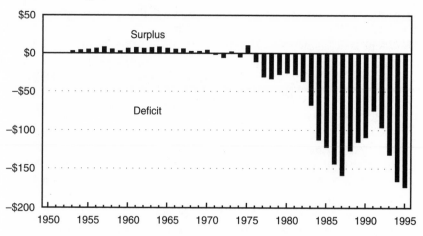

*Billions of dollars each year: merchandise trade, balance of payments basis
Data: IMF and MBG Information Services

Figure 8-2

The Shrinkage of Exports*

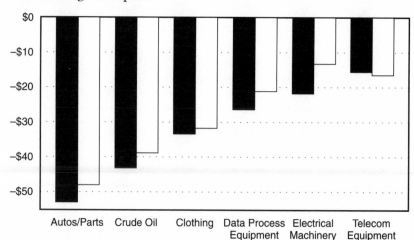

■ 1995 □ 1994

*Billions of dollars: net export losses each year
Data: U.S. Department of Commerce and MBG Information Services

Figure 8-3

A Sudden Deficit in Chips*

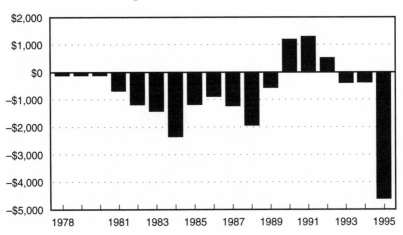

*Millions of dollars each year: net exports of semiconductors

Data: U.S. Dept. of Commerce and MBG Information Services

the deficit is larger for old-line industries such as autos, crude oil, and clothing, sizable deficits are also occurring in high-tech manufacturing, such as data processing equipment, electrical machinery, and telecommunications equipment. Figure 8-3 demonstrates the sudden appearance of a substantial trade deficit in semiconductors, even though the Japanese market is more open than it has been since the historic semiconductor trade agreement of the early 1990s.

The remaining charts bring home the growth in import penetration of the U.S. economy in a vivid way. As Figure 8-4 shows, imported goods have soared in importance relative to domestically produced goods, and export growth remains historically weak, despite the devaluation of the dollar. Finally, as is shown in Figure 8-5, the United States has developed startling trade deficits with the countries of the emerging world that have become major exporters: Argentina, Brazil, China, Hong Kong, India, Indonesia, South Korea, Mexico, Poland, South Africa, Taiwan, and Turkey. These data should leave no doubt that the exuberance that is often expressed about the increasing competitiveness of the U.S. economy, or of its increased efficiency, is at least partly misplaced. Sure, the United States is becoming more productive, but on the evidence the improvement in

Figure 8-4

Soaring Manufacturing Imports*

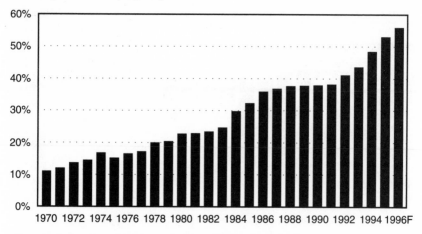

*Imported manufactured goods as % of U.S. manufacturing GDP
Data: U.S. Dept. of Commerce and MBG Information Services

Figure 8-5

Growing Deficits with Emerging World Countries*

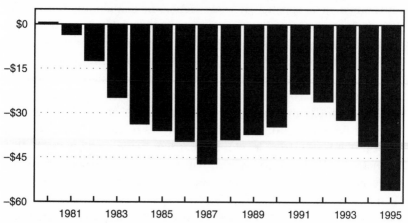

*Billions of dollars: annual U.S. merchandise trade deficits to BEMs
Data: U.S. Department of Commerce and MBG Information Services

competitiveness and the increase in exports is minor as compared to the startling gains made by many emerging world countries. There is simply no cause to celebrate the strength of the basic industries of the United States; even in the high-tech industries the competitive position of the U.S. is ending.

It is far more difficult to demonstrate America's growing financial hegemony than it is to document the chinks that have appeared in America's industrial armor. The problem is that some of America's chief financial houses are still privately held, and others are subsumed within larger international financial conglomerates, so it is difficult to discern the results of those sectors of the business that are involved in high international finance. But it is clear that the publicly held Wall Street giants are doing very well. At $814 million, the net income of Morgan Stanley averaged 80 percent higher in 1995 and 1996 than in the preceding two years. The firm with which it announced its intention to merge at the beginning of 1997, Dean Witter, Discover & Co., enjoyed an average net income of $671 million in 1995 and 1996, up 34 percent from 1993 and 1994.

Part of the explanation of the strength of financial institutions lies in the ability of Wall Street to exact huge fees from the rest of the business community. A vivid description of the results of this process has been provided for the year 1987 by Lawrence H. Summers (formerly a Harvard professor, now an undersecretary of the Treasury in the Clinton administration). Granted this was the year just before the end of the cold war, but by this time the financial sector was already demonstrating its dominance over the rest of the economy. Summers determined that the corporations listed on the New York Stock Exchange enjoyed a combined annual income of some $314 billion in that year. As an offset, he then calculated the basic cost to businesses of supporting the investment firms belonging to the exchange as being equal to the sum of these securities firms' annual receipts—a hefty $53 billion. Summers then added another $20 billion to represent what New York Stock Exchange firms spent on analysts, lawyers, and accountants, and investor relations programs to keep their stocks listed and traded. His conclusion: in 1987 the financial market, by directly or indirectly consuming about $73 billion, effectively ate up about a quarter of the profits of America's major corporations. The implication is powerful even if the mathematics are debatable. The more Wall Street earns, the less is left over for the rest of American business and consumers.

There is no doubt that the American financial community now benefits from the same business hegemony that once was inherent in America's industrial economy. Virtually every study that has been done shows that American financial companies are preeminent, clearly beating out the investment firms of Europe and decisively besting Japan's financial institutions in virtually every financial activity in the world—from the financing of privatizations, to the size of their trading profits, to the number of initial public offerings syndicated, to the volume of stock and bond trading, to the volume of commodity trading, to the creation and merchandising of all kinds of financial derivatives, to the securitization of every conceivable type of income stream from mortgages to auto loans.

There are two threats inherent in an economy where finance flourishes at the expense of industry. The larger the share of corporate income that ends up in the hands of the financial community, the smaller the share that is devoted to investment in real plant and equipment. As we have already seen (Chapter 4), there has been a fall in the capital/output ratio in the United States in recent years. Most of that decrease, as we have argued, is probably the result of America's cheap labor, but the need for companies to devote a substantial part of their income to keeping financial institutions fat and happy also limits the funds available for investment in new plants and equipment.

THE SUPPLY-SIDE FANTASY

In terms of economic policy, the great danger is that America has brushed aside reason to make room for faith. The country perceives that in winning the cold war it achieved a victory not over one "evil empire" but over two; it showed up the grotesque role of government in the Communist world, but it also stamped out any role for its own government in directing the American economy. In the Western industrialized countries, as we have seen, virtually every government activity other than defense and the provision of entitlements to middle-class voters is viewed with great suspicion; at the same time every activity of the private sector is celebrated, unless it is clearly illegal.

Supply-side economics, which champions the market to an extreme, has become the High Church of free enterprise and has drawn unreasoned faith.

In the early days of the Reagan administration, after the supply-siders captured tax policy, their view was that low taxes would so energize the economy—*incentivise* to use the ugly nonword that the supply-siders themselves use—that huge tax cuts would actually lead to a balanced budget, even without serious cuts in spending. This kind of thinking, of course, makes the populist yeoman entrepreneur, the true folk hero of the free enterprise system, a veritable Gary Cooper walking down Main Street at *High Noon*. The utopianism is touching and deserves some respect, especially when it is espoused by a supply-sider who really believes that it would help all Americans including minorities and the poor—someone like Jack Kemp. This is the bright side of extreme free enterprise.

But the basic tenet of supply-side economics that tax cuts will so stimulate income growth that government revenues will rise by enough, at the lower tax rates, to pay for the tax cut, is simply wrong, as the growth during the Reagan and Bush administrations amply demonstrates. The great supply-side defense against the accusation that their tax cuts ballooned the deficit is that control of the House of Representatives by the Democrats throughout Reagan's eight years in office prevented President Reagan from cutting government spending. Yet any serious analysis of the spending proposal in the budgets introduced during the Reagan years shows that the six budgets over which Reagan had most control produced deficits totaling over $1.1 trillion. Nor were these deficits primarily the responsibility of the Democrats. Even Reagan's staunch ideological ally and defender George Will has admitted, "The budgets Reagan sent to Congress proposed thirteen-fourteenths of that total [$1.1 trillion]. Congress added a piddling $90 billion a year."

Indeed, tax cuts do not stimulate income growth sufficiently to pay for themselves, no matter what is happening to government spending. The reason is simple: for while it is perfectly true that tax cuts increase the income available to the private sector and therefore stimulate spending and the growth of income, part of the money put into the hands of the consumers will go into private savings, and part—a large part in the new global economy—will go into paying for imports. That is why it wasn't only the deficit in the federal budget that escalated in the Reagan years; the trade deficit also quadrupled. Reagan's supply-side approach produced far greater benefits for Japan than it ever did for the United States. And acting on a similar fantasy now would provide far more economic stimulus in China than in the United States.

It's sad to think that America's victory in the cold war has created fertile ground for this kind of yahoo free market extremism. What is most tragic, moreover, is that any policy based on supply-side nostrums is particularly toxic in a global economy dominated by highly mobile capital that fears rising deficits.

There is also another dark side to extreme free enterprise. A careful reading of supply-side economics reveals that supply-siders have never met a tax they liked, or a tax cut they didn't like. That fault can be excused. No one in his or her right mind likes the thought of paying more taxes. But it is also true that the supply-siders have never met a tax they have felt is necessary. Equally important, they have never met a tax targeting the rich that they believe is anything but damaging. This view in the hands of cynical neoconservatives on the make is especially efficacious in soothing the conscience of the rich, and it makes supply-side economics a powerful tool for raising money for the Republican party and right-wing foundations. Give most people of property a socially acceptable excuse for accepting lower taxes, and they believe that they can use the extra income to protect themselves from any vicissitudes that may occur even if the tax cuts are a mistake. And that extra income was certainly forthcoming during the Reagan years. Between 1977 and 1987, the income of the bottom tenth of the population fell by 10 percent, while the income for the top 10 percent went up by 24.4 percent—and that for the top 1 percent by 74.2 percent. The invention of supply-side economics has therefore opened the coffers of the rich to a group of conservatives, fattened the campaign funds of politicians who make the right noises, and brought foundation grants and huge speakers fees for economists and journalists who sing the "Right" songs. Trouble is, they are the wrong songs:

- The supply-side view that tax cuts stimulate investment is simply not clearly demonstrated. The proportion of income applied to investment did not increase during the Reagan administration, except as a normal response to a business cycle upswing.

- There is no serious evidence that special savings incentives, such as IRAs and 401(k)s increase savings. The evidence is in fact mixed.

- There is simply no evidence that large government programs are inconsistent with spectacular economic performance. American agriculture is the eighth wonder of the world. And although government programs have their flaws, they are totally consistent with heavy government interference in agriculture.

The evidence that supply-side economics, in fact, works the way the supply-siders say it works is murky enough even though much of it goes back to an era when foreign trade was less important than it is now. But global interdependence makes supply-side economics even more toxic than the record of its past suggests, because its basic tenet—that low taxes stimulate income growth and therefore tax receipts in the United States—is undermined by the simple fact that a large proportion of tax cuts are spent purchasing goods and services that are produced abroad. We estimate that some 18 cents out of every dollar that Ronald Reagan gave up in tax cuts went abroad. That proportion would be even larger now.

Milton Friedman, George Stigler, and James Buchanan are all distinguished conservative economists. They are all Republicans. They have all won the Nobel Prize. And they all hold supply-side economics in contempt. They will not readily share this opinion, given Republican ties that bind. But the disdain of these accomplished economists for supply-side economics can easily be deduced from their writings and congressional testimony. And a similar disdain for supply-side economics can also be seen in the writings and testimony of two other distinguished Republicans: the late Arthur F. Burns, appointed chairman of the Federal Reserve by President Nixon; and Alan Greenspan, appointed to the Federal Reserve by Ronald Reagan, and still the chairman under Bill Clinton.

These economists all knew that supply-side economics is trash for one simple reason. It can easily be proven. And therein lies the danger. The swing to the Right in the United States threatens that economic policy will be based on a theory that is already discredited and that will do great damage in the increasingly globalized economy of the next decade.

CHAPTER 9

Conclusions

I T IS TIME FOR A REALITY CHECK FOR AMERICA. AS THE STOCK market soared and unemployment fell in 1995, 1996, and early 1997, American businesspeople and public officials alike were busily striding around the globe proclaiming victory in the great post-cold war economic battle, a victory that was readily accepted given that Europe and Japan seemed mired in economic rigidities of their own. After all, hadn't the United States of America accomplished the most successful adaptation of any of the advanced industrial countries to the new realities of the post-cold war economy? Was not America blessed by the most "flexible" labor market in the industrial world, the most technologically advanced industry, the most vigorous entrepreneurial spirit? Has not the dollar become the rising star of global currency markets in 1996 and early 1997?

With the American economy seemingly triumphant, a new sensibility had taken hold of a large part of the American public. As Americans watched the stock market catapult upward, they, in many cases, put their own wage stagnation and debt problems aside to become active cheerleaders—even at their own expense. Financial analysts repeated time and again to the media that any and all wage increases were bad for the stock market. Meanwhile, those who earn their living from work greatly outspent their incomes. Consumer debt soared to very high levels because people often thought the relentless rise in the Dow would somehow save them. And although wage gains were meager despite the strong economy, strikes began to be viewed as illogical, left-wing plots against the steady drumbeat of a victorious stock market that was raising the hopes of the boomer generation. Stocks, it seemed to many of them, could help create financial nest eggs large enough for the comfortable retirement that their scaled-back defined benefit pension plan would no longer include.

Those who earn their living from work in America certainly do have the right to be proud of the way they adapted to the needs of

197

the new economy. They carried on despite twenty years of wage stagnation and the emergence of an economic system that has produced by far the largest rewards to the very rich. They had willingly worked longer hours. They had lived through a period when more and more members of each household had to go to work seeking to maintain their accustomed standard of living.

Yet economic insecurity continued to be a fact of life for the average American even as the success of the American economy was being celebrated in the annual January rituals of the State of the Union message, the rosy forecast of economists and stock market analysts, and the early reports of corporate profits that were running higher than expected. As the market launched its assault on 7000 in the Dow in January of 1997, big companies announced plans to lay off some 43,595 employees, according to the outplacement firm of Challenger, Gray and Christmas. That figure was below the total for January of 1996, when AT&T announced plans to shed some 40,000 workers. But it was 12 percent more than in January of 1995 and the second-largest figure in a year.

Nor were the sources of economic insecurity confined to the continued erosion of good jobs in the private sector. There were also signs in 1996 and 1997 that many key trends in government also represented a continuation of the attack on the economic position of Americans who earn their living primarily from work.

The true nature of the proposal for Social Security reform that was circulating in those months represented an excellent example of the continued assault on work. There was, to begin with, wide acceptance of the conclusion that future Social Security payments should be scaled back because the cost of living adjustments guaranteed by the program were based on a Consumer Price Index (CPI) that considerably overstated the rate of inflation in the country. A commission appointed by the Republican majority on the Senate Finance Committee, and headed by Michael J. Boskin, chairman of the Council of Economic Advisers during the Bush administration, unanimously argued that the Consumer Price Index overstates the inflation rate by some 1.1 percent per year, mainly because it fails to make adequate adjustment for the improvement in the quality of products made available to the American public. Their conclusions were widely proclaimed as accurate by Federal Reserve Chairman Alan Greenspan. Implicit in their findings was the notion that the growth of Social Security benefits could justly be scaled back without doing any great damage to the living standards of those in the program. The commission was composed of economists with impeccable credentials. Yet its final report never mentioned the fact that procedures instituted by the Bureau of Labor Statistics (BLS), the agency that is the keeper of the CPI, had already taken enough account of quality change so as to reduce the 1996 inflation rate from 4.7 percent to the 2.8 percent that was reported. In 1996, the inflation rate had already gotten a 1.9 percentage point haircut. The Boskin commission's report contains no discussion of the adjustment already made to the CPI, yet the members of the commission must be aware that an adjustment has been made. Do they really think that an additional 1.1 percent adjustment is required?

The failure of the Boskin commission to adequately report on work already done by the BLS to cut the reported inflation rate is disturbing, but equally serious is the rather easy acceptance by not only the conservative but also the liberal wing of the intellectual establishment of a scheme to reduce the federal deficit over the long run, bringing federal outlays under control by scaling back Social Security benefits. Those who earn their living from work will be financing this scheme. The intellectual establishment conveniently neglected to mention that the kind of Social Security reform it favors reduces the long-term returns to those who earn their living from work, while leaving the richest Americans, the only group whose incomes have increased rapidly since the end of the cold war, essentially unscathed. The reason that the well-to-do are let off scot-free is, of course, that their retirement incomes are only trivially dependent on Social Security benefits. And evident in the plans for Medicare reform is a similar lack of appreciation of the way in which trends in income distribution have hurt those who earn their living from work.

Americans who earn their living from work are being told that what is good for the rich is also good for them, and they have not given serious examination to whether that comforting generalization fully squares with the facts. There are no better examples of the advice to behave like the rich do than what is being said of the stock market, where the top 1 percent of the population owned 49.6 percent of stocks outstanding, and the top 5 percent owned 85.9 percent in 1992 before the great stock market boom of the mid-1990s began in earnest (see Table 8–6 on page 173). Americans are not only being told that they should invest their money in stocks but also that the monies of the Social Security system should be invested in stocks. By inviting a large portion of the U.S. population to participate in the market—even in a small way, via the Social Security system—Wall Street has managed to take the eyes of many American workers off their own self-interest—earning a livable wage that reflects the profits that corporate America has been raking in during the mid-1990s.

And with limited options available to fulfill their longer-term goals, today's workers are putting their faith in private sector money managers to help them keep afloat financially; whereas a couple of generations ago, the labor movement and company-defined benefit pension funds were the main ones vested with the responsibility for keeping American families afloat over the long haul. As the stock market raced upward through the mid-1990s, the new faith—that the mutual fund industry would take the place of wage hikes and labor pressure to give workers a quality life—seemed to be vindicated. The American middle class, it seemed, backed their new passion for stocks with money. In 1996 Americans poured $226 billion into mutual funds, by far the most popular household investing vehicle. Nearly all of that money was placed in funds that invest in the booming stock market rather than bonds or money market instruments. In comparison, just $22 billion was invested in mutual funds in 1990. And today more than 63 million people own shares in mutual funds, up from 38 million four years ago.

The big financial news of early 1997 was the merger of the investment banks Dean Witter and Morgan Stanley, creating a company that offers 306 funds with assets of $146 billion. Consumers had been well schooled to keep their money in mutual funds over the long term because the industry had promoted the belief that the long-term trend of stocks is up. Dips, they were led to believe, were buying opportunities; the market would eventually retrace its steps and keep going up.

Inherent in this promise is a kind of security blanket; the union chief is replaced with a mutual fund manager. Since there is no longer much emphasis on a long-term career at one company with ongoing benefits, workers are pinning their long-term domestic financial hopes on financial managers who are seen as capable of conjuring up some future bliss. More and more, the mutual fund manager has become a kind of "new millennium mom" who will somehow manage to come up with enough profits for millions of families to ensure college tuition payments, retirement with comfort, and a lot left over for illnesses and other family crises.

But the odds are that this confidence will prove a cruel pipe dream. Passive investors who earn their living from work and are increasingly reliant on Wall Street for their future quality of life could very well find themselves in a financial market where stocks are not galloping upward. In the six years between 1990 and 1996, when inflows into mutual funds grew from $22 billion to $226 billion, stock prices, as measured by the S&P 500 Index, essentially doubled. It may be that no one is implicitly promising a doubling of stock prices in the six years between 1996 and 2002. But those who believe that it is the pace at which new monies are being put into mutual funds that explains the rise in the stock market should realize that in order for prices to grow at a pace equivalent to that achieved between 1990 and 1996, new monies being put into funds today would have to increase by more than ten times from $226 billion to $2,321 trillion in six years. Where is that money going to come from if wages continue to be sluggish and debt continues to pile up? And as a result the mighty millennium mom in the guise of a fund manager is bound to run into some trouble trying to take care of her expectant small investors. We wish those who are relying more and more on the stock market to take care of their long-term needs good luck. But every page of history, and every fiber of our being, leads us to believe that today's small investors in the stock market are being asked to put their faith in a system that could be much more fallible than they expect.

There is indeed abroad in the land a general tendency to "explain away" the difficulties of those who earn their living from work and to pretend that the problems of average workers are easily solved. Much evidence of this tendency is apparent in the earlier chapters of this book. Some of the most important examples are worth citing in this concluding chapter:

- The rapid growth in exports from America is endlessly celebrated, and America's export performance so far in the 1990s is indeed in some ways remarkable. This rapid growth is generally presented as evidence that American workers are benefiting from the emergence of the global economy. And many undoubtedly are. But the cold facts are that imports are growing faster than exports. If they weren't, the U.S. balance of trade would be improving, and the actual statistics would not be showing a continuing deterioration.

- Americans are constantly being told that the rate at which good jobs are being destroyed in large companies is overstated, and that there are in fact huge numbers of good new jobs being created in other parts of the economy. A perfect example is the report released by President Clinton's Council of Economic Advisers on April 23, 1996, unquestionably designed to bolster public perceptions of the administration's economic policy during the presidential primary season. That report went to great lengths to argue that more jobs were being created in fast-growing high-wage sectors of the economy than in more traditional and sluggish industries. For the four years covered by the report, 1993 – 1996, there is no question that the report's conclusion was true. But the same has been true in virtually any other period in economic history. What the report never analyzed were the pay levels for the new jobs that actually came onstream during the period. They could have been higher than the average wage prevailing in the economy, or they could have been lower. There is no way of telling from reading the report.

- There has been a tendency to assure the public that those employees who are downsized from large companies can easily find refuge in small business. Yet there is no evidence that the share of permanent new jobs being created by small business is higher now than it has been in the past (see Chapter 4).

- Another tendency is to assure American workers that their sacrifices have not been in vain because the new American corporation is emerging as a lean and mean competitor, although there is absolutely no evidence that the ratio of supervisors to production workers has fallen in recent years. Indeed, what evidence there is suggests that this critical ratio may, in fact, be rising, and this factor of the workplace may be one reason that there is no sign of a fundamental increase in the rate of productivity growth in the American economy. This despite the major sacrifice and the work speedups inflicted on most Americans who earn their living from work.

The one piece of good news for American workers in the 1990s is that there has been a decline in the unemployment rate. That is certainly a comforting fact. But American workers should realize that the primary reason that unemployment rates have fallen in the U.S.

economy in the 1990s is because U.S. labor has become cheap and is being widely substituted for capital. Unemployment has fallen in the 1990s because, contrary to the prevailing mythology in an age of triumphant capital, the United States has become a more labor intensive economy.

THE GREAT POST–COLD WAR DIVORCE I:
THE SEPARATE WORLDS OF WORK
AND CAPITAL

It is time once again for a reality check. Although those who earn their living from work in the U.S. economy have fared better in 1996 and early 1997 than they did in the earlier post-cold war years, the analysis in this book provides no solid ground for thinking that this relative good fortune will prove anything but ephemeral. For as we remember from Chapter 1, in the new global economy the industrial world is in a race without a finish line—where the competitive gains of one year or decade can, and most likely will, turn out to be the losses of the next year or decade.

To argue otherwise, and to accept the canons of the latest phase of American triumphalism, is to ignore the essential change in the relations between capital and work that occurred in the wake of the end of the cold war. A global economy in which those who earn their living from work in the developed world have, in effect, been divorced by the owners of the industrial world's capital has released forces that will, for decades, press down on the standard of living of the average American, European, and Japanese.

It is, to begin with, improbable that one of these three great regions can permanently best the other two in international competition. America looked like the great victor in international competition in the 1950s and early 1960s. Western Europe surged into the lead in the international economic marathon in the late 1960s only to be overtaken by Japan at some point in the 1970s. In the 1990s America has again surged into the lead.

It is likely that the economic regions of the developed world will continue to trade places, and perhaps at an even faster pace than in the past. With the opening of markets the forces that make for changes in the leadership of the industrial world will work with more intensity, with greater and greater speed, and at higher and higher cost to those who earn their living from work.

The way in which the United States has regained leadership in the 1990s is instructive in the following respects. As America's industrial position weakened in the 1980s, two forces were set in motion to reverse the trend. The first was, of course, the drive for greater efficiency by business in general and the great multinational corporations in particular. The drive for efficiency, as we saw in Chapter 4, forced the shedding of workers and the increase in hours of work for those who managed to stay employed, and virtually put an end to wage gains. Whether this drive for efficiency in fact increased the rate of growth of productivity of American industry is debatable—the statistics suggest that it did not. But there is little question that the power of capital increased. Witness the huge rise in CEO salaries and the surge in the stock market, accompanied by a decline in the power of those who earn their living from work. Witness the decline in the proportion of the U.S. labor force that is unionized and the failure of wages to increase significantly, even though profits were surging.

The second great process that was set into motion was the fall in the U.S. dollar. It made both goods produced in America relatively cheap and assets priced in American dollars more alluring, inducing foreign companies to locate more and more facilities in the United States, particularly the cheap labor areas of the South. The formula worked, but it worked by increasing the power of American capital at the expense of those Americans who earn their living from work.

The lessons of American revival in the 1990s have not been lost on either the Europeans or the Japanese. Both regions have launched drives that virtually guarantee that they will come back. Though the union movement is inherently stronger in Europe than in the United States, the mid-1990s have witnessed continued attempts by European capital to suppress wage growth. The process has been halting in Europe because of the strength of the unions there. But there is little doubt that European corporations will succeed in the long run.

Japan's industrial structure is, of course, paternalistic, and its unions are effectively company unions. Yet Japan has learned how to outsource. And, more significantly, it has also adopted a policy of currency devaluation. From its high in 1995, the yen had fallen by some 50 percent against the dollar by the end of the first quarter of 1997.

The inevitable result of these efforts in Europe and Japan will be another assault on the economic preeminence of the United States. It may take time for that assault to succeed. But by the end of 1996, for example, a cheaper yen and cost-cutting by Toyota, Honda, and other

Japanese auto companies had already reduced the relative prices of Japanese cars significantly enough to lead to a meaningful increase in Japan's share of the domestic U.S. auto market. And each time the market share of foreign corporations begins to increase, the result in America is more and more pressure on those who earn their living from work. For a critical element in the logic of the competition between the industrial world's key regions is the need to keep down the cost of hiring. And as American business begins to respond to the renewed challenges that will inevitably come from abroad, it will again seek to reduce the income of its employees. There is no real, clearly visible alternative given the way that the global economy now works.

So far we have described why those who earn their living from work in each of the important regions of the industrial world are trapped in a rivalry with other industrial world workers. But what is particularly ominous for developed world workers, whatever nation they live in, is that they face a common threat: the workforce of the less developed world. That workforce is huge, growing rapidly, becoming more skilled and more middle class, and it can be employed at relatively low wages. And above all, there has been a change in the attitude of industrial world capital toward the labor force of the less developed world. Through most of the four-hundred-year history of capitalism there was a reluctance on the part of the captains of industrial world capital to allow workers in the remainder of the world free access either to their money or to their technology. But with the end of colonialism and the dissolution of the Soviet empire, those attitudes have undergone a major change, resulting in a new relation between work and capital in the industrial world that we have termed "divorce post-cold war style," and have attempted to analyze in this book. It is a world in which the logic of production decrees that there shall be no difference between the wages earned in Seattle, Washington, in Osaka, Japan, or in Düsseldorf, Germany, and those earned in what are still the most backward regions of continental China and India, or in Borneo, for that matter. It is a backwardness that will be overcome, in a world in which capital has become highly mobile, and technology transfer a fact of industrial life.

Factor price equalization—the tendency of the factors of production to earn the same rates of return (wages in the case of work) no matter where they are located—is a force that works relentlessly, as Adam Smith recognized over two hundred years ago (Chapter 2). As Smith wrote in 1766, a major reason that any group of workers can earn higher incomes than any other group of workers is that that group is advantaged by relatively favorable access to the other factors of production.

So as capital has emerged as an equal opportunity employer throughout the post-cold war world, the tendency of wages to become equal at all points on the globe will work with great force. For workers in the emerging world the prospects are the ascent of their relative wages toward a new heaven. For workers in the developed world the prospects are for a descent in their relative wages toward a new hell. At the end, relative wages, heaven and hell, will fuse. But not before the twenty-second century. The implications of this new set of global demographics are that huge new pools of workers in China, India, and the former Soviet empire will be assimilated relentlessly into the world labor pool, creating a daunting set of problems for those who earn their living from work in developed nations.

THE GREAT POST–COLD WAR DIVORCE II: IS RECONCILIATION POSSIBLE?

It appears highly unlikely that the old marriage between Western labor and capital will ever reappear in its former post-cold war form, given the remarkable vitality of such places as Bangalore, India, and Shanghai, China, where sophisticated workers are just beginning to become truly innovative. There is probably no way that the traditional relationship between industrial world capital and industrial world work that has existed throughout most of the history of modern capitalism can be restored. Yet Americans, indeed the entire industrialized world, are of a pragmatic cast of mind, demanding solutions to perceived problems. And it is to a discussion of our hierarchy of solutions that we now turn.

Our policy recommendations are predicated on the view that policy as well as politics must be grounded in the possible. Should out-of-control financial markets create a crisis of the proportions of the great crash of 1929—a possible but by no means certain result of the financial excesses of the current stage of world capitalism—it would be feasible to envisage a new set of economic policies that seems as implausible now as the New Deal would have seemed in the period prior to the great crash. But that is not an outcome that we either desire or that we can confidently predict. The current stage of financial exuberance is just as likely to end with a whimper as to end with a bang. Nor do we have any desire to institute any measures designed to raise up those who earn their living from work in the industrial world by holding down their counterparts in the developing world. What we primarily seek is a better balance between the interest of labor and the interest of capital in the industrial world.

Much stands in the way of even modest changes in policy. The same kind of myopia of capital that fought the New Deal tooth and nail even in the wake of the stock market crash, and the Great Depression that followed, still exists. And in a world of capital triumphant, the ability of business to block legislation that limits the sway of the free market works with greater force than ever, particularly in an environment where politics depends on outsized campaign contributions.

Yet the 1996 election, with a Democrat reelected to the White House and a reduced Republican majority in the House of Representatives, made it clear that there is much political resistance to the untrammeled power of free market ideology. So far that resistance has created little in the way of meaningful change to increase the power of those who earn their living from work. The current euphemisms emanating from the White House having to do with improving the average family's quality of life are just that—roundabout measures to relieve the symptoms of economic stress: workers trying hard to maintain pensions and health insurance as they move from job to job, new mothers needing a few extra days in the hospital after giving birth, agitated children sitting home alone watching too many hours of violent television. These symptoms merely demonstrate that the mass of the population is having a hard time keeping up emotionally and financially, no matter how hard they work. Families and communities are falling apart, and there is just not enough money being made by hardworking parents to keep the family afloat because there have been such tight controls placed on wage hikes by those who control capital. When it comes to the low real wages that are at the root of the problem, the administration, as we have seen, tends to trumpet meager gains using vague statistical analysis. Much credit was taken by President Clinton for the small wage gains that occurred in late 1996. But when data became available showing that average weekly wages had fallen by 1.8 percent in January 1997—the biggest decline since August of 1973—no high-ranking official from the Clinton administration appeared to tell the world that a good part of the weekly income gains of 1996 had eroded in one month. And, most important, the Democratic administration has proved unwilling to take steps to stand up to capital.

Policy as euphemism is so popular because it involves the weakest and least threatening kind of attack against global capital. But to prove effective in redressing the grave imbalance the administration would have to act on policy changes that would represent a real challenge both to the interest of capital as it perceives them and to the ideology of the free market. We will discuss these policies in an order inverse to the challenge that they pose to the existing hierarchy of economic power in the United States, recognizing that those policies that require the biggest changes are the least likely to be adopted without the onset first of a serious economic crisis.

MAKING AMERICAN WORKERS MORE COMPETITIVE

"Capitalism is myopic and cannot make the long-term social investment in education, infrastructure, and research and development that it needs for its own future survival. It needs government help to make those investments, but its own ideology won't allow it to recognize the need for those investments or request government help." These words written by MIT economist Lester C. Thurow are an apt description of some of the ways in which capitalism must be saved from itself. Thurow calls capitalist resistance to appropriate government investment in these three areas "the ideological paradox of our time." That, of course, is what it is, yet there are at least some signs that Thurow may be too pessimistic about the chances that the programs that he deems most vital will be adopted.

There is evidence, for example, that a broad American consensus is developing on the need for at least some kind of education reform. In his State of the Union address, at the beginning of 1997, President Clinton proposed tax subsidies for families who wish to send their children to college. And for their part, the Republicans have talked of special tax breaks for monies saved for education. These are certainly a better use of tax money than is cutting the capital gains tax, which gives relief to the rich who need no relief, or subsidizing a middle-class housing market that already benefits from massive government subsidies in the form of income tax deductions for home mortgage interest and property taxes.

Yet blaming American workers for their plight because they are either dumb or uneducated is an egregious insult to them. For as we showed in Chapter 2, the educational accomplishments of the American workforce have increased and increased significantly throughout the entire period in which their incomes have been stagnant. George Bernard Shaw once observed that the curse of the poor is their poverty. In the same way, a lack of good new jobs is the curse of the jobless. The future of most Americans depends far more on economic growth than on increased spending for education and training.

That, indeed, is the lesson that is provided by the experience of the United States, and the rest of the industrial world as well, with job retraining—the other important aspect of improving education. In the new post-cold war economy, job training has met with a success rate that can charitably be described as "mixed." When economic growth is not robust, even the most highly skilled workers have trouble finding well-paying jobs. A recent analysis of dislocated defense workers in New England showed that they hardly had an easy time finding new jobs, even though they had significant experience with computers, precision tools, and quality control. Even when they did find a job, one in five had to work at wages that were 40 percent or more below their previous levels. Indeed, over 60 percent of all dislocated workers had noticeably lower hourly earnings.

Elsewhere, highly skilled workers who need retraining often cannot afford the cost of appropriate programs, and others have difficulty matching training opportunities to projected new job requirements. For still others, the lack of good job prospects in even distantly related industries raises questions about whether retraining is really a good investment. Difficulties with retraining programs are legion. Even the World Bank's 1995 *World Development Report* expressed skepticism regarding the value of training in helping unemployed workers to find new jobs. The reality is that neither ignorance nor lack of skills is the chief job problem of the American workers, and, indeed, lack of training is probably overrated as a cause of the job problems of workers in the industrial world as a whole.

It is also conceivable that substantial public support could be mobilized for accelerating spending on public infrastructure. Business does, after all, benefit from this kind of spending, and Wall Street would surely welcome the significant fees generated by municipal bond financing (both commercial and investment banks can underwrite municipal bonds). A growing body of research suggests that each dollar spent on infrastructure makes a greater short-run contribution to productivity growth than does any other form of spending, or tax cuts. The reason is that the entire first round of infrastructure spending occurs in the home country. When taxes are cut, by contrast, the public spends over 25 percent in a way that immediately puts money in the pockets of foreign countries through buying more imported goods. In the long run public spending has much the same effect, but at least the first round of spending occurs at home, meaning that imports of consumer goods only begin to increase when the money spent to improve the infrastructure begins to be paid out as wages and other forms of consumer income. Indeed, large tax cuts are a key reason that the U.S. balance of payments has deteriorated, particularly during the Reagan years. Neither Truman nor Eisenhower nor Kennedy nor Johnson nor Nixon nor Carter were quite as ideologically blinded to the need for infrastructure.

Important as public spending on education and infrastructure is, it pales in comparison to the need for increased spending on research and development. A program to increase government spending on R & D would run counter to the spirit of the times, but would not be deeply threatening to the business apostles of the new global capitalism. The argument is often made that the newly emerging countries of Asia are growing fast because government spending is a lower proportion of gross domestic product (about 20 percent) than in Europe (about 50 percent) or the United States (about 35 percent). But the difference lies in bigger social programs in the west, where the role of the family has diminished. When it comes to government subsidies to research and development, the governments of the fast-growing countries of Asia are by far the leaders. Indeed, R & D spending as a proportion of real GDP is higher in Asia, and in Europe for that matter, than in the U.S.

The United States is different from those countries that have declined in the past because it has generally been open to immigration and has therefore refreshed its creative capacities. Technical progress in this country has often been immigrant based; the United States has an enormous advantage compared to more homogeneous countries such as Germany, Japan, and Korea in its ready access to immigrant workers. South Korean immigrants provide an example of how immigrants trained in top U.S. graduate schools will help the U.S. economy. In that dynamic country newly assembled Korean technical teams often retain their strong links to the U.S. universities where they trained. These relationships are already leading to joint ventures and long-term project commitments between U.S. and South Korean firms. The U.S. store of diverse student populations on the undergraduate and graduate level, often encouraged by liberal government policies, is now beginning to pay off for the United States economically.

Any objective study of U.S. economic success inevitably recognizes the role played by government in technological progress. This includes the key importance of the work done by the Department of

Defense's Advanced Research Projects Agency (ARPA), the Pentagon's research agency, which has been critical in inventing everything from the computer chip to the Internet. Current spending for this effort is being cut ruthlessly; it must be reaccelerated, perhaps with a less overtly military mission.

Sustaining productivity in research also depends on the health of the roughly fifty top American universities. Whatever the faults of U.S. education, there is general agreement that the top universities in the United States are the best in the world, particularly at the graduate level. It is madness to cut back federal funding for these institutions. Funding must be expanded, doubled or tripled, or the United States will lose its lead in the emerging sciences of biotechnology and superconductivity, fields that will dominate innovation over the coming decades.

Measures to improve education, rebuild the public infrastructure, and accelerate R&D will depend for their success not just on government, but on the *federal* government. We are no subscribers to what the *Washington Monthly* has disparagingly called "devolution chic"—the widespread passing of power and funding issues to the states. The fact is concentrating power in the federal government increases efficiency. The parallel functions of state and federal government are inherently wasteful, leading to a bloated legal system and the duplication of spending in many areas, including education and law enforcement. In the economies of our major competitors, the trend has been toward centralization, not decentralization. Passing power to the states also virtually guarantees that capital will prosper, compared to work: competition for capital among the states is certain to lead to special concessions for American and foreign corporations.

Alexander Hamilton, a hero of the political Right in his time but a man who understood the advantages of centralized power, would have aggressively resisted devolution, even though he knew it had popular support. The United States must relearn many things that he understood in the eighteenth century.

TOWARD ECONOMIC COOPERATION IN THE INDUSTRIAL WORLD

Needed policy changes do not end at national borders within the developed world. Measures to increase the productivity of workers in individual countries will not, in themselves, do a great deal to restore an equitable balance between work and capital. Macroeconomic policy must also be reformed, on some cooperative basis, in the developed world.

The reason is simple but usually overlooked. In recent years the industrial world has, in effect, ceded policies that would yield rapid growth to the countries of the developed world. They don't take the same view of such policies in the developing world. Although rapid inflation in any country of the world draws fire from international economic organizations and is swiftly punished by the financial markets, it is generally true that those who move money usually cheer when countries such as Brazil, Argentina, Malaysia, or Indonesia manage to grow at 6 to 7 percent per year, even if their inflation rates remain higher than the average for industrial countries.

In sharp contrast, the conventional view among economists is that neither the United States nor the other industrial countries can pursue policies aimed at rapid growth without risking an ignition of inflation because the rate of productivity growth in these countries has slowed down. It is a view that has put the industrial world's economic policy into a straitjacket. This abandonment of growth goals explains why giant holes have appeared in the social safety net of the United States, why there are strenuous efforts to cut back on social programs in virtually all the other industrial countries, and why wage gains continue to be so meager throughout the developed world.

This fundamental economic dichotomy has far-reaching implications. Developing countries can grow rapidly without provoking immediate retaliation by the financial markets. But any deviation from slow-growth policies has severe economic consequences for the nations of the developed world. As those who dispose of capital survey the total global scene, they see clear-cut investment implications: they are motivated to invest greater and greater proportions of their capital in the developing world, and smaller and smaller proportions in the developed world.

The effect is, of course, to turn what ought to be a fair and square economic race between the countries of the world into a handicap derby. Those who earn their living from work in the developed world have to carry the weight of restrictive economic policy. Those who earn their living from work in the developing world need not bear an equivalent weight. It is only those who dispose of mobile capital who can fully take advantage of this growth differential.

The burdens imposed on the industrial countries by slow-growth policies do not weigh heavily on the minds of central bankers or currency traders. But they have not gone unnoticed by investors. As we know, the S&P 500 Index measures the performance of the stock prices of the five hundred most heavily capitalized companies in the world that are traded on the American stock exchanges. In 1995 and 1996, years of stock market boom, the thirty largest companies in the index accounted for some 65 percent of the index's total gains. What these companies have in common is global reach: the ability to locate facilities and develop markets in any part of the world. And an increasing proportion of these companies' investments are, of course, in the developing world. The corporations understand that.

We believe economic policy in the developed world is fundamentally flawed. In contrast to the conventional view that argues that slow productivity growth dooms the developed world to slow economic growth, we argue that the productivity slowdown is not the cause but a symptom of the new economic order. Specifically, the most elementary analysis suggests that productivity growth is strongest when high demand pushes up business volume. But when receipts are stagnant, companies often respond by rewarding cost-cutting and consolidation through merger rather than innovation and the introduction of new products. For all these reasons the primary agenda for the next century should be to move economic growth to the top of the policy agenda, and in a creative fashion.

If the United States could have been put back on a rapid growth path by waving a magic wand, it would have been done a long time ago. The triumph of capitalism in the cold war has made the restoration of rapid noninflationary growth extremely difficult. The reason, as we saw in Chapter 7, is that any country in the developed world that aims at fast growth immediately invites the ire of the bond and currency market vigilantes who foresee rising inflation as a consequence. "I told you so," say the grizzled central bankers and fuzzy-cheeked currency traders alike. "You have no alternative but to move back to a slow-growth policy." That is the great dilemma facing the United States and the other countries of the developed world.

There is, in principle at least, a way out of the dilemma. It was shown to the world by John Maynard Keynes, the Cambridge don who was perhaps the greatest political economist of the twentieth century. Keynes's reputation as an economist is, of course, based on his theoretical work in economics. But his public reputation has grown out of his more passionate, and more accessible, analysis of the needs and failures of world economic policy after the two great world wars of this century.

No figure is more thoroughly disliked by the apostles of market extremism than is Keynes. He is blamed for being the father of the welfare state, for supporting ever-growing government spending, and for endorsing inflationary policies. He is called a socialist. Yet no one understood better the vitality of the market economy, and no one could have better outlined the dire consequences of a capitalist system that loses its momentum. Keynes firmly believed that his entire career had been devoted, not to putting the world on the road to socialism and central planning, which he loathed, but to saving capitalism from itself.

The brilliant and well-connected Keynes was in a unique position to observe the aftermath of both world wars first hand. He was a very junior member of the British delegation that participated in formulating the Treaty of Versailles that ended World War I. His early fame was based on his analysis of the fatal economic faults of the international economic order that emerged from Versailles, which he published in 1919 in a book called *The Economic Consequences of the Peace.*

Keynes's most important work was his analysis of the causes and cures of the Great Depression of the 1930s, in a book called *The General Theory of Employment, Interest, and Money,* published in 1936. That book revolutionized the thinking of economists, but apart from some minor influence on the second Roosevelt administration, this work had little effect on economic policy until after World War II.

It was then that Keynesian economics flowered. Its influence was brief but vital in explaining how the world economy could be put back together. Keynes himself was a senior member of the British delegation to the Bretton Woods Conference that set up the International Monetary Fund and the World Bank after World War II, institutions that formed the basis for over forty years of international economic cooperation. At the same time, Keynes's *General Theory* provided the rationale for the adoption of full employment policies in virtually all of the countries that belonged to the United Nations, most important, of course, in the victorious developed countries of the industrial world. In the United States those policies were embodied in the Full Employment Act of 1946, which for the first time committed the United States to an active government policy designed to generate enough growth to make jobs widely available. To set such policies it mandated a Council of Economic Advisers to the president. That system, the financial underpinning of the golden age for industrial world workers, performed brilliantly for many years.

But since the total victory of the market, made final in 1988 with the end of the cold war, the system has failed. Workers are the chief victims of this global dynamic, with its combination of increasingly fierce competition on the one hand and fiscally conservative governments on the other. There are only two ways to attack the problem. One—restricting competition with a new round of tariffs and quotas—was the route followed during the catastrophic 1930s. The other can be seen in the tack Keynes set out on after World War II: establishing new ground rules for international economic cooperation. Some analysts today are developing a similar line of thinking: "States must now reorient their economic policies toward growth, but it should be done as part of a coordinated economic effort. Calling for such might seem utopian in the current political environment, but it has been done before." These are the words of Ethan B. Kapstein, former director of studies at the Council on Foreign Relations, a center of establishment thinking. Absent a new era of cooperation, he goes on to say, governments will continue to "break their deal with workers while maintaining their commitment to an open economy. They cannot have it both ways, and instead, the policy focus should be on negotiating a package that helps workers adjust to ongoing changes."

International cooperation between the advanced industrial countries is the only way to depose the tyranny of the central banks and the markets. Such cooperation would short-circuit the usual punishing transfers of capital away from countries that stray from fiscal orthodoxy. Whatever risk there might be that such growth-oriented coordination could be undermined by massive capital flight to East Asia or other regions would be limited, since the United States and other Western countries still dominate the global financial marketplace. According to the Organization for Economic Cooperation and Development (OECD), in 1994 their member nations (including Japan) were still home to 90 percent of world stock market capitalization and bond issues.

Furthermore, as we have argued in this book, the link between more rapid economic growth and inflation no longer need be such a serious concern. To summarize our views:

- A world with a growing labor pool willing to work for low wages (Chapter 3) provides some insurance against inflation that did not exist when the economy of the industrial countries was more self-contained.

- A world in which labor organizations are weakened by the threat of outsourcing and low-wage competition from abroad is hardly the kind of world threatened by the reemergence of the so-called wage-price spiral of the 1970s and 1980s.

- A world in which the main engine of growth—the high technology sector—is characterized by rapidly falling costs and prices also carries insurance against the reemergence of the wage-price spiral.

- A world in which central bankers and currency traders continue to have influence under any feasible new set of rules for economic policy reform is hardly a world that will create a new inflationary dragon that will have to be slain.

There are, indeed, some fragile indications that the economic establishment itself is beginning to realize that the inflationary threat posed by more rapid growth has receded. The years 1995 and 1996 provided reasonably clear evidence of the change. Throughout the 1980s and in the earlier years of the 1990s there was a belief that the unemployment rate in the United States could not fall below roughly 6 percent without resulting in rapid wage growth and accelerating inflation. Yet unemployment moved toward 5.3 percent in 1996 without causing any increase in inflation.

And, in fact, there is some glimmer of hope for the new international pro-growth arrangements that have sprung from this new behavior of the U.S. economy. Despite the warnings of the bond market vigilantes, America's central bank, the Federal Reserve, refrained from tightening money throughout 1996 and early 1997. And it is particularly heartening to those who see the need for faster industrial world growth that in his Delphic way Federal Reserve Chairman Alan Greenspan in effect admitted that the forces apt to bring about inflation in the developed world have waned. Is it too much to hope that this lesson could provide the basis for a new system of international cooperation in which nations will be willing to take more risks for growth? We believe the real lesson of the 1990s is that the threat of global deflation is far more credible than the threat of a resurgence of global inflation. We can only hope that the policy establishment recognizes these new realities soon.

TOWARD A NEW WORKPLACE

To those with some sense of history, it is difficult to grasp the degree to which the power and influence of the American labor movement has declined in the new global economy. Looking back at the key events in labor history, it almost feels as if most of the major episodes that marked labor's rise to a position of great influence occurred in another century, rather than within the past forty years.

The American labor movement, of course, came under assault long before the global march of the market began. Unions representing workers in the private sector had ceased to grow well before the 1980s, although they experienced enormous expansion at all levels of public employment after President Kennedy's 1961 executive order sanctioning union recognition and bargaining for federal employees. Yet in financial and banking services, and among the rapidly growing scientific and technical categories, organized labor has made almost no inroads. Labor's presence disappeared almost completely from the federal government during the Reagan administration and has not, to anyone's surprise, resurfaced in a significant way during the Clinton years.

That is not to say that labor has stopped supporting the Democratic party, which union leaders regard as by far the lesser of two evils. But the first Clinton administration saw something profoundly new in a Democratic administration: it, to say the least, was reluctant to have its own labor secretary discuss falling real wages openly. Organized labor gave strong financial support to Clinton during the 1996 presidential campaign—support that was critical to his reelection—only to see the resignation of Robert Reich as labor secretary. This left no prominent person with workers' needs in mind to balance the pro-bond market counsel of Treasury Secretary Robert Rubin, who in any case had always been more of an "insider" than Reich.

There is little reason to expect that it will be easy for unions themselves to become effective in the workplace anytime soon. Too many workers, at all levels of skill, have been profoundly shaken by the decoupling of their interests from those of capital, and as a consequence many have become passive (Chapter 4). And although the new president of the AFL-CIO, John Sweeney, has promised massive new organizing, depending more on heavy participation by unionized workers themselves and less on paid union organizers, it is still to early to know if the effort will succeed. People are extremely skeptical of joining organizations that do not deliver and that seem weak. Yet the United States has had other periods of what the authors of *Who Built America?*, a history of the American labor movement, called "unexpected popular insurgencies," when there has been a sense that corporate power was out of control. One such period was in the first decade of the twentieth century, when the Progressive movement—made up of a combination of the working class and middle-class professionals—joined together to change a climate they found, in the words of *Who Built America?*, to be "chaotic, inefficient, and inhumane." Who would have thought a few years ago, for example, that young physicians would be a beehive of union activity in mid-1990s?

This insight should provide hope to those who would like to see a union revival in the United States in the near future. There is lots of evidence that unions do indeed have some influence when they back legislative programs that find middle-class support such as environmental protection, the reform of pension legislation, and the protection of the basic elements of the social safety net, Social Security and Medicare.

But in the absence of a strong resurgent union movement, it falls to the federal government to take certain actions. We recommend the following measures:

- Make it easier and less costly to change jobs. Americans need programs that provide some protection from the rapid change forced on the production process by the workings of the global economy. The government has already mandated more portable health insurance; it should do the same for pensions by eliminating the wait that most companies require for workers to be fully vested.

- Impart a sense of movement to those who work. Americans still think of themselves as living in a frontier society that allows those who yearn for change to move to a new frontier. Our guess is that workers in the industrial world, and especially in the United States, feel they are stuck in place compared both to capital and to their own idea of how much mobility they should have. In his *Studies in Classical American Literature,* D. H. Lawrence, who understood the working class, argued that the essential characteristics of those who emigrated to America was a desire to be "masterless." This still holds true, and it explains much of what goes on in the United States, from our unique brand of populism to the popularity of the National Rifle Association to fears of bureaucracy. Workers must feel that they can move and use the government to help them move. To this end we suggest that moving costs be given even more generous tax treatment than that provided by the existing tax code.

- Government ought also to subsidize job listings, to ease the process of finding a new job. National job listings already exist in the private sector, both on the Internet and in other forums. Their expansion should be subsidized, just as capital investment receives tax subsidies.

- Create a new safety net to socialize those risks inherent in a global capitalism that threaten workers. No matter what is done to increase worker mobility, those who earn their living from work will remain relatively immobile in a world of quicksilver capital. That means that there should be catastrophe insurance for those who are totally laid low by the sudden and unexpected loss of a job. The insurance should include the financing of continued health care and protection against the loss of retirement benefits.

CREATIVITY: THE AMERICAN EDGE

For all the difficulties that the new global economy has caused for those who earn their living from work, Americans do have a unique advantage as their country moves toward the twenty-first century.

It is now about one hundred years since the United States became the economic leader of the developed capitalist world, in the estimate of Angus Maddison, among other economic historians (as we have seen in Chapter 2). Most count only two other dominant powers prior to the United States in the four-hundred-year development of modern capitalism: the Netherlands, at the beginning of the seventeenth century, and Great Britain in the eighteenth and most of the nineteenth century. The Netherlands is usually characterized as the first truly capitalist nation state to dominate the world economically.

Maddison's critique of Dutch technological and agricultural innovation in the seventeenth century demonstrates that Dutch innovation was just as creative (in its own way) as American inventiveness was at the beginning of its economic ascent around the turn of the century. Britain's economic ascendancy, by contrast, had a much stronger imperialistic framework than that of the Netherlands or the United States, although, of course, Britain too introduced many important technological innovations.

We believe that the history of U.S. capitalism is unique. Largely because of an enlightened immigration policy and the technologically progressive industrial policy of the Pentagon during the cold war, the United States today is once again at an innovative peak, just as creative as the Dutch were in the seventeenth century, the British were during the early eighteenth century, and just as creative as the United States itself was during its own first period of economic and technological leadership. Historically such periods of intense innovation and creativity in a nation are extremely rare, and most such eras don't last long. That the United States is now well into another major wave of technological breakthroughs exactly a century after becoming the world's economic leader says something about this country's indelible creativity: the United States has far more creative stamina than either of the earlier economic giants because it still leads in the most dynamic industries—computers and software, telecommunications, and biogenetics.

Dutch innovators worked hard to secure water-centered Holland a place in the world economy. But they did so by working hand in hand with Dutch capitalists, as did British inventors, who went to British financiers to underwrite their breakthrough technological products. Similarly, America's latest innovative wave had its genesis in the cradle of its most well endowed universities—places like Stanford, MIT, and Carnegie-Mellon—and government grants ensured early on that research took place, which came to fruition years later.

Today, as U.S. technology companies struggle to ensure that creative spurts will continue, it is unclear whether the newly emerging generation of elite workers will have the psychological "space" and security to continue to produce a stream of innovative products in the wake of the great post–cold war divorce between work and capital. In contrast, Bangaloreans, who have yet to fully prove themselves as technologically creative, are currently operating in a protected environment, partly under the auspices of the government.

The dangers of a capital-worker divorce have paradoxically been described by Joseph A. Schumpeter, the Harvard economist who is a hero to many on the political Right. It has become an established view that in the new global economy, capitalism is changing in "a perennial gale of creative destruction" just as Schumpeter had forecast that it would. But as we have examined these forces—reengineering, outsourcing, megamergers and spinoffs, all happening simultaneously—we have raised questions about whether the changes taking place are downright destructive, rather than creatively destructive, as Schumpeter believed. Schumpeter himself warned that "Capitalism creates a rational frame of mind which, having destroyed the moral authority of so many other institutions, in the end turns against its own." Observing the world in the wake of the great divorce brought on by the end of the cold war we have raised the question of whether America can continue to innovate and grow, remaining capitalism's most creative leader at the same time that its labor force—and increasingly its managerial and intellectual labor force—exists in a truly global environment, an unprotected environment in which capital sheds its most trusted managers and workers at the whim of every new CEO that takes over a new company.

Fortunately there are signs that the virtues of unchecked global capitalism are being questioned, and in the most unexpected venues. The need to place limits on global capital was a basic theme at the early 1997 meeting of the august Davos Conference, which brings together economic and political leaders from around the world. Reporting on the thrust of the conference, Thomas Friedman of the *New York Times* raised the following possibility: "the backlash against those who would like to construct the world on a one-dimensional basis, where commerce is everything, where only financial accounting matters," he writes, could easily encounter a potential moral backlash against globalization.

A similar conclusion has been reached by George Soros, the hedge fund operator who has made billions of dollars by taking advantage of the irrationalities in markets and government policies and is accordingly feared and respected by government officials around the world. A great debate is beginning about whether some new rules are needed for global capitalism. It has started none too soon.

Endnotes

Note: Unattributed quotes are based on authors' interviews.

CHAPTER 1
Introduction: The Race Without a Finish Line

Page 2. "in the Dutch Republic during the early 1600s." Jan de Vries, *The Economy of Europe in an Age of Crisis, 1600-1750* (Cambridge: Cambridge University Press, 1976).

Page 3. "the fifth year of an economic upswing." The most comprehensive statistics on the current American labor market are to be found in Lawrence Mishel, Jared Bernstein, and John Schmitt, *The State of Working America,* published semiannually by the Economic Policy Institute. The statistics in this chapter are taken from the 1996-1997 edition. Copies of the book can be obtained from the Economic Policy Institute, 1660 L St. NW, Suite 1200, Washington, D.C. 20036.

Page 5. "has apparently reached its maximum capacity." Data in this paragraph and the two following paragraphs are from Mishel, Bernstein, and Schmitt, *The State of Working America,* 1996-1997.

Page 6. "the elite top 20 percent would be spared." Robert Reich, *The Work of Nations* (New York: Vintage Books, 1992), 234-40; Richard J. Herrnstein and Charles Murray, *The Bell Curve* (New York: The Free Press, 1994), 25-50; Alvin and Heidi Toffler, *Creating a New Civilization: The Politics of the Third Wave* (Atlanta: Turner Publishing, 1994), 54-61.

Page 6. "a widespread restructuring of the economy." Data on past productivity growth and projections of future productivity growth are taken from *The Economic Report of the President* (Washington, D.C.: U.S. Government Printing Office, 1996), 58.

CHAPTER 2
Capital versus Labor: Divorce, Post–Cold War Style

Page 13. " 'The change in world history' " J. M. Roberts, *History of the World* (New York: Penguin Books, 1988), 587.

Page 14. " 'saw a new integration' " Eric J. Hobsbawm, *The Age of Capital* (London: Abacus/Little, Brown, 1977), 356.

Page 15. "in the entire second half of the nineteenth century." Data on population movements for this paragraph and the next two paragraphs are from U.S. Census Bureau, *Historical Statistics of the United States, Colonial Times to 1970*, Bicentennial edition, part 1 (Washington, D.C.: U.S. Government Printing Office, 1975), 93.

Page 16. "with membership confined mainly to white ethnic Europeans." America Social History Project, University of New York, *Who Built America?* vol. 2, *From the Guilded Age to the Present* (New York: Pantheon Books, 1992), 7-58.

Page 16. "*The Wealth of Nations* was published" Adam Smith, *The Wealth of Nations* (New York: Modern Library Edition, Random House, 1937), 531-32.

Page 18. "increased by less than 1 percent per year." Angus Maddison, *Dynamic Forces in Capitalist Development* (Oxford: Oxford University Press, 1991), 48-84, and U.S. Census Bureau, *Historical Statistics of the United States*.

Page 22. " 'a lot richer than it is today.' " "Twentieth Century Capitalism," Christopher Farrell, *Business Week,* 1994 special edition, 16.

Page 22. "continue to be dismal." *Economic Report of the President,* February 1996, 402.

Page 25. "quintupled to about $150 billion a year." U.S. Census Bureau, *Statistical Abstract of the United States: 1996* (Washington, D.C.: U.S. Government Printing Office, 1996), 857.

Page 28. "appears to have become very immobile." Ibid., 32.

Page 29. "about 800 in 1980." Pam Belluck, "Healthy Korean Economy Draws Immigrants Home," *New York Times,* August 22, 1995, 1, B4.

Page 32. " 'We're not geographically bound' " Erle Norton, "Alcoa Has Remade Itself," *Wall Street Journal,* September 26, 1996, R14.

CHAPTER 3
The New Leviathan: The Global Labor Pool

Page 33. "The serious nature of the decline" Data in this chapter on world population growth and on the size of the middle class were prepared for *Business Week* magazine by DRI/McGraw Hill. Inevitably, statistics and projections of the size of the world middle class cannot be precise. However, these data and projections appear reasonable despite the uncertainty of demographic numbers for the countries of the emerging world.

Page 36. "in the years to come." Saul Hansell, "The Ante Rises in East Asia," *New York Times,* July 14, 1996, section 3, 1, 12-13.

Page 40. "As of 1996 the cost per square foot" *Global Economic Prospects and the Developing Countries* (Washington, D.C.: World Bank, 1995).

Page 40. "because labor could be bought cheap" Jane Jacobs, *Cities and the Wealth of Nations* (New York: Vintage Books, 1985), 102.

Page 44. "of highly skilled labor." Mike Mills, *Washington Post,* September 17, 1996, 1, A7, col. 3.

Page 49. "the difference was only 42 percent." Christopher Farrell, "Productivity to the Rescue," *Business Week,* October 9, 1995, 134.

Page 49. " 'America is a house divided.' " Jeremy Rifkin, *The End of Work* (New York: G. P. Putnam's Sons, 1995), 177.

Page 49. " 'We are on our way to becoming' " Reich, *Work of Nations,* 282.

Page 49. "argued in *The Bell Curve*." Herrnstein and Murray, *The Bell Curve.*

Page 51. "in *The Organization Man*," William H. Whyte, *The Organization Man* (London: Jonathan Cape, 1956).

CHAPTER 4
Downsizing or Cultural Revolution?

Page 59. "who had power over his career." Ningku Wu, *A Single Tear* (Boston: Little, Brown, 1993), 39.

Page 59. "that ran the bureaucracies and universities." Lucien W. Pye, *China, An Introduction* (Boston: Little, Brown, 1984), 252–87.

Page 60. "The new Holy Grail" Michael Hammer and James Champy, *Reengineering the Corporation* (New York: Harper Business, 1994), cover.

Page 60. "is dramatic improvement in cost, quality, and customer satisfaction." Kirk Johnson, "A Giant in Motion—Surviving Corporate Reinvention," *New York Times,* May 12, 1996, 1.

Page 61. "would be helped along by 'facilitators.' " Edmund L. Andrews, "Don't Go Away Mad, Just Go Away," *New York Times,* February 13, 1996, D1, D6.

Page 63. "for the next forty years." Wu, *A Single Tear,* 7.

Page 64. "my head ached day and night." Ibid., 36.

Page 64. " 'who knows contentment with his lot.' " Ibid., 182.

Page 64. "Comparably, in the book *White Collar Blues*" Charles Heckscher, *White Collar Blues* (New York: Basic Books, 1995), 49.

Page 67. "reengineering programs achieve 'shoddy results.' " Phillip Zweig, "The Case Against Mergers," *Business Week,* October 30, 1995, 126.

Page 68. "I've since learned that's critical." Joseph B. White, "Reengineering Gurus Take Steps to Remodel Their Stalling Vehicles," *Wall Street Journal,* November 26, 1996, A1, A13.

Page 69. " 'most of it is wrong' " Hammer and Champy, *Reengineering the Corporation,* cover.

Page 69. "to remain dispassionate under such circumstances" Ibid., xii.

Page 69. "so vividly described in *Barbarians at the Gate.*" Bryan Burrough and John Helyar, *Barbarians at the Gate* (New York: Harper Collins, 1991).

Page 71. " 'For most Americans, do you think' " *Business Week,* March 11, 1996, 64.

Page 73. "an annual rate of 1.1 percent" All the data on productivity growth are from *The Economic Report of the President,* 1996; and Maddison, *Dynamic Forces in Capitalist Development,* 48-60.

Page 79. "the 16 percent increase for average workers" Business Week Executive Pay Survey, *Business Week,* April 22, 1996, 100.

Page 81. "by *fattening,* not flattening, their administrative apparatus." The data in this paragraph are from David Gordon's *Fat and Mean* (New York: Martin Kessler Books/The Free Press, 1996), 82.

Page 83. "hence productivity." Heckscher, *White Collar Blues,* 49.

Page 84. " 'more isolated and looking to be left alone.' " Ibid., 49.

Page 84. " 'work very well together.' " Ibid., 11.

CHAPTER 5
A Passage to India: The Case of Bangalore

Page 87. "In his exuberant, much-celebrated novel," Salman Rushdie, *The Moor's Last Sigh* (New York: Pantheon Books, 1995).

Page 88. "with their American counterparts." Reich, *The Work of Nations,* 235.

Page 92. "and lush cascades of bougainvillea." Introductory essay "Reminiscences of a Bangalorean," written by Professor M. N. Srinivas, *Bangalore: Scenes from an Indian City* (Bangalore: Gangarams Publications Private Limited, 1994), 6-27.

Page 92. "Bangalore and its environs today boasts three universities," John Stremlau, "Dateline Bangalore: Third World Technopolis," *Foreign Policy,* Spring 1996, 152–68.

Page 100. "As Jane Jacobs has argued" This is an essential insight of Jane Jacobs, *Cities and Wealth of Nations* (New York: Vintage Books, 1985).

Page 105. "low- or medium-tech goods" Sylvia Ostrey and Richard R. Nelson, *Techno-Nationalism and Techno-Globalism* (Washington, D.C.: Brookings Institution, 1995), 21.

Note: All other material in this chapter came from direct interviews the authors did in Bangalore, India, in April 1996.

CHAPTER 6
Have the Elite Workers Had It?

Page 107. "Books like *The Winner-Take-All Society*" Robert H. Frank and Philip J. Cook, *The Winner-Take-All Society* (New York: The Free Press, 1995).

Page 108. "afflicted by a 'skills mismatch' " Paul R. Krugman, *Peddling Prosperity* (New York: Norton, 1994), 140–45.

Page 108. "Conservative writers such as" Richard J. Herrnstein and Charles Murray, *The Bell Curve.*

Page 108. "The economist Joan Robinson," To the authors' knowledge, Joan Robinson used the term *idiosyncratic factors of production* in lectures at Cambridge University in the mid-1930s. William Wolman learned of some of the content of these lectures from Professor Lorrie Tarshis of Stanford University when he was a graduate student there.

Page 110. " 'principally set one man above another.' " Smith, *Wealth of Nations,* 673.

Page 112. " 'This plan involves not only the obvious loss of income' " Heckscher, *White Collar Blues,* 168–76.

Page 115. "currently taking place in Poland." Jane Perlez, "It's Yuppie Heaven in Poland," *New York Times,* September 4, 1996, D1, D4.

Page 118. "its reproductive cycle is so rapid." Quotes in the next four paragraphs are drawn from Paula Dwyer, "The New Music Biz," *Business Week*'s International Edition, January 15, 1996, 20.

Page 120. "no longer afford to work in New York City." Kathleen Becket, *New York Times,* May 6, 1992, C10.

Page 121. " 'For more than a decade,' " Bennett Harrison, *Lean and Mean: The Changing Landscape of Corporate Power in the Age of Flexibility* (New York: Basic Books, 1994), 12.

Page 122. "David L. Birch, a business consultant," David L. Birch, *Job Generation in America* (New York: The Free Press, 1987). The article that made Birch's undeserved reputation as a maven on job generation is "Who Creates Jobs?" *Public Interest 65*, Fall 1995, 3-14.

Page 122. "James Hamilton and James Medoff." Charles Brown, James Hamilton, and James Medoff, *Employers Large and Small* (Cambridge, Mass.: Harvard University Press, 1990), 21.

Page 123. "widely dispersed locations to work together" "The Networked Corporation," *Business Week,* June 26, 1995, 90-91.

Page 124. "In their classic work *The Modern Corporation and Private Property*," Adolf A. Berle and Gardiner C. Means, *The Modern Corporation and Private Property* (New York: Harcourt, Brace & World, 1968).

Page 124. "the nineteenth and early twentieth centuries." John Kenneth Galbraith, *The New Industrial State* (Boston: Houghton Mifflin, 1971).

Page 124. " 'brings its own specialty' " Harrison, *Lean and Mean,* 150-88.

Page 127. "but weren't actively pursuing employment." Bernard Wysocki, Jr., "Missing in Action: About a Million Men Have Left the Workforce," *Wall Street Journal,* June 12, 1996, A, 1.

Page 130. "There have been penetrating analyses" Milton and Rose Friedman, *Capitalism and Freedom* (Chicago: University of Chicago Press, 1962), 137-60; C. Wright Mills, *White Collar* (New York: Oxford University Press, 1951), 239-58.

Page 131. "the early phases of the development of modern capitalism." de Vries, *The Economy of Europe in an Age of Crisis, 1600-1750,* 94.

CHAPTER 7
Can We Depend on Wall Street?

Page 141. " 'over the monetary system of a country.' " Milton and Rose Friedman, *Capitalism and Freedom,* 50.

Page 141. " 'You can intimidate everybody.' " Kevin Phillips, *Arrogant Capital* (Boston: Back Bay Books, 1995), 95.

Page 142. "will likewise be shown to be in error." Fernand Braudel, *Perspective of the World* (New York: Harper & Row, 1984), 245.

Page 143. "and several other top financial firms." Joel Kurtzman, *The Death of Money: How the Electronic Economy Has Destabilized the World's Markets and Created Financial Chaos* (Boston: Little, Brown, 1994).

Page 146. "when we think about central banking." Comparing the Federal Reserve chairman to the Wizard of Oz in the way that is done in this chapter may not be too far from the true spirit of Baum's book. A good argument can be made that *The Wizard of Oz* is replete with symbols of the populist politics of the 1890s. The author briefly saw agrarian unrest firsthand working as a journalist in South Dakota in the late nineteenth century. He wrote the book in the aftermath of the pivotal 1896 election and published it in 1900.

The backdrop for the 1896 election was economic and social unrest related to the farm-to-factory shift. The Republican candidate, William McKinley, and his campaign manager, Marcus Alonzo Hanna, the Cleveland industrialist (who has drawn favorable comments from Newt Gingrich) created a coalition of the winners of the new industrial age. The nominee of the Democratic and populist parties, William Jennings Bryan, defended rural interests.

So what does Oz have to do with this? Start with the witches—the good ones were from the North and South, while the wicked ones were from the East and West. Or consider Dorothy's companions. The Scarecrow represents the farmers that were made to think that they were brainless. The Tin Woodsman symbolizes the "heartless" industrial workers. (Baum's view of the dehumanizing Eastern influences was not too subtle—the woodsman started off as a human who was put under a spell by the Wicked Witch of the East, so that each swing of the ax cost him a body part, which was replaced by tin.) The Cowardly Lion was William Jennings Bryan himself, whose bellicose nature was insufficiently intimidating.

There's more. The Wizard was McKinley, who projected a benign image but because he represented the industrial interests ("Mark Hanna wears him like a watch fob," said the commentators of the day), had no intention on delivering on his promises to Dorothy.

Then there are the slippers. Unlike the ruby slippers in the 1939 movie version, Baum's slippers were made of silver. The bimetallic symbolism is obvious. Before Dorothy realized the power of silver, she sought her goal by traveling the "yellow brick" road, replete with all its hazards. Once the Good Witch of the South showed her the power of the silver slippers, she achieved her goal of returning to Kansas. But the silver slippers fell off during the flight and "were lost forever." Baum apparently agreed with Bryan's powerful oratory that saw the common people being crucified on a cross of gold—the late nineteenth century's version of tight money. Reprinted from Thomas D. Gallagher, "Lions, Tigers . . . and Bear Markets?", Lehman Brothers, Washington Report, April 8, 1996. Copyright © 1996 by Lehman Brothers, Inc. Used with permission of Lehman Brothers, Inc.

Page 152. "resigned in frustration, explaining in an article" John Cassidy, *The New Yorker,* February 19, 1996, on Alan Blinder, 38-46.

Page 161. "The years between the end of World War II" Maddison, *Dynamic Forces in Capitalist Development,* 121-24.

Page 162. "much reduced or entirely overthrown." Doris Kearns Goodwin, *No Ordinary Time* (New York: Simon & Schuster, 1994), 624-25.

Page 163. "the accompanying unemployment rate averaged 10 percent." J. M. Keynes, *Essays and Sketches in Biography* (New York: Meridian Books, 1956), 163–74. His essay on Winston Churchill's role as chancellor of the exchequer is the classic description of the follies of the gold standard in the 1920s.

Page 164. " 'all businessmen were sons of bitches' " Theodore C. Sorenson, *Kennedy* (New York: Harper & Row, 1965), 461.

CHAPTER 8
A New Crisis of Capitalism?

Page 175. "Pension coverage, as Harvard economists" David Bloom and Richard Freeman, "The Fall in Private Pension Coverage in the United States," *American Economic Review,* May 1992, 539–42.

Page 176. "A study by Robert Smith shows" Robert S. Smith, "Have OSHA and Workers' Compensation Made the Workplace Safer?" in D. Lewin, O. Mitchell, and P. Sherer, eds., *Research Frontiers in Industrial Relations and Human Resources* (Madison, Wis.: Industrial Relations Research Association, 1992).

Page 180. "By 1994 there were already 2.4" Saul Hansell, "Spending It; We Like You, Now Pay Up," *New York Times,* January 26, 1997, Section 3, 1.

Page 186. " 'If ten or twelve businessmen in Amsterdam' " Braudel, *The Perspective of the World,* 245.

Page 186. "In Holland, as the mid-eighteenth" Phillips, *Arrogant Capital,* 111.

Page 186. "Instead of putting money into new technology" Lectures by Columbia University historian Jacobus Smit in his course "Origins of Capitalism," in 1986.

Page 187. "A prominent critic" Phillips, *Arrogant Capital,* 112.

Page 187. " 'Granted you are the clearing house of the world,' " Aaron L. Friedberg, *The Weary Titan: Britain and the Experience of Relative Decline, 1895–1905* (Princeton: Princeton University Press, 1988), 75–76.

Page 191. "A vivid description of the results" The Summers calculation is taken from Kevin Phillips's *Arrogant Capital,* 109–10.

Page 192. "The country perceives that " The notion that domestic government is an evil empire comes from Gary Wills's "Reagan Country: It's His Party," *New York Times Magazine,* August 11, 1996, 30.

Page 193. "Congress added a piddling $90 billion a year." Ibid., 32.

CHAPTER 9
Conclusions

Page 208. "or request government help." Lester C. Thurow, "The Revolution Upon Us," *The Atlantic Monthly,* March 1997, 100.

Page 209. "have trouble finding well-paying jobs." Yolanda Kodrzycki, "Laid-off Workers in a Time of Structural Change," *New England Economic Review,* July-August 1996, 3 – 26.

Page 210. "when it comes to government subsidies" Sylvia Ostry, *The Post-Cold War Trading System* (Chicago: University of Chicago Press, 1997), 132 – 72.

Page 211. "has called 'devolution chic' " Gareth Cook, "Devolution Chic," *The Washington Monthly,* April 1995, 9.

Page 215. "but it has been done before." Ethan Kapstein, "Workers and the World Economy," *Foreign Affairs,* May-June 1996, 16 – 37.

Page 215. "adjust to ongoing changes." Kapstein, ibid., 15.

Page 215. "capitalization and bond issues," Ibid.

Page 220. "breakthrough technological products." Based on lectures by Columbia University historian Jacobus Smit in his course "Origins of Capitalism," in 1986.

Page 221. "capitalism is changing in" Joseph Schumpeter, *Capitalism, Socialism, and Democracy* (New York: Harper & Bros., 1942), 163.

Page 221. "raised the following possibility" Thomas L. Friedman, "The Neutrality Myth," *New York Times,* February 5, 1997, A23.

Page 221. "has been reached by" George Soros, "The Capitalist Threat," *The Atlantic Monthly,* February 1997, 45.

Index

A

Advanced Research Projects Agency
(ARPA), 144, 211
Aetna Life and Casualty, 66
AFL-CIO, 217
Allen, Robert E., 60
Aluminum Co. of America (ALCOA),
32
American Association of University
Professors, 134
American Depositary Receipts
(ADRs), 25
American Management Association,
67, 85
American Quality Foundation, 67
Arbitrage, 47
Arthur D. Little, 67
Ashok, D. (Dash), 98, 99
Ashok, Revathy, 98, 99, 100
Asian countries, 4, 34-35, 36, 210
middle-class, 38, 39, 47
technology in, 44, 167
See also China; India
A Single Tear, 59
Assets, x, 30, 175
AT&T, 60, 61, 70, 103, 116
Automobile companies, foreign, 27,
204-205

B

Babbitt, 130
Balances, economic, ix, 206-208
Barbarians at the Gates, 69
Baverish, Nariman, 127
Bell Curve, The, 6, 49
Belli, Melvin, 135
Berle, Adolf, 124
Bell Labs, 116
Berlin Wall, x, 3-4, 71
Berry, Ken, 119
Bhagwati, Jagdish, 101

Birch, David L., 121-122
Blinder, Alan, 152
Bloom, David, 175
Boesky, Ivan, 179
Boskin, Michael J., 198-199
Braudel, Ferdinand, 186
British elite, 142, 187, 219-220
Brown vs. Board of Education, 164
Buchanan, James, 195
Buchanan, Pat, 3, 79, 84-85
Bureaucratic burden, 81
Burns, Arthur F., 151, 160, 195
Business Week, 70, 71, 79

C

Capital, 54, 109-110, 142, 204
in developing countries, 23-26
European, 14-17
vs. labor, 76-79
mobility of, 45, 15, 18, 23-24,
194, 212, 213
outflow of, 25, 26-27, 30
rate of profit, 171-172
Western, 13-14
vs. work, divorce of, 13-32,
203-208, 221
Capitalism, ix-x, 1-2, 76, 220
global, 6-7, 17-20, 221
history of, 109-110
Capitalism and Freedom, 130
Capital/output ratio, 77, 192
Card, David, 53
Carnegie, Andrew, 75
Carter, Jimmy, 146, 151, 210
Caterpillar Corporation, 98
Central banks, 160, 215
interests of, 148-150
policies, 141-143, 146, 163,
212-214
See also Economic policy;
Federal Reserve

Century 21, 133
Champy, James, 60, 61, 65, 66, 69
Charles Schwab, 133
China, 35, 47, 117-118
  Cultural Revolution, 59-65, 67
  middle-class, 38-39
Chubb Insurance, 66
Churchill, Winston, 163, 165
Citibank, 36-37, 44, 64, 103, 113
Citicorp, 133, 143
Cities and the Wealth of Nations,
  40
Citi Islamic Investment Bank, 37
Civil War, 18
Clavell, James, 79
Clinton, Bill, 145, 152, 167, 195,
  202, 217
  wage gains, 207-208
Clinton administration, 71
Cochran, Johnny, 135
Cold war, post-, ix-x, 9, 25, 205
  capital vs. labor, 29-32
  global economic growth, 20-23
  real wage gain, 169-170
  victory in, 12
  See also Economy, U.S.
College graduates, earnings of, 6,
  43, 49
Colonialism, 110
Communism, fall of, 19, 110
Competition, 215
  international, 203-206
  U.S. workers and, 208-211
Computer industry, 31-32, 53-54,
  75-76
  See also Technology
Conner Peripherals, 31-32
Consumer Price Index (CPI), 154,
  198-199
Convergence, 45-48, 115
Cook, Philip J., 107
Coolidge, Calvin, 163
Coopers and Lybrand, 90, 127
Corporate community
  downsizing, 57-59
  lay-offs and comebacks, 125-129
  networking, 123-125
  practices, 84-85

Council on Economic Advisers
  (CEA), 126, 198, 202
Council of Foreign Relations, 215
Creativity, 48
  centers of, 116-118
  protection of, 219-220
CSC Index, 60, 66, 68
CS First Boston, 143
Cultural Revolution, 59-65, 67

D

Dean Witter, 200
DeBakey, Michael, 134
Debt, 142, 149
  consumer, 57, 180-183, 197
  foreign, 183-185
  vs. income, 178-183
Debtor nation, 184-185
Demographics
  middle-class, 42-43
  productivity growth and, 73-74
  worker, 2-3, 33-35, 46-47
Dertouzos, Michael, 51
Developing countries
  capital in, 23-26
  economic growth rate, 21-22,
    25
  vs. industrial countries,
    212-214
  middle class in, 110-111
Devolution, 211
Displacement, 125-129
Douglass, Paul H., 149
Downsizing, 83-85, 202
  See also Reengineering
DRI/McGraw Hill, 25, 26, 42, 127
Drucker, Peter F., 60
Dutch elite, 142, 186, 219-220

E

Earnings differentials, 7, 107
Eastman Kodak, 31, 66
Ebert, Fredrich, 19
*Economic Consequences of the
  Peace, The,* 214
Economic decline, symptoms of,
  142, 186-187, 220

Economic growth, 5
    global, 20-23
    rapid, 161-165
    slow, 165-166, 178, 212-214
Economic insecurity, 6, 198
Economic policy, 150-159
    changes in, 206-208
    competitive workers and,
        208-211
    current, 213-215
    international cooperation in,
        211-216
    protection of creativity and,
        219-220
    supply-side, 192-195
    workplace support by, 217-219
Economic Policy Institute, 57
Economic Report of the President,
    74, 158
Economy, global, 4, 7, 16, 35
    cooperative, 211-216
    effect on U.S., 203-206
    post-WWII, 161-162
    specific growth rates in, 20-23
Economy, U.S., 3, 7
    1920s, 162-163, 165
    deficits, 193
    foreign debt, 183-185
    post-Cold war, 67, 205
    post-WWII, 161-165
    rate of growth, 22-23
Education, 73, 211, 220-221
    cost of, 134
    trends in, 53, 111, 208-209
    wages and, 56, 51
Eisenhower, Dwight D., 164, 210
Electric Power Institute, 67
Electronic Industries Association,
    123
Elite workers, x, 2, 6, 50
    displacement of, 125-129
    future of, 107-115
    global, 7, 17-18, 33-36, 41-45
    income of, 135-138, 170
    in India, 89-91, 98-102
    small business and, 120-123
Enron, 35
Entertainment, 118-120

Ernst and Young, 67
Expectations, 112

F
Factor price equalization, 205-206
Family
    home, 175
    income, 5, 57, 170
    mobility, 28, 219
Federal Open Market Committee,
    147
Federal Reserve, 146-148, 163, 177,
    179, 216
    policies, 150-158, 160
    See also Central banks
Feldstein, Martin, 158
Financial hegemony, 191-192
Financial institutions, 143, 149
    interest rates, 179-183
    vs. industry, 186-192
Ford, Gerald, 152
Ford Motor Company, 66
Foundation on Economic Trends, 49
Frank, Robert H., 107
Freeman, Richard, 175
Free market economy, 47, 207
    in developing countries, 21-22
    supply-side, 192-195
    victory of, ix, 2, 3-4, 8, 19-20,
        125
Friedman, Milton, 130, 195
Friedman, Rose, 130
Friedman, Thomas, 221

G
Galbraith, John Kenneth, 51, 124
Gap, the, 66
Gates, Bill, 75, 93, 94, 99
General Agreements on Tariffs and
    Trade (GATT), 19
General Electric, 35, 103, 113
General Theory of Employment,
    Interest and Money,
    The, 214
Goldin, Claudia, 51
Gompers, Samuel, 163
Goodwin, Doris Kearns, 161
Gorbachev, Mikhail, x

Gordon, David M., 81
Government, role of, 167-168
  in technology, 210-211
  support of workplace, 218-219
Great Depression, 1, 54, 162, 172, 214
Greenspan, Alan, 151-152, 158-159, 177, 195, 198, 216
Griffey, Ken, Jr., x
Gronet, Radek A., 115
Gross Domestic Product (GDP), 25
Gross National Product (GNP), 18
Groupware technology, 123
Groves, Andy, 99

H

Hamilton, Alexander, 211
Hammer, Michael, 60, 61, 65, 66, 68-69
Harding, Warren G., 162
Harrison, Bennett, 121, 124
Hayes, Samuel B., 81
Health insurance, 131-133, 175-176, 218
Heckscher, Charles, 64, 83-84, 111-112
Herrnstein, Richard J., 49, 108
Hewlett-Packard (HP), 31, 44
Hobsbawm, Eric, 14
Hoover, Herbert, 163
Hyman, Edward, Jr., 153

I

IBM, 31, 118
Idiosyncratic work, 48, 107, 108-109, 117
Immigrants, 27-28, 210
  U.S. population of, 14-15
Imported goods, 189-191, 201
Income
  mean, 136-138
  vs. debt, 178-183
  work vs. capital, 168-172
  See also Wages
India, 35
  Bangalore, 91-93
  middle-class and elite workers of, 38-39, 98-102

software industry in, 87-91, 93-98, 102-106
Industrial countries
  vs. developing countries, 212-214
  economic growth, 20-21
  monetary growth rates, 153-154
  real interest rates, 154-156
Industrial Revolution, 15-16, 50, 52, 160
Industry vs. finance, 186-192
Inflation, 142, 151, 154-156, 212
  post-WWII, 149
  punishment for, 145-146
  threat of, 215-216
  in U.S., 159-160
  See also Economic policy
Information technology, 6, 37, 53-54, 74, 124
  See also Technology
Infosys, 93, 94-95, 103, 106
Infrastructure, public, 164, 209-210
Injury rates, 176
Insurance business, 133
Intel, 31
Interest rates, 179-180, 183
  prime, 182
  real, 155-156, 180-182, 185
International Monetary Fund (IMF), 19, 22, 26, 165, 214
Internet, 1, 75, 97, 144, 219
Internet Society, 31
Intranet, 97
Investment, 166
  direct, 24, 30, 113
  foreign, 26-27, 184
  portfolio, 24, 26
  worldwide, 25
  See also Debt, foreign

J

Jacobs, Jane, 40, 100
Job market, 5, 219
Jobs, Steve, 94
Johnson, Lyndon B., 19, 165, 210

K

Kapstein, Ethan B., 215
Kemp, Jack, 193

Kennedy, Joe, 8
Kennedy, John F., 164-165, 210, 217
Keynes, John Maynard, 108, 213-215
Keynesian economics, 214
Krugman, Paul, 158
Kumar, Vijay, 90, 97, 100
Kuznets, Simon, 172

L

Labor, x, 7, 24, 47, 53
  vs. capital, 76-79
  divorce of, 13-32, 203-208, 221
  global, 14, 33-35
  participation rate, 126-127
  shortages, 16-17
  See also Work; Worker
Labor pool, global, 29-30, 33-35
  competition of, 36-37
  convergence and, 45-48
  elite workers of, 41-45
  middle-class workforce of, 38-41
  technology impact on, 48-54
Lawrence, D.H., 218
Lay-offs, 61, 125-126, 198
  See also Reengineering
Lazard Frères, 152
Lean and Mean, 121, 124
Lee, Suk K., 28
Legal profession, 133
Lenin, V.I., 19
Lewis, Sinclair, 130
Lewis, William, 127
L.M. Ericsson, 123-124
Local area networks (LANs), 123
Lotus Development Corporation, 123

M

Maddison, Angus, 161, 162, 219
Malone, John, 61
Management remake, 62, 66, 72
Managers, middle, 29-30, 51-52, 83-84
  reengineering, 62-63, 64
Mantech program, 144
Mao Tse-tung, 59, 60, 61, 69

Markets, globalization of, 107, 150
Marx, Karl, x, 19
Matsushita, 70
MCA, 70
McKinsey and Company, 67
McKinsey Global Institute, 127
Means, Gardiner, 124
Means, Grady E., 127
Medicaid, 132, 164
Medical profession, 131-133
Medicare, 19, 132, 164, 178, 199, 218
Mencken, H.I., 163
Mercer Management Consulting Inc., 70
Mergers, 69-70, 145, 200
Merrill Lynch, 133
Microsoft, 117
Middle class
  demographics of, 42-43
  developing world, 110-111
  global, 33-36, 38-41
  in India, 98-102
Milken, Michael, 179
Miller, Ann, 72, 112
Miller, G. William, 146, 147, 151
Mills, C. Wright, 130
Modern Corporation and Private Property, The, 124
Monetary growth rate, 152-153, 157, 160
  of industrial countries, 153-154
Money, creation of, 146-148
Monitor, 84
Morale, 111-112
  productivity and, 82-85
Morgan Stanley, 200
Morse, Samuel F.B., 75
Motorola, 31
Multinational corporations, 30, 44, 113, 121
Murray, Charles, 6, 49, 108
Murthi, N.R. Narayana, 93-95, 103, 106

N

National Association of College Placement Officers, 135
National Association of Colleges and Employers, 43

National Association of Securities
Dealers Automated
Quotations (NASDAQ), 3
Natural rate of employment (NRE),
157-158
NCR, 70
Nehru, Jawaharlal, 92
Nelson, Richard R., 105
Networked organizations, 123-125
New Industrial State, 51
New School for Social Research, 81
New York Stock Exchange (NYSE),
31, 191
Nixon, Richard M., 151, 159, 160,
164, 165, 195, 210
No Ordinary Time, 161
Nordstrom, 103

O

Occupational Safety and Health
Administration (OSHA), 176
Oliner, Stephen D., 67
O'Neill, Paul, 32
OPEC (Organization of Petroleum
Exporting Countries),
73, 160, 169, 179
Organization for Economic Coopera-
tion and Development
(OECD), 215
Organization Man, The, 51
Ostry, Sylvia, 105
Outsourcing, 44-45, 102-106, 133,
134, 204, 216

P

Patman, Wright, 149
Pension coverage, 175-176, 218
Phillips, Kevin, 186, 187
Pop culture, 118-120
Population, 38, 110-111
urban, 39-40
Power, 81, 124, 127, 204
of financial institutions, 145,
149-150
over money creation, 147-148
Presidential campaign, 1996, 3
Privatization, global, 26, 34
Procter and Gamble, 113

Productivity
creativity and, 116-118
growth rate, 73-74, 82-83, 202
morale and, 82-85
reengineering and, 70-74
stagnation of, 75-82
Professions, 43
assault on, 129-134
mean incomes of, 136-138

R

Rao, P.V. Narasimha, 35, 101
Reagan, Ronald, x, 151, 193, 194,
195, 210
Real estate business, 133-134
Red Guards, 62, 64
Reed, John S., 36
Reengineering, 58-59, 60-66
failures of, 66-69
productivity and, 70-74, 83-84
Reengineering the Corporation, 60,
66, 68-69
Reich, Robert B., 6, 49, 88, 217
Research and development,
210-211
Rifkin, Jeremy, 49
Rivlin, Alice M., 152
Robert Half Associates, 43
Robinson, Joan, 108
Rohatyn, Felix, 152
Roosevelt, Franklin Delano, 19, 54,
161, 214
Rowan, Henry S., 22
Rubin, Robert, 145, 217
Rushdie, Salman, 87

S

Sachs, Jeffrey D., 22
Safety net, 160, 163, 212, 218, 219
Sasaki, Kuniyoshi, 127
Savings and loan industry, 144, 179
Schmidt, Helmut, 19
Schumpeter, Joseph A., 221
Securities Data Corporation, 69
Semiconductor Association, 31
Shaw, George Bernard, 209
Shaiken, Harley, 41
Shogun, 79

Sibson and Company, 67
Silicon Graphics, 96, 102
Singh, Manmohan, 101
Small business, 120-123
Small Business Administration (SBA), 180
Smith, Adam, 16, 17, 110, 172, 205-206
Smith, Robert, 176
Smith Barney, 37
Social infrastructure, 114-115
Social Security system, 8, 176-178, 198-199, 200, 218
Software industry
  competition in, 102-106
  in India, 87-91, 93-98
  See also Technology
Solow, Robert A., 72
Soros, George, 221
South America, 35, 36
South Korea, 28-29, 210
Soviet Union, 2, 4, 19
Star Wars, 79
Stigler, George, 195
Stiglitz, Joseph E., 74
Stock market, 3, 5, 24, 57, 197, 213
  holdings in, 8, 174-175, 199-201
  See also Wall Street
Strong, Benjamin, 163
Studies in Classical American Literature, 218
Summers, Lawrence H., 191
Supervisory workforce, 81-82, 202
Supplyside economics, 192-195
Sweeney, John, 217

T
Taiwan, 40
Taxes, 176-177, 193, 194, 209, 219
TCI, 61
Technology, 6, 75-76, 128, 216, 220
  erosion of jobs and, 31, 43-45
  global labor and, 48-54
  migration of, 116-118
  networks, 123-125

transfer of, 102-106
  See also Information technology
Tenure, 134
Textron, 151
Thurow, Lester C., 208
Tight money. *See* Economic policy
Toffler, Alvin and Heidi, 6, 121
Trade
  balance of, 46
  deficit, 39, 183-184, 187-189, 193, 201
  ratios, 105
Training, job, 53, 209
  See also Education
Transnational corporations, 121, 124, 127
  See also Multinational corporations
Truman, Harry S., 210
Tseng, John, 31

U
Underemployment, 57
Unemployment rate, 3, 5, 158, 197
  decline in, 197, 202-203, 216
  industrial world, 22
  U.S., 57, 58, 78-79
Union of Radical Political Economists (URPE), 81
Unions, 130, 163, 217-218
United Nations World Investment Report, 30
Universities, 211, 220

V
Varadan, N., 93, 95-96, 97
Virtual corporation, 114
Volcker, Paul A., 151
von Wittfogel, Karl August, 79

W
Wage-price spiral, 216
Wages
  CEO vs. worker, 79-81
  college graduate, 6, 43, 49
  competition for, 47-48
  education and, 135-138
  gains of, 5, 24, 207, 212

Wages (*continued*)
  growth of, 6, 78-79
  real, 18, 169-170
  stagnation of, 46, 71, 160,
    197-198
  See also Convergence; Income
Wall Street, 4, 110, 152, 191-192,
    209
  strength of, 143-146
  See also Stock market
Wal-Mart, 66-67, 117
Wascher, William L., 67
Wealth, distribution of, 79-81,
    172-175, 178, 194
Wealth of Nations, The, 16, 110
White Collar, 130
White Collar Blues, 64, 83, 111
Who Built America?, 218
Whyte, William H., 51
Wide area networks (WANs), 123
Will, George, 193
Winner-Take-All Society, The, 107
Women, 53, 74
  income of, 5, 43, 138
Work
  assault on, 168-170, 197-199
  betrayal of, 84-85, 159

psychological attack on, 59-66
  reengineering, 68-69, 70-74
  vs. capital, 13-32, 203-208, 221
  See also Labor
Worker, x, 8
  benefits, 175-176
  betrayal of, 12, 67, 9, 54, 71-72
  college-educated, 56, 43, 49
  competitive, 208-211
  demographics, 23, 33-35,
    46-47
  mobility, 27-28, 219
  status of, 49-50
  See also Elite workers
Workforce
  global, 33-35
    middle-class, 38-41
  supervisory, 81-82, 202
Workplace, 67, 77
  deterioration of, 176-178
  support of, 217-219
World Bank, 19, 26, 31, 106, 165,
    209, 214
World Development Report, 209
World War I, 18
World War II, 19, 73, 110, 215
Wu, Ningkun, 59, 60, 63-64, 65